SOCIAL CAPITAL AND PUBLIC POLICY

Social Capital and Public Policy

By

Satya Prakash Dash

ANMOL PUBLICATIONS PVT. LTD.
NEW DELHI - 110 002 (INDIA)

ANMOL PUBLICATIONS PVT. LTD.
4374/4B, Ansari Road, Daryaganj
New Delhi - 110 002
Ph.: 23261597, 23278000
Visit us at: www.anmolpublications.com

Social Capital and Public Policy

First Published, 2004

ISBN 81-261-1978-0

ICSSR Consultant: Prof. R.B. Jain

PRINTED IN INDIA

Published by J.L. Kumar for Anmol Publications Pvt. Ltd., New Delhi - 110 002 and Printed at Mehra Offset Press, Delhi.

CONTENTS

PREFACE

The idea social capital simply means 'social skills' or 'social connections'. Of late, it has gained a lot of significance and is regarded as a vital component in developmental activities. Now it is proclaimed by the World Bank to be 'the missing link' in international development. The World Bank has taken recourse to social capital in a number of instances and has achieved a high degree of success. Social capital also paves the way for an egalitarian and responsible society.

The book is primarily based on the concept of social capital and its uses to the society. It has been divided into five chapters. The first chapter introduces the topic and the significance of the study. It also contains objectives of the study and the hypotheses framed. A review of literature is included in this chapter. The sample, coverage and area under study is included in this chapter.

The second chapter presents a conceptual analysis of social capital. It deals with the meaning and interpretations of social capital and it varied uses for human development.

The third chapter discusses the link between social capital and public policy and how social is utilized to reap the benefits from various public policies. It also discusses how the voluntary associations, in the areas selected, are involving in the public policies implemented by the Government and assist the latter.

The fourth chapter deals with the role of voluntary associations in the implementation of the Total Literacy Campaign (TLC). As far as practicable, the analysis has been illustrated on the basis of the responses of the respondents through tables. In pursuing a study of this kind, the author has tried to make use of questionnaire and interviews. The author mostly depended on the field study and responses provided by the respondents.

The fifth chapter is on the concluding observations. The suggestions derived from the members of the voluntary associations and the neo-literates are provided in it for the better implementation of the TLC policy. It also discusses how the civil society is engaged in the promotion of the welfare activities for the people.

From the research work undertaken it is evident that social capital does have a significant role in the promotion of literacy. The voluntary associations and informal associations have involved themselves in the implementation of various welfare policies and programmes of the Government and have achieved success. Human Capital and Social Capital, to a large extent, determine the level of social development in general, and economic development in particular.

—Satya Prakash Dash

ACKNOWLEDGEMENTS

The book is based on an empirical research Project on "Democracy & Social Capital in Segmented Societies" funded by SAREC (Swedish Agency for Research Cooperation in Development Countries) and under the auspices of Uppsala University, Sweden. I am grateful to the selection Committee for awarding me fellowship to undertake research. My association in the international research project and in the present work is due to the blessings of Prof. Amareswar Mishra, Utkal University, Dr. Ashok Swain, Uppsala University; Dr. Hans Blomkvist, Uppsala University and Prof. Brahmananda Satapathy, Utkal University, who was also my supervisor. Prof. Satapathy has also taken all the pains of reviewing the draft and suggesting valuable comments.

I also take this opportunity to express my deep gratitude to Indian Council of Social Science Research (ICSSR), New Delhi for granting financial assistance for publication of my research work. I am also thankful to Prof. R.B. Jain, Consultant for ICSSR, for his positive comments and encouragement.

I am indebted to Prof. C.P. Bhambhri, Prof. Aswini K. Ray, Prof. Sukadev Nanda, Dr. S.N. Misra, Mr. Somen Chakraborty, Mr. Umakanta Mishra, Mr. Pritam Mohanty and Mr. Deba Prasad Dash for their constant encouragement and interest in my research.

Further, my sincere, thanks are also due to my life-partner Ms. Susmita Acharya for her silent support in every work I do and to my mother Annapurna Dash for her moral support and constant nagging to complete every work that I undertake.

—Satya Prakash Dash

1

INTRODUCTION

In the present time much reliance is given on resurgence, revitalization and reinvigoration of the civil society for better and effective articulation and deliverance of common good. The aim is to 'roll back' the overarchical state, which has marginalized the civil society. It centers around the basic assumption "More the Social Capital, better the democratic governmental performance". Civil society believes in the principle of collective action and this collective action can be brought if there is high level of social capital in the community. In the *Communist Manifesto,* Marx hinted upon this collective action on the part of the proletariat for the overthrow of the bourgeoisie and their exploitation. However, the concept of social capital was not used by him. Social capital basically refers to trust, belief, faith, norms of reciprocity, associationism, voluntarism and networks of engagement that facilitate coordinated actions. Social capital gives the community a sort of bargaining power so as to achieve community welfare and this community welfare is brought by the involvement and cooperation of the living in the community. It can be said that "understandings of civil society are often unthinkingly transposed from the west to the rest of the world, both for conceptual purposes and for ideals to be emulated. Second, civil society has been regarded as a panacea, a source of positive-sum outcomes, if only appropriately organized, embraced and participated in by its citizens. Third, a corollary or summary of the two previous points taken together, civil society is recognizably complex and diverse, not least because it is the outcome of associations, organizations, institutions, networks, cultures and so on that have been forged out of equally diverse and complex interests and conflicts".[1] Civil society, usually is defined as a sphere of what may be called 'self-constitution and self-mobilisation', aside from the family and independent of the state.[2] It consists of voluntary organization and public (though privately controlled) communication.

In its narrow view social capital refers to the social skills of individuals – one's prosperity for cooperative behaviour, conflict resolution, tolerance and the like. Social capital can be associated with families and local community associations and the underlying norms (trust, reciprocity) that facilitate coordination and cooperation for mutual benefit. This view highlights the positive aspects of social capital for members of these associations but remains largely silent on the possibility that social capital may not impart benefits to society at large and that group membership itself may entail significant costs.

A more nuanced meso view of social capital recognizes that group membership can have both positive and negative effects. This approach broadens the concept of social capital to include associations in which relationships among members may be hierarchical and power sharing unequal. These forms of association and networks address a wider range of objectives: some of them serve only the private interests of members, while others are motivated by a commitment to serve broader public objectives. This view emphasizes that groups, in addition to providing benefits to members, can make significant non-economic claims on them.

A macro view of social capital focuses on the social and political environment that shapes social structures and enables norms to develop. This environment includes formalised institutional relationships and structures, such as government political regime, rule of law, the court system, and civil and political liberties. Institutions have an important effect on the rate and pattern of economic development.

An integrating view of social capital recognizes that micro, meso and macro institutions coexist and have the potential to complement one another. Macro institutions can provide an enabling environment in which micro institutions develop and flourish. In turn, local associations help sustain regional and national institutions by giving them a measure of stability and legitimacy—and by holding them accountable for their actions.

While the mechanisms by which social capital operate are generally well understood, there is less consensus on whether they qualify social capital as 'capital'. In many cases norms and institutions have the durability and lasting effects associated with capital. Some argue, however, that the sacrifice of a present for a future benefit, typical of traditional forms of capital, is not present in social networks – to the extent that these network are built for reasons other than their economic value to participants. Even so, social networks and organizations are clearly key assets in the portfolio of resources drawn on by poor people to manage risk and opportunity. They are also key assets for the rich, who advance their interests through such organizations as country clubs and professional associations, but their relative importance is greater for poor people.

In short, it can be said social capital refers to societal capacity in working together through networking in communities, in associations with each other based on norms, procedures, tradition, memories, culture and similar features that makes possible the subordination of individual interests to those of the larger groups of the society. This societal capacity needs to be nurtured and continuously developed. This is especially true in society with diverse religion, ethnicity, race, political ideology, dialects and other possible disintegrating factors. This diversity could become the major factor for social conflicts, but it can also become the major source of strength and stability as it is demonstrated in nature's bio-diversity. Social capital, in a way, affects the quality of interactions among individuals.

The basic argument in this work is that horizontal structure of civil society organisations, the relationships between members, play an important role in making democracy work. Social capital is an asset for political and economic development: without it, physical and human capitals are often squandered. It is particularly important in countries where resources are inadequate, as these are not essential for creating social capital, and the stock of social capital increases rather than decreases with use. And it is, in this view, an important factor determining citizens' willingness and ability to participate in public life. An important aspect of civil society in this respect is, therefore, whether associations here are sources of the social capital, which may underpin democratic participation.

The aim of this study is to focus on responsiveness of government to popular opinions and interests and whether the policy implementation process can be seen as fair, adhering to universalistic principles rather than patronage. We will also study the extent of popular participation in policy formulation, adjustment and implementation. The attitudes and needs of citizens will be assessed, and implications for participation in the continuing process of democratization will be drawn.

In the process of governance, expecting total success of plans and realization of developmental objectives by any government, irrespective of its form or ideology, is almost a utopia. This is mainly due to the fact that the phenomenon 'power corrupts' (absolute power corrupts absolutely) comes into full play as the political executive, bureaucracy, elites and even opposition quickly develop (or are widely suspected to be so) vested interests in continuation or perpetuation of a governmental system of which they are a part. As a natural corollary thereof, they allow themselves gradually to get sucked into the vortex of evils like corruption, nepotism, apathy, etc., exposing the system to the wrath of the surging disaffected masses. The grimness of this reality has constantly spurred and goaded the political thinkers and right-thinking political leadership to devise ways and means to invoke greater and greater voluntary participation of the people themselves to get optimum results from developmental programmes. It is for this reason that the civil society organisations have always been looked upon as saviours of democratic spirit and also the instrument for accomplishment of developmental goals. Voluntarism, thus, becomes an approach as well as a technique.

Public policy under the democratic political system is implemented by a complex of administrative institutions, functions of which affect the life of citizens. Policy analysts would not concern themselves with public administration but for the fact that in the countries, which have become independent, the bureaucracy has come to play a decisive role in the formulation and implementation of public policies. Although the primary implementators of public policy are the administrative agencies, there are several others, including voluntary organisations, involved in their implementation. While the action of the public or the state agencies is in response to the constitutional or statutory mandate, that of voluntary agencies stems from the non-formal, reflecting the people's will as is ought to be in participatory democracy. Voluntarism is to be welcomed, especially in a democracy, because voluntary organisations are usually formed to fulfill the emerging needs of the community at large. Their relation with the statutory authorities are not governed by a conflict model but by a complementary model.

Research Problem

The present study is taken up to examine and analyse the role of social capital in giving a better democratic governmental performance. Here democratic government is represented by the public policies and for the convenience of our study we have selected the national literacy policy i.e. Total Literacy Campaign (TLC) of both the national and state Government. An empirical study was undertaken to examine how the literacy policy is being implemented at the ground level and whether the voluntary associations and informal associations are involving themselves in the policy for the community welfare as a whole or not. The TLC policy also requires the involvement of the civil society and is designed to move on a basis of voluntarism rather than a State-sponsored programme. The subsequent chapters exhaustively deal with the subject matter.

Indian society is a multi-dimensional and segmented society and is composed of different castes, religion, language, customs, traditions, ethnicity and cultures. This division of the society makes it an appropriate condition for the study of the existence of social capital and whether it promotes a better and effective democratic governmental performance. Here, we are deliberately using the term 'segmented' society and we refer it to a society "where political divisions follow very closely, and especially concerns lines of objective social differentiation, especially those particularly salient in a society".[3] As mentioned earlier, Indian society is composed of various social cleavages. Such cleavages do not have an "objective" role in politics; they need to be politicized before they matter in political contestation.[4] So, the study attempts to focus on the presence of social capital in spite of the various social cleavages prevalent. Indian society is often remarked to exhibit 'unity in diversity' and this phenomenon can also be utilized for a responsive democratic government thereby bringing community welfare.

The study is undertaken in the district of Cuttack, Orissa and it makes a comparative analysis of the rural and urban areas of Cuttack district. Specific focus is also given on the activities of the Women associations functioning within the Cuttack Urban area i.e. Cuttack Municipal Corporation.

Objectives

Basically the present research is a comparative study of social capital, being exhibited in the voluntary and informal associations, in the Cuttack rural and urban areas in the promotion of better effective and responsive democratic governmental performance. The main focus is how the voluntary and informal associations are involving themselves in the public policies so as to attain communitarian welfare.

Briefly the objectives of the study are as follows:

a) To give a conceptual clarity to the concepts of 'social capital' and 'public policy';

b) To examine the role of voluntary associations in the formulation and implementation of public policy;

c) To investigate and analyse the role of voluntary associations / informal associations involved in the process of the implementation of the national policy of TLC;

d) To make a comparative assessment of the rural and urban areas of Cuttack district in the implementation of TLC Policy;

e) To identify the constraints/deficiencies in the process of implementation of TLC policy; and

f) To derive some suggestions for the improvement of the TLC Policy.

Review of Literature

Although the concept of 'civil society' and 'social capital' are much in vogue today and experts and authors frequently refer to these concepts in their intellectual discourse in India, there has been no significant work at the ground-level or at the empirical level. Theoretically, it is often repeated to resort to civil society for the deliverance of 'good' governance, particularly at implementation stage of public policies, but practically no work has been done to study the feasibility of this approach. There has been a few works on this field outside India but within India, and that too in a relatively under-developed State like Orissa, no empirical work has been done on this particular subject.

Based on available studies, a brief review of literature of contemporal relevance is presented here.

Robert D. Putnam in his book *Bowling Alone: The Collapse and Revival of American Community*[5] studies the state of contemporary American society and writes that Americans are now much less sociable, both formally and informally, than they were in the 1960s. Their 'civil engagements' in the present times has drastically declined and this applies to persons of all statuses, races and religions. To support his theoretical conclusions Putnam has elaborately conducted social surveys and empirical studies and has given statistical evidence to it. The decline of civic participation is attributed due to the generational change. The older generation had an obligation to the community life while the younger generation are more inclined to individualistic and materialistic values. The increased pressures on time and money in the 1970s and 1980s, the increased participation of women in the workforce, the consequences of sub-urbanisation, and the amount of time spent on viewing television programmes, are responsible for the decline of sociability and social capital. Putnam by his empirical analysis shows that with regard to low social capital places, people need to attend church two more times a month, or increase their turnout in presidential elections by 50 per cent.

Putnam with his seminal work *Making Democracy Work: Civic Traditions in Modern Italy*[6] set rolling the Bandwagon of 'social capital'. *The Economist* (London) described the book in a review as "the most important work of social science since Pareto and Max Weber".[7] The book focusses on the civic traditions and civic engagements in the context of the Italian society. In this book, Putnam through detailed empirical evidence concludes that there is better democratic government performance in north Italy in comparison to south Italy and this is attributed to the civil society functioning and the presence of social capital. The author very articulately traces the presence of social capital and how people, in general, get a responsive government. He also traces the historical roots of the Italian society in order to strengthen his arguments. The book also gives empirical findings at the grass-root level. The first chapter of this book goes through studying institutional performance and the concluding chapter is social capital and institutional success and in all the six chapters, Putnam very convincingly explores how presence of social capital gives better democratic governmental performance. The book has been referred in the subsequent chapters.

Charles Hardy in his book *Understanding Voluntary Organisations*[8] discuss the ways in which non-profit-making groups can function most efficiently. Voluntary Organisations can vary greatly in their aims and structure; some, for example, provide a service, others range from charities to self-help groups. The book deals with the management processes of such organisations in order to operate successfully. In the first part of the book, Charles Hardy deals with the staff, who works for Voluntary Organisations and looks at how they communicate and influence each other. Part two examines the culture and structure of the organisations themselves. This book provides an opportunity to have a first hand experience of working with the voluntary sector. In addition, the author suggests ways in which voluntary bodies might organise themselves that will influence others as patterns of work in our changing society. The book provides a bird's eye-view to Voluntary Organisations and a theoretical understanding to such organisations.

The book *Street Vendors: Organising Strategies – NIDAN*[9] relates Nidan's (a NGO) experiences with street vendors, the difficulties and achievements in organising the unorganised poor, both in urban and rural areas. The book deals with how the NGO was formed and it rendered service to the street vendors by creating self-help groups, arranging loans from SIDBI, convincing the Administrator of Patna Municipal Corporation to issue licences to the Vendors, beginning a census of all Vendors / Hawkers of Patna Municipal area limit and providing them with other income-generating sources. The book also deals how the NGO took up the course of eviction of five thousand slum-dwellers of Adalatganj and taking of legal recourse. The NGO also provided training on Co-operative Act and legal issues to the street vendors. In other words, the book describes how Nidan was completely dedicated for the upliftment and development of the street vendors/hawkers of Patna Municipal Corporation. The book is a short book but is a narration of the ground-level work undertaken by the NGO.

D.K. Oza in his book *Voluntary Action and Gandhian Approach*[10] studies three voluntary movements in India viz. the *Chipko* movement started by Shri Sunderlal Bahuguna for conservation of forests; the *Anandwan* by Baba Amte against leprosy; and the SEWA (Self-Employed Women's Association) by Smt. Ela R.Bhatt against exploitation of women workers, and how each of these movements were influenced by Gandhian thought and practical realities. The author very comprehensively analyses the role of Gandhi and gives examples of his activities and movements during the freedom struggle. Each of the leaders and their movements had traces of Gandhian voluntary approach. The author very minutely deals with the movements and while reading the book one observes that he mentions even the smallest activity undertaken by the leaders of the said movements.

Neera Chandhoke in her book *State and Civil Society: Explorations in Political Theory*[11] has dealt very exhaustively on the concept of Civil Society *vis-à-vis* the State. She analyses the role and importance of civil society in the present time. The book also gives a conceptual history and the theoretical groundwork for civil society. The author in the concluding part describes the usefulness of civil society to the individual and how civil society is being squeezed by 'particularistic loyalities' and the 'state'. The author says that to counteract it, the 'civil society has to constantly and consciously recreate spaces of freedom and equality'. She is of the view that the stabilisation of civil society is a pre-condition for the practices of democracy, and the existence of civil society is certainly one of the essential factors for democratic life. The author very lucidly analyses the different notions of civil society and states the relevance of civil society to 'collective projects' of human life. After going through the book one realises the immense impact of civil society on a community and the benefits of knitting the isolated individuals.

Alfred C. Tandau's book on *Policy Implementation in India: A Case Study*[12] deals with public policy and its stages of implementation. The book includes not only the role of executive but also that of legislative, judiciary, civil society and the citizens. The book contains primary data-based analysis of the policy implementation process. The problems confronted by the implementors on various course have been highlighted. The author, in the concluding chapter, draws some broad suggestions and key strategies so as to improve the policy implementation process. While concluding, he is of the view that policy implementation is not the end of policy-making but is rather a continuation of framing of policies through other means. Consequently, all efforts must be made to improve upon the implementation process so that not only the best results of the existing policies made could be attained but the exercise proves to be more fruitful for making the best policies in the times to come. It is praiseworthy to mention that even though the author is a Tanzanian, he has acquired a thorough and in-depth knowledge of Indian policy implementation process.

Peter John in his book *Analysing Public Policy*[13] studies the various approaches to public policy. The book suggests that there are two main sets of phenomena in public policy, which seek an explanation; policy variation and policy change. The book also analyses the causes of policy successes and failures and how democratic and accountable is public-policy making. The five main chapters of the book investigate each approach or theory. All offer compelling accounts of the policy process. Institutional approaches examine the constraints actors face, and take account of the norms and habits of policy-making in different political systems and policy sub-systems. Group accounts analyse alliance building, networking and mobilisation in public decision-making. Macro socio-economic accounts focus on the importance of socio-economic factors, both in terms of practical constraints on action and as ideologies. Rational choice theory investigates the preferences and choices of the actors themselves in the situations they face. Ideas based approaches appraise actors' beliefs and conceptions about policy. The book argues that the rational choice theory is capable of linking action to structure by explaining how agents respond to a range of constraints and more problematically, the theory seeks to understand how actors seek to shape those constraints. The book suggests that rational choice theory has the potential to offer a better explanation of the policy process than the others. The text draws on policy-making in local authorities in national governments and in the European Union, and selects some of the public policies. The implication of the book's argument is that the five approaches and their synthesis are applicable in any time or place as they are likely to be present in various combinations wherever policy is being made and implemented.

The book *Literacy and Empowerment*[14] co-authored by Venkatesh B. Athreya and Sheela Rani Chunkath is a brilliant exposition of literacy policy implementation in a backward district of Tamil Nadu (a South Indian State). The authors were directly involved in the literacy policy implementation in their official capacity as the first author was the State Co-ordinator of *Bharat Gyan Vigyan Samiti* (a leading NGO involved in literacy campaigns) and the later was the Collector and Chairperson of District Literacy Society and belongs to the IAS. They have not only described the literacy policy implementation but have also analysed it as well within the overall context of strategies for literacy and empowerment. The book is divided into three section. The first section traces India's adult education efforts within the larger framework of mass literacy campaigns. The authors present a detailed picture of literacy trends in India, both nationally and for Tamil Nadu in particular. The second section deals with the process of implementation. The final section is based on personal experience and critical evaluation of the district's literacy policy implementation. The authors are of the view that the combined energies of activists and a supportive administration helps to make a campaign successful as it has happened in the district of Pudukkotai, Tamil Nadu. The book is a blend of historical analysis, contemporary narrative and critical reflection of the literacy policy implementation. However, it seems that only because of the author's direct involvement in the literacy policy implementation process, it could be successful. Then, it also seems true for the reverse, i.e., direct involvement at the literacy policy implementation stage makes it successful.

The book *Social Change through Voluntary Action*[15] edited by M.L. Dantwala is a collection of essays written by experts and authors associated with voluntary activities. In the present gloomy and deteriorating situation in India's social and political ethos marked by apathy and cynicism, the contributors to this book maintain that there is reason to believe that voluntary action can be a potent instrument for bringing about social transformation, for eliminating poverty, and for building an egalitarian and humane society. To this end, they present convincing examples of successful socio-economic transformation brought about by a determined application of these ideals. Case studies like that of *Swadhyaya* Movement, Ralegan Siddhi, Aga Khan Rural Support Programme (a NGO in Gujarat), Sumangali Seva Ashram (a NGO working for women in rural and urban Bangalore), the Self-Employed Women's Association (in Gujarat) have been traced in the book. These case studies serve to highlight the viability of voluntarism as a social impulse suffused with the values of service and sacrifice; the significant change in the attitude of the people from apathy to active involvement when presented with unselfish leadership; and the evolution in the priorities of voluntary organisations from welfare and development to advocacy and the struggle for rights and entitlements, without giving up the earlier goals. The book emphasise that NGO's must evolve mechanisms to ensure transparency and accountability so as to maintain people's confidence on them. Rajni Kothari's reflective essay locates the larger phenomenon of voluntarism in the civilisational ethos of the Indian sub-continent and favours giving priority to civil society over the State. The book advocates voluntarism to be an alternative model of development.

Gaylord George Candler in a paper "The Professions and Public Policy: Expanding the Third Sector"[16] writes on the

Brazilian experience in order to broaden the focus of the international third sector literature. The paper studies the public-interest nature of social movements and NGO's. The first part of this paper seeks to show that numerous policy-relevant groups beyond the NGO/social movement ambit have long existed in Brazil and introduces the reader to the professional associations that are discussed throughout the article. The next section discusses the autonomy of these professional associations by demonstrating that, contrary to the traditional elite, they have often acted in the broader public interest. The final section shifts to the local level, using the activities of these groups in the State of Santa Catarina to show that the Brazilian third sector is best seen not in opposition to the State, but as working with the State as part of the dense policy networks that include business and non-profit groups as well. The paper describes how professional associations along with NGO's and social movements associate themselves by networks so as to influence policy decision.

Kenneth Newton's article on "Social Capital and Democracy"[17] starts by picking out three different aspects or dimensions of the concept of social capital, viz., norms (especially trust), networks and consequences. It then considers three models of social capital and the forms of trust and democracy associated with them, viz.: (a) communal society, mechanical solidarity, "thick" trust, and primary democracy; (b) voluntary associations, organic solidarity, and "thin" trust; and (c) modern democracy, imaginary communities, abstract trust, education and the media. Finally it discusses the role of voluntary associations as a foundation for social capital, arguing that their importance may be overstated in the classical Tocquevillean model of the 19th century and that, in any case, modern democracy may be increasingly based on different forms of trust and association.

Vimala Ramachandran in an article "Adult Education: A Tale of Empowerment Denied"[18] outlines the efforts of the Government for adult education through National Adult

Education Programme (NAEP) and which later assumed adult literacy due to the Total Literacy Campaign (TLC). He attributes the failure of these programmes due to corruption and grants-in-aid besides the stress on the commitment of individual administrators rather than on system reform. The paper briefly describes the literacy programme and process. The author, however, agrees that the literacy programme had a spin-off effect and that was the empowerment of women and their consciousness. The Anti-arrack movement of women in Nellore district of Andhra Pradesh in 1992 was a result of the literacy classes and this movement completed the State Government to declare prohibition in April 1993. The self-help groups among women, which led to the birth of the savings movement, were also an offshoot of literacy classes. In Tamil Nadu, the literacy campaign enabled the women to ride bicycles and it became an instrument of empowerment for women in this area. The author writes that the literacy campaign changed the lives of women in Nellore (Andhra Pradesh) and Pudukkotai (Tamil Nadu) districts and the classes opened the window to the outside world for women, in general. However, the author is in a pessimistic mood and blames the Government and the bureaucrats for not sustaining the tempo for literacy campaigns as they lack dedication to their service. The author, while concluding, is of the view that today we need dedicated accountable bureaucrats, transparent processes and systems, programmes that are not dependent on the individual commitment but on group commitment.

Sudha Sundararaman in her article "Literacy Campaigns: Lessons for Women's Movement" [19] attributes the literacy campaign for an unprecedented national mobilisation of women and rural youth. The literacy campaign had an effect not only on literacy and primary education but also in a number of other development areas. She focuses on five themes, which are relevant for further study and these are (i) mobilisation of women in the literacy campaign; (ii) opposition to literacy campaigns; (iii) impact on women's empowerment; (iv) decline of Total Literacy Campaign; and (v) lessons for the future. She writes that the literacy groups, in a way, acted as women's first experience of organisation in a myriad number of ways. She also gives some empirical evidences in support of her themes like decline of wife beating in Podicherry, Anti-arrack movement in Andhra Pradesh and Tamil Nadu. Credit Co-operatives for economic development of women, conversion of the literacy movement into a women's employment generation programme in Madurai, larger women representation in the Panchayati system in Madhya Pradesh. Women development through literacy campaign also took place at Madhepura in Bihar State. For the decline in the campaign, the author blames lack of political will except in West Bengal, dedication on the part of NGO's and volunteers, bureaucratisation of the campaign programe, and lack of committed bureaucrats. However, she is optimistic about the campaign, if NGO's are more involved in it. To her, literacy is a learning skill, a tool to unlock many wide areas of knowledge and capabilities that are essential for survival as well as for building a society without discrimination.

Chandan Sengupta and M.N. Roy is an article "Sociological Impact of Total Literacy Campaign – The Case of Midnapore"[20] write about the social consequences of a total literacy campaign in Midnapore, the largest district of West Bengal in terms of both area and population. The paper mainly examines the impact of the TLC on the collective consciousness of the people as well as on the political consciousness, social awareness and functionality among the neo-literates. The Midnapore literacy programmes was conceived and launched voluntarily by the district planning committee and it was a people's programme i.e. the need should be felt by every participant and she should not only accept it as her own programme but would also enrich and sustain the same till the ultimate objective is achieved. The authors discuss the role of the various political parties in making the programme successful. They write that there was collective consciousness at political party level, at administrative level, and at the grass-roots level. The formation of village committees was one of the important features in this campaign. It was through these village-based organisational power that the mass movement for the literacy campaign could be utilised for socio-economic development of the villages. They also acknowledge that the sociological impact was too much higher in the case of women, SCs and STs but it was lower in the case of the artisan and similar backward castes.

S.P. Punalekar in an article "On Dialectics of Voluntary Organisations and Social Change"[21] writes on relationship between Voluntary Organisations (VOs) and social change, and covers briefly an overview of role and relevance of VOs in the context of changes occuring in the Third World including Indian sub-continent. He draws a historical review of the emergence of VOs in India. He writes that the institutional arrangement of the State failed to reach very nook and corner for which VOs were necessitated and there also existed a conducive environment for the growth of VOs. He writes that the emergence and growth of VOs in recent times are largely attributable to serious disjunctions and distortions in the development paradigm itself, where the poor and marginalised received the least attention. There was a breakdown of communication between them. The VOs having financial support and grants and believing in the tasks of mobilisation and conscientisation of the masses or their specific target groups, work for development and welfare of people. He writes on the problems and prospects of Asian VO's in general, how there is increasing alliances and networking among the VO's in the Third World. He is of the view that VOs have vital and somewhat decisive presence on the Indian soil which may be due to serious and critical flaws in political governance and management of economy by the state and its ruling interests. VO's are also helping the government to save its face and to keep its legitimacy unchallenged and untainted. While concluding, he writes that the success of VO's committed to emancipatory goals lies in evolution and consolidation of mass politics, the disclosure of politics cannot be disentangled from the politics of discourse. Social transformation must be the task willfully chosen by the masses themselves. It should be their agenda and aspiration; their mandate and mission.

Gurpreet Mahajan's article "Civil Society and its Avatars– What Happened to Freedom and Democracy ?"[22] analyses the debate around state-civil society relationship in modern Western and Indian political discourse, and points out the gap between the 18th and 19th century political thinking and later 20th century political thought. The second half of the 20th century, the author writes, is characterised by a loss of faith in the institutions of the state and looks towards civil society to preserve essential human and democratic rights. As against this, the paper advocates a return to an earlier right-based conception of civility by enforcing universal laws through the instruments of the state. Since the state alone can create conditions necessary to protect the institutions of civil society from internal disruptions, the paper argues against detachment of civil society from the State. Instead, the author writes, the institutions of civil society are very much part of democratic constitutional State, which alone will ensure social equality and non-discrimination along with individual liberty.

John Harriss in his book *Depoliticizing Development:The World Bank & Social Capital*[23] explores the origins of the idea of the social capital and its diverse meanings. His book asks why it is that such an apparently commonplace idea should have been elaborated and made complicated and mystifying – in the way that it has been, and it explores the purposes that are served by it. In the end, the book aims to show how the work of often very clever and well-intentioned social scientists derives from and contributes to a hegemonic social science that systematically obscures, power, class and politics. The book argues, "Social capital and the closely related idea of 'trust', and the ideas and activities around 'civil society' (held to be the sphere of association, outside the state, in which people freely participate), 'participation', and non-governmental organisations have come to constitute new weapons in the armoury of 'the anti-politics machine' that is constituted by the practices of 'international development'. They are clever ideas which suit the interests of global capitalism (or in other words, present-day, US-centered imperialism) because they represent problems that are rooted in differences of power and in class relations as purely technical matters that can be resolved outside the political arena. They are directed in particular, therefore, against movements of the political left for progressive socio-political and economic change, that do identify the roots of poverty and social deprivation in class differences". In conclusion, Harriss writes that in the contemporary discourse on development articulated in international agencies, notably the World Bank, there is a good deal of emphasis upon the virtues of 'participation', sometimes taken as implying also 'empowerment', and upon 'decentralisation', which is seen either as the key means of realising participation or sometimes as being more or less equivalent to it. These three buzz-words are used in close alliance with 'social capital' and 'civil society'. He writes, "these ideas are painted as being 'progressive' and they are deceptively attractive. They are attractive because they imply active support for the ideas and the needs and the aspirations of the common people. Can one possibly be against participation and empowerment? But these ideas are deceptive because they are used to veil the nature and the effects of power, and—as I have argued in this book—they hold out the prospects of democracy (in 'civil society') without the inconveniences of contestational politics and of the conflicts of ideas and interests that are an essential part of democracy". He quotes Michael Edwards and David Hulme, who concede that, "there is increasing evidence that NGOs and grass-roots organisations do not perform as effectively as (has) been assumed in terms of poverty-reach, cost-effectiveness, sustainability, popular participation (including gender), flexibility and innovation"[24] and –as avowed partisans –they recognise that NGOs must address the problems surrounding their democratic accoutability, and their relations to the political process. While being highly critical of 'social capital', Harriss is of the view,

"A good deal of the policy literature on social capital reflects the idea of 'people pulling themselves together from below without much help from government or their privileged fellow citizens' –which is so convenient for those who benefit from cuts in social expenditure"[25]

Methodology

Considering the nature of the theme, an empirical method was adopted for the present attempt and two areas viz.: Tangi Block and Cuttack City were selected from the district of Cuttack, the former representing the rural area and the later the urban area. To get indepth understanding at the grassroot level, the study concentrated in two Gram Panchayats of Tangi Block and four Wards at Cuttack Municipal area.

The methodology to carry out this study was through open-ended structured schedules with the members of Voluntary Association and Informal Associations and with the neo-literates (the beneficiaries) covered under the TLC Policy. Interviews, group discussions and observation techniques were also adopted. Also, available secondary data from various sources have been made use wherever it was necessary for this study.

Hypotheses

1) Social Capital facilitates co-ordinated actions.
2) It helps formulating public policy.
3) The success of the implementation of the public policy depends to a large extent on the articulation and mobilization of Social Capital.
4) Human Capital and Social Capital reinforce one another.
5) Social Capital promotes the implementation of the public policy.

AREA UNDER STUDY: SAMPLE AND COVERAGE

The total population of undivided Cuttack district is 5,522,659 out of which 2,814,589 are males and 2,708,070 are females, according to 1991 Census. The number of females per 1,000 males is 964. The rural sex-ratio is 987, while urban sex-ratio is 820. The total population was distributed into 48,44,040 as rural and 678,619 as urban. There are 6,030 inhabited and 539 uninhabited villages in the district. There are 13 towns and one city in undivided Cuttack district. The Scheduled Tribes population according to 1991 Census is 1,82,188 in undivided Cuttack district. The major tribes found are Bhumij, Kandha, Kolab, Matya, Ho, Santal and Shabar. The Scheduled Castes population of the undivided district is 1,124,160. Some of the SCs include Adi Andhra, Baghuti, Bauri, Chambar, Pana and Tiar. The Literacy percentage according to 1991 census is 53.36% in the undivided Cuttack district. Among males it is 63.7% and among females it is 42.63%.

The Total urban Scheduled Caste (S.C.) population of undivided Cuttack district is 90,273 of which 59,591 persons i.e. 12.27% live in divided Cuttack district. Jajpur has the lowest S.C. population in comparison to other districts.

The urban Scheduled Tribe (S.T.) population of undivided Cuttack district is 20,431. Jagatsinghpur district has the highest S.T. population i.e. 8531 persons of which 4470 are males and 4061 are females. It is closely followed by divided Cuttack district which has 8253 S.T. persons of which 4647 are males and 3606 are females. The overall data show that the divided Cuttack district is the most urbanised area and the other three districts have more or less the same level of urbanisation. All the four districts have a healthy male to female urban population ratio. Compared to the overall urban population of the four districts, we note that the ST population is very less. This shows that the urban areas of Cuttack have attracted few tribals.

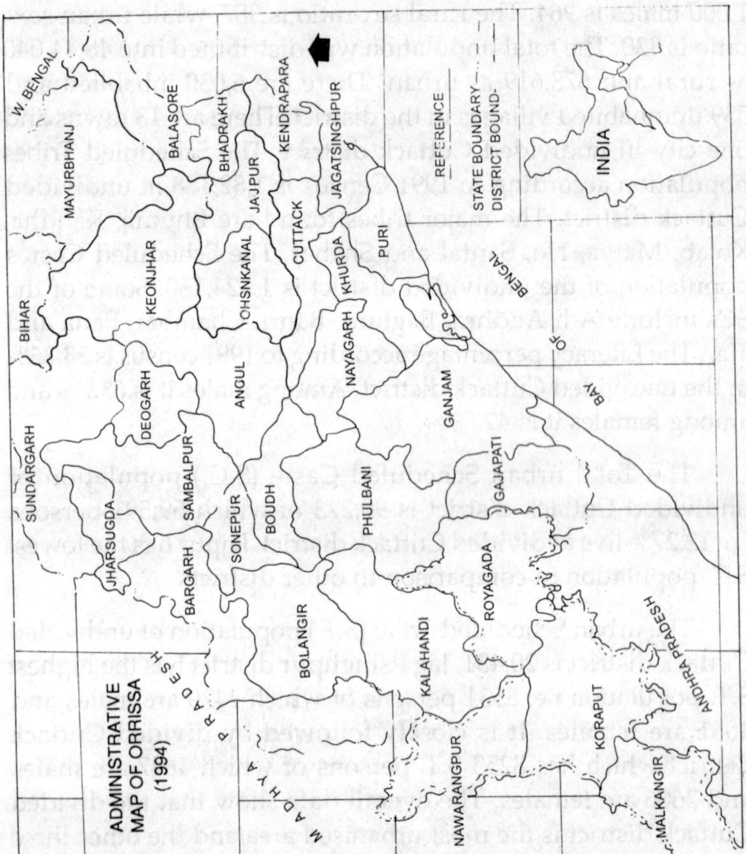
ADMINISTRATIVE MAP OF ORRISSA (1994)
W. BENGAL
MAYURBHANJ
BALASORE
BHADRAKH
KENDRAPARA
JAGATSINGHPUR
JAJPUR
CUTTACK
KEONJHAR
OHSNKANAL
KHURDA
PURI
BIHAR
DEOGARH
ANGUL
NAYAGARH
GANJAM
SUNDARGARH
SAMBALPUR
JHARSUGDA
BARGARH
SONEPUR
BOUDH
PHULBANI
GAJAPATI
ROYAGADA
BOLANGIR
KALAHANDI
NAWARANGPUR
KORAPUT
MALKANGIR
ANDHRA PRADESH
MADHYA PRADESH
BAY OF BENGAL
REFERENCE
STATE BOUNDARY
DISTRICT BOUND-
INDIA

Fig. 1

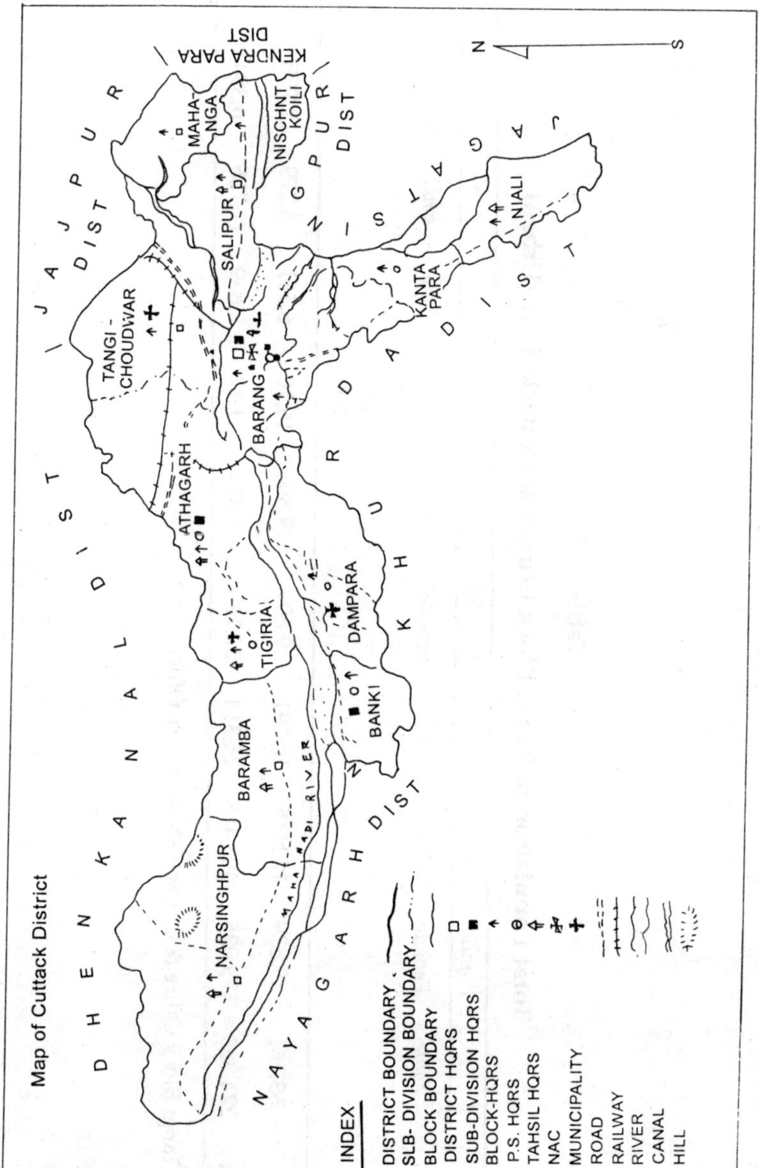
Map of Cuttack District
DHENKANAL DIST
JAJPUR DIST
KENDRA PARA DIST
JAGATSINGHPUR DIST
KHURDA DIST
NAYAGARH DIST
NARSINGHPUR
BARAMBA
TIGIRIA
ATHAGARH
TANGI-CHOUDWAR
BARANG
SALIPUR
MAHANGA
NISCHNT KOILI
KANTA PARA
NIALI
DAMPARA
BANKI
MAHA NADI RIVER
N
S
INDEX
DISTRICT BOUNDARY
SLB- DIVISION BOUNDARY
BLOCK BOUNDARY
DISTRICT HQRS
SUB-DIVISION HQRS
BLOCK-HQRS
P.S. HQRS
TAHSIL HQRS
NAC
MUNICIPALITY
ROAD
RAILWAY
RIVER
CANAL
HILL

Table-1

Total Population of Tangi Block (Rural) & Cuttack City (Urban)

Area	*Population*			*SC*				*ST*			
	Male	*Female*	*Total*	*Male*	*Female*	*Total*	*% to Total Population*	*Male*	*Female*	*Total*	*% to Total Population*
Tangi	63,161	59,839	122,999	10,191	9,609	19,800	16,10	6,511	6,279	12,790	10.40
Cuttack	224,383	179,035	403,418	25,314	22,160	47,474	11.17	3,639	2,755	6,394	1.58

Source : Tangi Block Office & Cuttack Municipality Office.

The overall S.C. and S.T. population of the undivided Cuttack district is about 22% of the total population of which the majority are SC persons. The same holds true for all the four divided districts. Jajpur district has a greater concentration of ST population compared to the other three districts. The male-female ratio of the SC's and ST's are more or less the same throughout the undivided Cuttack district.

For both Cuttack urban and rural areas we have selected, from each area 100 sample respondents who are members of voluntary associations both formal and informal. Stratified random sampling of the members of voluntary associations involved in TLC program has been adopted for the selection of sample respondents. The voluntary associations involved in TLC program were obtained from the TLC Control Room Office, Cuttack. Out of the 100 sample respondents for urban area we have specifically selected 40 female members of Women's Voluntary Associations as our respondents. For rural area, even though there are a number of existing voluntary associations but none of them are actively involved in TLC program. Their involvement is limited up to mobilisation and motivation of the illiterates. However, during our interaction with block level officials and Master Trainers (MT), we knew that informal associations like village committees, religious associations, youth associations, peasant associations, women associations and political party activists get themselves involved in TLC program. So, we have included them as our respondents in rural area. We have also included the informal association of Voluntary Teachers (VT) involved in TLC program. These informal associations act as voluntary associations and the members volunteer themselves for any community work. Contact with the members was established in their association office and also in their residences. The respondents responded to the open-ended structured questionnaire supplied by us for necessary information. Question regarding personal profile were also inquired.

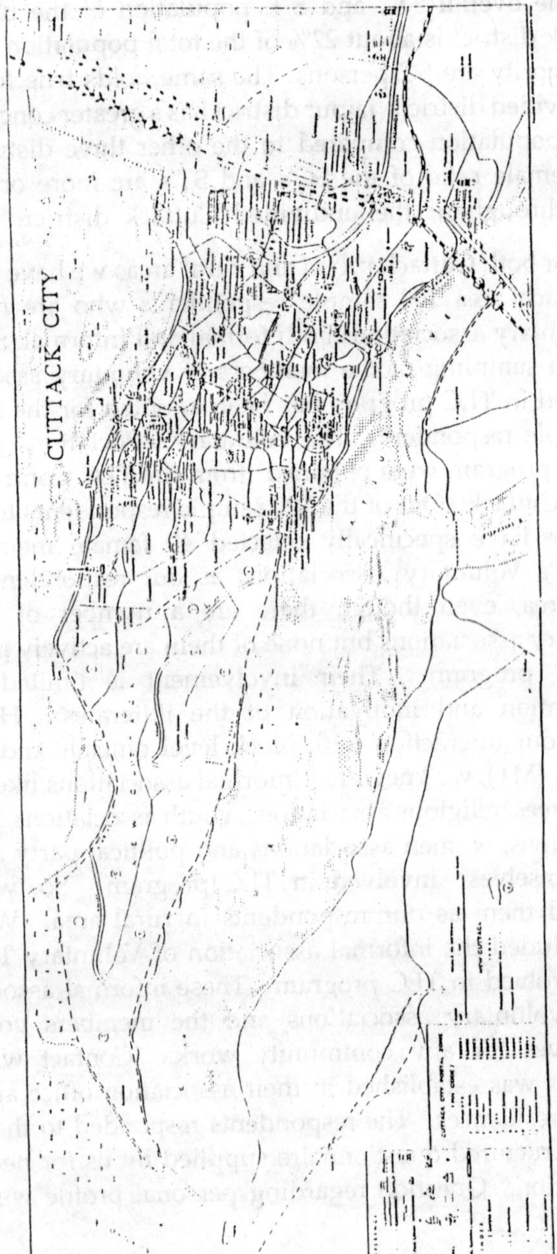
CUTTACK CITY

TANGI BLOCK

The Block is one of the fourteen blocks of the Cuttack district. On 2nd October,1960 the Block was carved out of the district. It has a total geographical area of 324.78 Sq. Km. The total number of Gram Panchayats is 20 and the total number of villages are 177 out of which 152 villages are inhabited and 25 villages are uninhabited. The total population of the Block as per 1991 census is 122,999 persons out of which 63,161 persons are males and 59,838 are females. The total number of Scheduled Caste (SC) persons is 19,800 out of which 10,191 are males and 9,609 are females. The total Scheduled Tribe (ST), population in the block is 12,790 out of which 6,511 persons are males and 6,279 are females. The percentage of SC & ST population to total population of the block is 16.10% and 10.40% respectively. Out of the total twenty Gram Panchayats, we have selected two Gram Panchayats viz. Kotasahi Gram Panchayat and Safa Gram Panchayat for our empirical study.

CUTTACK CITY

Cuttack City is one of the seven urban areas of the district. It has a total geographical area of 121.91 Sq. Kms. The total number of municipality wards of the city is 48. The total population of the city as per 1991 census is 403,418 persons out of which 224,383 are males and 179,035 are females. The total number of Scheduled Castes (SC) are 47,474 persons out of which 25,314 are males and 22,160 are females. The total Scheduled Tribe (ST) population is 6,394 out of which 3,639 persons are males and 2,755 persons are females. The percentage of SC & ST population to the total population of the City is 11.77% and 1.58% respectively. Out of the total 48 Municipal Wards of Cuttack Municipal Area we have selected 4 Wards viz; Ward No. 6, Ward No. 9, Ward No. 18 & Ward No. 32.

Table 2 shows the literacy rate to the total population, SC population & ST population in the Tangi Block (Rural) and Cuttack Municipal Area (Urban). It is seen that Cuttack City has a high literacy rate in comparison to Tangi Block.

Table - 2

Literacy Rate

Area	*Total*			*SC*			*ST*		
	Male	*Female*	*Total*	*Male*	*Female*	*Total*	*Male*	*Female*	*Total*
Tangi	74.16	48.83	61.84	61.04	30.44	46.25	27.62	06.37	17.28
Cuttack	85.57	71.86	79.57	65.84	42.69	55.18	53.54	23.77	41.23

Source : Tangi Block Office & Cuttack Municipality Office

Table 3 shows the total number of Primary Schools, Middle Schools, Secondary Schools and Colleges in Tangi Block and Cuttack City. Primary Schools have teaching facility upto Class-V, Middle School have teaching facility upto Class-VII, Secondary School have teaching facility upto matriculation i.e. Class-X and Colleges have teaching facility upto Post-Graduation/M.Phil level. In Tangi Block the Colleges have teaching facility upto Graduation level.

Table 3

Number of Primary , Middle & Secondary Schools & Colleges

Area	*Primary School*	*Middle School*	*Secondary School*	*Colleges*
Tangi	139	41	27	04
Cuttack	118	42	38	14

Source : Tangi Block Office & Cuttack Municipality Office.

Table 4

Health Facility in Tangi & Cuttack City

Area	*Hospital*	*Dispensary*	*P.H.C &.*	*P.H.C Addl. P.H.C*
Tangi	01	--	03	01
Cuttack	10	02	05	--

Source : Tangi Block Office & Cuttack Municipality.

The above Table 4 shows the availability of health facility in the Tangi Block and Cuttack City.

Table 5

Classification of Main Workers in Tangi Block & Cuttack City

Area	*Total Population*	*Cultivators*	*Agricultural Labourers*	*Livestock*	*Mining / Quarrying*	*Manufacturing Processing, Servicing & Repairs*	*Construction*	*Trade & Commerce*	*Transport, Storage & Communicate*	*Other Services*
Tangi	122499	11840 (9.63%)	10387 (8.44%)	624 (0.51%)	249 (0.20%)	4365 (3.55%)	396 (0.32%)	2435 (1.98%)	754 (0.61%)	3303 (2.69%)
Cuttack	403418	849 (0.21%)	1705 (0.42%)	2665 (0.66%)	141 (0.04%)	22177 (5.50%)	3758 (0.93%)	33301 (8.26%)	12757 (3.16%)	44956 -11.14%

Source: Tangi Block Office & Cuttack Municipality Office.

Table 6

Population of the Selected Gram Panchayats in Tangi Block

Area	*Population*			
	General	*SC*	*ST*	*Total*
Kotasahi G.P	6652	1329	215	8196
Safa G.P	4000	405	4051	8453

Source: Tangi Block Office & Cuttack Municipality Office.

Table 7

Population of the Selected Municipal Wards in Cuttack City

Area	*Population*			
	General	*SC*	*ST*	*Total*
Ward No. 6	8021	496	18	8535
Ward No. 9	5683	3168	08	8859
Ward No.18	11214	1146	24	12384
Ward No.32	11954	1546	798	14298

Source: Tangi Block Office & Cuttack Municipality Office.

Table 8

No. of Schools & Colleges in the Selected Gram Panchayats

Area	*Primary School*	*Middle School*	*High School*	*College*
Kotasahi G.P	07	--	01	01
Safa G.P	07	03	02	01

Source: Tangi Block Office & Cuttack Municipality Office.

Table 9

No. of Schools & Colleges in the Selected Municipal Wards

Area	*Primary School*	*Middle School*	*High School*	*College*
Ward No.6	02	03	01	01
Ward No.9	03	01	02	00
Ward No.18	02	05	02	01
Ward No.32	02	02	01	00

Source: Tangi Block Office & Cuttack Municipality Office.

We have also selected 100 neo-literate as sample respondents from each urban and rural area, who have been covered under TLC program. Responses were obtained in a similar manner.

Table 10
Socio-economic Data of the Members of Voluntary Associations

Variables	*Particulars*	*Urban*		*Rural*	
		Number	*Total*	*Number*	*Total*
Gender	Male	60	100	90	100
	Female	40		10	
Marital-Status	Married	62	100	86	100
	Unmarried	14		04	
	Widow	18		00	
	Divorcee	06		10	
Religion	Hindu	58	100	86	100
	Muslim	16		14	
	Christian	14		00	
	Sikh	04		00	
	Buddhist/Jain	08		00	
Caste	General	52	100	28	100
	OBC	34		34	
	SC	10		14	
	ST	04		24	
Occupation	Govt.Service	46	100	22	100
	Private Service	20		08	

(Contd.)

	Professional	16		60	
	House wife	18		10	
Age	30-40 years	10	100	24	100
	40-50 years	44		54	
	50-60 years	34		12	
	60 and above	12		10	

Source : Field Survey.

Table 11

Socio-economic Data of the Neo-literate Covered under TLC Policy

Variables	*Particulars*	*Urban*		*Rural*	
		Number	*Total*	*Number*	*Total*
Gender	Male	60	100	100	100
	Female		40		
Marital Status	Married	64	100	92	100
	Unmarried	20		00	
	Widow	08		08	
	Divorcee	12		00	
Religion	Hindu	58	100	80	100
	Muslim	30		20	
	Christian	12		00	
	Sikh	00		00	
	Buddhist/Jain	00		00	
Caste	General	36	100	26	100
	OBC	40		24	
	SC	20		18	
	ST	04		32	
Occupation	Daily-Labourer	54	100	58	100
	Child-Labourer	08		00	
	Private-Service	12		12	
	House Wife	26		30	
Age	9-15 years	16	100	00	100
	15-25 years	12		16	
	25-35 years	30		50	
	35-45 years	28		20	
	45-55 years	14		14	

REFERENCES

1. Fine, Ben, (2001), 'Social Capital and Realm of the Intellect', *Economic and Political Weekly*, Vol. XXXVI, No. 9, 3rd March, p. 741.

2. Tornquist, Olle (1999), *Politics and Development*, Sage, London, p. 94.

3. Lijphart, Arend (1977), *Democracy in Plural Societies*, Yale University Press, Yale, p. 3.

4. Blomkvist, Hans (1996), *Democracy and Social Capital, Agora Project*, Deptt. of Government, Uppsala University, Uppsala, p. 19.

5. Putnam, Robert D. (2000), *Bowling Alone: The Collapse and Revival of American Community*, Simon and Suchuster, New York.

6. Putnam, Robert D. (1993), *Making Democracy Work: Civic Traditions in Modern Italy*, Princeton University Press, New Jersey.

7. Quoted by H John Havris in *Frontline* (2000), November 10, Vol.17, No. 22, Kasturi & Sons Ltd., p. 77.

8. Hardy, Charles (1990), *Understanding Voluntary Organisations*, Penguin, London.

9. *Street Vendors: Organising Strategies - NIDAN* (1998), Published by Friedrich Ebert Stiftung, New Delhi.

10. Oza, D.K. (1991), *Voluntary Action and Gandhian Approach*, National Book Trust, New Delhi.

11. Chandhoke, Nerra (1995), *State and Civil Society: Explorations in Political Theory*, Sage, New Delhi.

12. Tandau, Alfred C. (1996), *Policy Implementation in India: A Case Study*, Vikas Publishing House, New Delhi.

13. John, Peter (1998), *Analysing Public Policy*, Pinter, London.

14. Athreya, Venkatesh B., & Chunkath, Sheela Rani (1996), *Literacy and Employment*, Sage Publications, New Delhi.

15. Dantwala, M.L. *et al.* (1998), *Social Change through Voluntary Action*, Sage Publications, New Delhi.

16. Candler, Gaylord George (2000), "The Professions and Public Policy: Expanding the Third Sector", *International Political Science Review*, Vol.21, No.1, London, pp. 43-58.

17. Newton, Kenneth (1997), "Social Capital and Democracy", *American Behavioural Scientist*, Vol. 40, No. 5, Sage Publication, California, pp. 575-86.

18. Ramachandran, Vimala (1999), "Adult Education: A Tale of Empowerment Denied", *Economic and Political Weekly*, Vol. XXXIV, April,10, pp. 877-882.

19. Sudararaman, Sudha (1996), "Literacy Campaigns: Lessons for Women's Movement", *Economic and Political Weekly*, Vol. XXXI, May,18, pp. 1193-1197.

20. Sengupta, Candan, & Roy, M.N. (1996), "Sociological Impact of Total Literacy Campaign—The case of Midnapur", *Economic and Political Weekly*, Vol. XXXI, February, 24, pp. 484-88.

21. Punalekar, S.P. (1997), "On Dialectic of Voluntary Organisations and Social Change", *IASSI Quarterly*, Vol. 15, No. 4, pp. 67-90.

22. Mahajan, Gurpreet (1999), "Civil Society and its Avatars: What Happened to Freedom and Democrcy?", *Economic and Political Weekly*, Vol. XXXIV, May 15, pp. 1188-96.

23. Harriss, John (2001), *Depoliticizing Development: The World Bank & Social Capital*, Left World, New Delhi.

24. Edwards, M. & D. Hulme (eds.) (1995), *Non-Governmental Organisations—Performance and Accountability: Beyond the Magic Bullet*, Earthscan Publications, London, p. 6.

25. Harriss, J., *op. cit*, p. 122.

2

SOCIAL CAPITAL—A CONCEPTUAL ANALYSIS

The relationship between 'social' and 'capital' is neither divergent not antithetical. It is complementary, reciprocal and mutually reinforcing. The word 'social capital' captures the imagination of many with plural meanings in different contexts. It is common for many to understand the terms 'social' and 'capital' but becomes a bit baffling to analyse the concept social capital – a compound. It is an intrinsic component of civil society. It is an essential motivating force for action. If we add 'ism' to both the words it becomes antithetical. Every social system subscribes a political system and an economic system. The political system may be based on Weber's classification of rational-legal, traditional or charismatic legitimacy. The economic system may be based on from the ancient barter system to the present market system. Hence the three systems are inter-dependent in one form or another and cannot be separated from one another. In this perspective, the term 'social capital' creates confusion in the minds of people who are not aware of it. An adequate understanding of the concept requires a systematic analysis of its meaning, types and forms in relation to civil society.

The term 'social capital' may be new to some and might create some amount of confusion in them. They might consider it to be an ambiguous term and dub it as a camouflaged intention. The term 'social and capital' are easily understandable but an integration of both, which is considered to be antithetical by some, may lead to some sort of suspicion. 'Social' and 'Capital' are the central key concepts in the disciplines of Sociology and Economics, respectively. The distance between these two disciplines, as they have developed in the post-war world, was pithily expressed as long ago as 1960, when James S. Duesenberry commented, after hearing the young Gary Becker, the Nobel prize-winner and a leading advocate of neo-classical approach, that 'Economics is all about how people make choices. Sociology is all about why they don't have any choices to make'.

To begin with, in simple terms, we can say that social capital refers to the communal resources that a community possesses which is very much intangible but which yields tangible results when effectively utilised. Thus differing from human capital and physical capital. Robert Putnam in his path-breaking study on modern Italian society writes, "social capital refers to features of social organisation, such as trust, norms and networks, that can improve the efficiency of society, by facilitating coordinated actions".[1] The concept of social capital refers to three features of social life–interpersonal trust, networks and shared norms – that enable people to act together more effectively to pursue shared objectives.[2] It is the set of resources that inhere in the family relations and in community social organisation.[3] According to Coleman, "social Capital is defined by its function. It is not a single entity, but a variety of different entities having two characteristics in common. They all consist of some aspect of social structure, and they facilitate certain actions of individuals who are within the structure....Unlike other forms of capital, social capital inheres in the structure of relations between persons and among persons".[4] Coleman gives the credit of introducing the term 'Social Capital' to Glenn Loury. In Loury's usage social capital is that set of resources that inhere in family relations and community social organisation and that are useful for the cognitive or social development of a child or young person. These resources differ for different persons and can constitute an important advantage for children and adolescents in the development of their human capital. The forms of social capital are the relations of authority, of trust and of the norms.[5] Loury introduced the concept of 'social capital' into economics to identify the social resources useful for the development of human capital. Human capital signifies the talent and knowledge an individual has or acquires and this is further enriched by social capital. Social capital is not locked in the actors themselves but in structures of relations among the actors, making otherwise unattainable ends within reach.[6] Social capital facilitates cooperation and coordination among individual or groups of individual for achieving the greater common interest among them through voluntary initiatives. For this, Putnam writes, "voluntary cooperation is easier in a community that has inherited a substantial stock of social capital, in the form of norms of reciprocity and networks of civic engagement".[7] Social capital, in this sense is a set of structural requisites that refines or strengthens the functional ability of a social system. Every society has a certain degree of social capital present in its members in the form of family relationships, kinships, friendships, the typical ancient Indian system of *Jajmani*, which is present even today in some parts of India. These features of social system are however individual-oriented and not group-oriented. It gives personal benefits to the person's concerned ignoring the mass of the society. When the question of the mass arose, their welfare/wellbeing, the above-mentioned features remained silent. In a way it can be correct to mark these features as selfish and self-oriented features. It looked after the petty gains of the persons concerned and not to the larger interests of the society.

Social capital cannot exist in a vacuum. It is a subjective phenomenon depending on the citizen's values and attitudes towards a sense of trust, reciprocity and mutuality leading to cooperation among them. "Treated in this way, social capital focuses on those cultural values and attitudes that predispose citizens to cooperate, trust, understand, and empathize with each other – to treat each other as fellow citizens, rather than as strangers, competitors or political enemies. Therefore, social capital is important because it constitutes a force that helps to bind society together by transforming individuals from self-seeking and ego-centric calculators, with little social conscience or sense of mutual obligation, into members of a community with shared interests, shared assumptions about social relations and a sense of the common good. Trust and reciprocity are crucial aspects of social capital".[8] Social capital in this way broadens the horizon of the people and ordains a feeling of goodwill and mutual preservation. It has thus a quality of integration and helps to the growth of the unity and brotherhood of people. Social capital is primarily defined as inter-personal trust that makes it easier for people to do things together, neutralise free riders, and, for instance, agree on sanctions against non-performing governments.

The sense of reciprocal feeling generating trust and networks among individuals necessitates the presence of a civil society for the growth of social capital. Putnam concludes that long-standing norms of reciprocity among the citizens and networks of civic engagement is what is making democracy work in northern Italy. To him, reciprocal and trustworthy relationships between citizens, supported by mores and free associations make democracy strong. He stresses on the importance of civil society for government performance and development. Unless people obey the civic virtues and act according to certain norms and mutuality, social capital is bound to deteriorate and fade. Liberal democracy, adopted by many nations, both developed and developing, needs not only elections but also is connected to various rights and liberties and constitutional privileges. The Constitution of such countries prescribes certain rights and duties to the citizens and these cannot be violated by the State or more particularly by the persons running the administration. Remedial measures are also provided in the Constitution so that a citizen is not deprived of his rights and liberties. The presence of a strong civil society *suo-motto* guarantees unhindered rights and liberties to the citizens thereby forbidding the State to act against the citizen.

Various scholars have defined the term 'Civil Society' and it remains a debatable question whether the 'Civil Society' is within the purview of the state or outside its purview. According to Axel Hadenius and Fredrik Uggla, the concept of civil society denote (a) a certain area of society, which is (b) dominated by interaction of a certain kind.[10] The area here refers to the gap between the State and the individual citizen. The activities undertaken are organised, collective and coordinated and have a positive consequence on the citizens. They opine that the civil society is free and independent and outside the realm of the State. Whenever people form a group to achieve some common objective a civil society is formed. It may manifest in different forms starting from a sociable nature to cultural activities or may be political or apolitical with a variegated membership and organisational structure. Certain external factors help for the growth of civil activities. One of those is cooperation and trust leading to civil networks. Once they are established then, social networks can set a dynamic, self-reinforcing process in motion.[11] The coming together of people enable them power resources and the ability to bargain for their interests against other groups and the State. An advanced civil society – one characterised by a multiplicity of well-developed popular associations – forms a bull-work against despotic tendencies in political life and serves as well as defense against oppression and discrimination in the intercourse of social groups.[12] The organisations must be autonomous and plural, have a democratic structure, which will lead to the democratisation process in the country, a broad popular base, an open recruitment of members and the ability to balance between different power centres, interests and opinions. If these criteria are in a large part fulfilled – which signifies a high degree of civicness on part of the organisation in question, a critical support for the development of political democracy is furnished thereby.[13] Organisations networking people prove the later with power and skills necessary for controlling the state that wields control over them. However, according to them, it is not uni-directional but the "relationship between state and civil society is of a mutual (or recursive) nature".[14] The primary requisite for civil society is autonomy but this autonomy is relative due to direct cooperation, funding, facilitation and may also be due to patriotic and nationalist feelings inherent in citizens. The state also requires the assistance of organisations to pursue its developmental and welfare policies and programme. A healthy partnership between the two can yield better results and can make things, which organisations want for the betterment of the collectivity. The two, therefore, should be evenly poised and the state should try to seek the cooperation of such organisations, which have genuine interest for development and thereby can transform the idea of "developmental state" into a reality. Many times this has taken place and there are also instances where the State has calculatively succeeded in suppressing and eliminating the development of civil society. State and Civil Society cannot be viewed as binary categories. They reinforce each other.

Michael Foley and Bob Edwards write, "a 'dense network of civil associations' is said to promote the stability and effectiveness of the democratic polity through both the effects of association on citizens ' habits of the heart' and the ability of associations to mobilise citizens on behalf of public causes. Thus civil society, understood as the realm of private voluntary association from neighbourhood committees to interest groups to philanthropic enterprises of all sorts, has come to be seen as an essential ingredient in both democratisation and the health of established democracies" .[15] Here they try to bring out how the voluntary associations facilitate and smoothen the democratic process thereby making the roots of democracy stronger. They present two versions of civil society. One of them includes Alexis de Tocqueville, and who further draws from Adam Smith, Adam Ferguson and Francis Hutcheson. This approach puts special emphasis on the ability of associational life in general and the habits of association in particular to foster patterns of civility in the actions of citizens in a democratic polity.[16] The other version stated by Jacek Kuron, Adam Michnik and their associates lay special emphasis on civil society as a sphere of action that is independent of the state, and that is capable precisely for this reason – of energizing resistance to a tyrannical regime. The difference between the two is that the former helps the state for governance by their positive attitude while the latter possess the civil society as a counterweight to the state. The second version is also supported by the economist Mancur Olson, who perceives the 'dense webs of association' as enduring threats to the smooth and equitable functioning of modern states and markets alike.[17] However, Robert Putnam supports the former version and writes the more dense the networks in a community, the more chance of mutual benefit. Countering Olson's view, he writes, "social capital, as embodied in horizontal networks of civic engagement, bolsters the performance of the polity and the economy, rather than the reverse: strong society, strong economy; strong society, strong state" .[18] Putnam in his empirical study on US writes, that since 1960's the 'civil community' is eroding and hence a decreasing level of social capital is observed in US. This results in a reduction of mutually beneficial collective action and so he writes; "weakening society, weakening economy; weakening society, weakening state".[19] By this comparative empirical analysis, Putnam shows the importance of civil society for building a stronger state and also its benefits to the collectivity. For Putnam, the chief virtue of civil associations lies in their capacity to socialise participants into the 'norms of generalised reciprocity' and 'trust' that are essential components of the 'social capital' needed for effective cooperation.[20] Prior to Putnam, Bellah and his colleagues on their work of US also reported a decline of 'civic culture'.[21] The civil association generates networks of civic engagement and trust among citizens facilitating communication and patterns of collective action. The associations are, horizontally structured establishing equality and thus differing from the traditional vertically structured organisations, which perpetuates inequality.

"Dense, but segregate horizontal networks, sustain cooperation within each group, but networks of civic engagement that cut across social cleavages nourish wider cooperation.... If horizontal networks of civic engagement help participants solve dilemmas of collective action, then the more horizontally structured an organisation, the more it should foster institutional success in the broader community. Membership, in horizontally ordered groups (like sports clubs, cooperatives, mutual aid societies, cultural associations & voluntary unions) should be positively associated with good government".[22]

Coleman in his attempt to bring economics and sociology closer stressed on the concept of 'social capital'. He put forth the economics' principle of rational action into the social systems analysis without discarding social organisation in the process. He defines social capital "by its function not a single entity but variety of different entities, with two elements in common: they all consist of some aspect of social structures and they facilitate certain actions of actors – whether persons or corporate actors – within the structure. Like other forms of capital, social capital is productive, making possible the achievement of certain goals that in its absence would not be possible. Like physical capital and human capital, social capital is not completely fungible but may be specific to certain activities. A given form of social capital that is valuable in facilitating certain actions may be useless or even harmful for others. Unlike other forms of capital, social capital inheres in the structure of relations between actors. It is not lodged either in the actors themselves or in physical implements of production".[23] According to him, trust and trustworthiness in a group facilitate certain productive activity, in a similar manner to physical capital and human capital.

For the generation of social capital in social structures, Coleman lists some aspects. If any of these aspects are present in a social structure then we can very well conclude the presence of social capital.[24] These are:

1) Obligations, expectations and trustworthiness of structures – ex-rotating credit associations of South-East Asia;
2) Informational channels – such as networks that provide data about available jobs;

3) Norms and effective sanctions – such as those against crime in certain neighbourhoods;
4) Closure of social networks, in which all actors interact, one with another; and
5) Multiplex relationships, in which resources of one relationship can be appropriated for us in a second relationship – such as in the context of different roles an individual plays.

For Coleman it was immaterial whether the social capital he spoke of produced positive results or not on the society. His social capital is neutral. It provides a perspective for looking at human social structures that enables the analyst to look for the work of this powerful social resource in human relationships, effecting either human capital or profit.[25] Thus, Coleman did not visualise that the social capital he was talking about could bring negative consequences on the citizens and is a morally and ethically neutral resource, which facilitated all types of collective activities.

Debra C. Minkoff in an article "Producing Social Capital – National Social Movements and Civil Society" refutes the decline of civil society and argues how national social movement organisations, rampant in US, are producing social capital.[26] These national Social Movement Organisations (SMO) serve an effective antidote to the segmentation of the society on the basis of residence communities, religious or ethnic affiliation or even race and clans. He is of the view that these organisations provide the necessary infrastructure for collective action and act as visible proponents of group claims, producing a kind of symbolic affiliation and social integration which enables even the ostracised groups like – gays, lesbians, disabled etc. – an opportunity to be in the collectivity. In elaborating the role of national SMOs in promoting social capital and civil society, Minkoff list four reasons. "First, they provide trace evidence of denser social networks and social infrastructures of the sort applauded by analysts of civil society. Second, the expansion of the national movement sector contributes to an enduring opportunity structure for activism by marginalised groups. Third, national SMO's serve a critical linkage function for movements with 'weak infrastructures' and have the potential to promote the diffusion of collective identities, providing atleast a minimal degree of solidarity and integration for otherwise isolated members of society. Fourth, national SMO's promote public discourse and debate, strengthening the 'public sphere' and the formation of 'counterpublics'[27]. These are reasons, which contribute to the growth of social capital and diminish the segmentation of the citizens leading to the process of integration and fulfilling desired beneficial actions for the citizens.

Taking the example of US, Minkoff writes that though protest movements have receded, their place is taken over by social organisations, which put pressure on the Government for mutually beneficial actions. He gives the example of contemporary women's organisation movement, whose number, rose from 40 in 1960 to more than 330 in 1971.[28] Similar consequences were also observed for national social organisations engaged in other sectors and the number of active organisations is relatively stable since 1990's. This suggests that this sector of national movement activity has become institutionalised and relatively protected against changing political conditions.

Minkoff is of the view that rather than emphasising on local dimensions of civil society and social capital such as face-to-face social networks, voluntary associations and community institutions, bringing norms of reciprocity and trust we should incorporate social movements, which help the growth of grass-roots participatory movements. He gives instances of civil society advocates who overlook the role of social movements. One relates to the concern of factionalism that undergrids elite and pluralist theories of State power. The other relates to democratic mechanisms needed for integrating individuals and managing competing interests and its absence may give priority to individual interests over public good. Voluntary associations such as churches, social clubs, choral societies and other forms of civic engagement are integrative mechanisms that bridge particularistic concerns and involve citizens in networks of social interaction around common activities and presumably shared goals. Social movements rather tend to sharpen the conflict and so are organised around existing social cleavages, which lead to generate new ones.

A second concern centres on the national movement organisational form in contrast with grass-roots movements and local organisations that involve intense commitment and interaction with other members of the group, national social movement organisations tend to be centralised and bureaucratic with a great deal of distance between leaders and members. Secondly, membership is retained only by financial contributions and there is very rare face-to-face contact by members.

From all these, Minkoff gathers that such organisations are marked by hierarchy as a mode of decision-making, sharpen existing social inequalities by allotting leadership positions to favoured classes i.e. white middle class members and also are not necessarily participatory institutions. By implication, such organisations cannot contribute to the development of models of democratic participation and norms of equalitarianism that are central to the vision of civil society advocated by analysts of recent democratic transitions.

Countering these allegations, Minkoff writes that without local mobilisation and community based institutions and organisations, national social movements would not have been possible. He gives instances of feminist movement, gay liberation movement, anti-apartheid movements and New Right movements to strengthen his point.[29] National social movement organisations are, more directly, vehicles for the accumulation and mobilisation of social capital that can be deployed for collective action. Such movements disseminate the protest models and also draw up picture plans to sustain such activities by creating a resource and institutional space to the otherwise powerless collectivity to claim for their rights and privileges. Protest is important not only because it can put pressure on elites, but also because in the process of direct political engagement, collective identity and solidarity are formed and strengthened[30]. In this way national social movement organisations have a crucial role to play in civil society and in the production of social capital by providing an infrastructure for collective action, facilitating the development of mediated collective identities that link otherwise marginalised members of society and shaping public discourse and debate.

According to Coleman, in every social relations certain degree of social capital exists and its existence is dependent on the resources the social relations produce for any action. He does not conceive social capital to be of metaphysical character nor is it explicitly connected to the functioning of democracies. Social capital certainly helps individuals and collective actors in getting things done however this may or may not apply to society as a whole. We must remember here that Coleman's concept of social capital is 'neutral'. Individuals alone, their immediate circles, their communities, the polity as a whole, or transnational networks may all benefit from the relatively richer social settings in which social capital is typically available; but access to such capital may be unevenly distributed throughout a society, and its uses may range from asocial to anti-social to broadly prosocial.[31]

Robert Putnam contradicts Coleman's conception of social capital as neutral. He relates social capital to the economic growth and democratic governmental performance of a country. Putnam writes. "the more social capital a society possesses the better will a democratic government work". This social capital depends on the quality of associational life of people. He emphasises on a dense network of associations as it can bring norms or reciprocity and civic engagement, leading to social trust, and providing networks of social relations that can be mobilised for civic action. Associations provide structural resources and promote self-consciously attitudes and values to the citizens thereby strengthening civic engagement and democracy. It is this attitudes and values, the associations disseminate which help the growth of the civil society.

Alexis de Tocqueville argues that there exists a rich associational life in America and this is mainly due to social and political conditions. Americans, he said, were forever forming associations. Such associational activity is a cornerstone of the theory of social capital contributing as it does to the forging of horizontal networks of reciprocal trust. This strengthens the sustenance of civic engagement and the democratic process. It was only because of the force of voluntary associations that individuals in America co-operated for collective purposes despite the absence of an aristocracy and the remoteness of the federal state. By social condition he implies the egalitarian character of American Society. The citizens there also enjoy a greater amount of political freedom. These two conditions have contributed to the growth of associational life. According to him, associations were necessitated due to the inaction of the political representative to take up public works and initiatives. Individuals or rather citizens joined together to accomplish the greater public needs and their efforts also had a positive impact on the private needs. Tocqueville notes that associations spring up to meet public (and private) needs and take initiatives; and associational life trains citizens in participation and the virtues of citizenship, preparing leaders for public life. Thus his model of associational life was broadly based on structural and functional perspective. The ends generate the means to achieve it.

Tocqueville in his study of American society of 1830, highly praised the role of associations. He felt voluntary associations act as a democratic buffer against state power. Such associations are an antidote to the overbearing and centralised bureaucratic power in the State. Americans were intense in forming associations of all types so as to bring vibrancy in civic life. He saw this art of association to be a key virtue of democracy in the 19th century America, which moderated the American tendency towards individualism and schooled people in cooperation.[32] The freedom of association, leading to the increase of voluntary organisations, is considered by him as "semi-constitutional political circumstances which contribute to the safeguarding of liberty".[33] He was of the view that liberty and equality are incompatible. But in democracy, equality is a basic pre-requisite and without it democracy cannot be thought of. So in order to protect the liberty of citizens he stressed upon voluntary associations to guard against the encroaching state controls. To paraphrase Tocqueville, whether it is a case of building a hospital in a small town or of investigating the cause of war or abolishing war, whatever its order of magnitude, a voluntary organisation will emerge to devote its free time and especially its money to studying the problem.[34] Freedom of the press was also advocated by Tocqueville for a good democracy. He was of the view that American citizens had a good knowledge of civic education and this is one of the reasons for a successful democracy in America. Associations also bring together the isolated citizen, in an individualistic society and thus the society is saved from being doomed to despotism. Associations, according to him, are interposed between the solitary individual and the all-powerful state. The 'art of association' he said, contributes 'super-abundant force and energy' to the body politic which constitutes political society. He argues that civil associations lead to political ones. It is through civil society that the potential excesses of the centralised state in democratic societies can be controlled.

Social capital also promotes the economic condition of the citizens and this is achieved through co-operative activities. Many writers have acknowledged the role of cooperation in different forms for a healthy economy. Putnam attributes this to the role of social capital i.e. 'trust'. Trust in other words also means that people obey the norms, customs, mores and conventions. It reduces unnecessary hassles and uncalled altercation between citizens. Trust also increases the moral dignity of the citizens and they begin to know each other more intimately. This has a direct correlation to the social networks among them. Once trust is established among people, the chances of prisoner's dilemma like situations are virtually wiped out.

Lane Kenworthy lists nine chief types of economic cooperation, which can lead to enhance economic welfare and progress.[36] For each type, institutional arrangements are designed to bring in economic cooperation without relying on trust.

ECONOMIC COOPERATION AND INSTITUTIONAL INCENTIVES

Sl. No.	*Actors Cooperating*	*Economic Benefits*	*Institutions Promoting Cooperation*
01.	Firms across industry	Reduced rent seeking	Centralised business federation
02.	Unions	Wage restraint	Centralised and/or concentrated labour movement
03.	Govt.'s interest groups	Coherent productive govt. policy	United Govt. and centralised interest group organisation
04.	Investors & Firms	Extended time horizons for times	Long term commitment by investors a product of investor having large ownership stakes and a means of effectively influencing company decision making.
05.	Purchaser & Supplier Firms	Heightened communication, greater supplier willingness to invest and raise productivity.	Long-term commitment by purchasers.
06.	Competing Firms	Greater investment in R&B of employee training, quicker agreement on standards, assistance with prancing, tech, diffusion, design accounting marketing and so on.	Industry trade associations or Govt. incentives.

07. Labours Management	Greater willingness on the part of workers to share valuable knowledge, accept productivity enhancing tech. & upgrade skills.	Long term commitment by employers (employment guarantee)
08. Workers	Heightend work efforts.	Participatory work teams.
09. Fractional Departments within firms.	Quicker, more effective transition from R&D to production.	Multidivisional teams that link departments along the production chains.

Kenworthy writes that even though trust promotes economic cooperation, it is not a necessary factor. The self-sustaining process often reinforces on the economic system and this reduces the role of trust. She gives examples of Japanese and German firms, which have achieved considerable economic progress without relying much on trust.

Kenworthy disputes Putnam's argument that civic engagement is a key source of economic cooperation and prosperity. For this, she resorted to two indicators of civic engagement. One is citizen's participation in atleast one voluntary organisation and the second is the average voter participation. Although voters turn out seems less clearly linked to trust and economic cooperation, the degree to which citizens are willing to participate in the electoral process may tell us something about the prominence of civic participation norms that foster trust.[37] In the eighteen richest industrialised democracies there was no correlation between the two indicators and for three major components of economic performance – productivity growth, unemployment and inflation from the period 1960 to 1994. There was only a marginal direct proportion between volunteering and inflation.

According to Kenworthy, civic engagement does not promote economic cooperation or trust among economic actors. For this institutional arrangements, as is mentioned before, is required.

Putnam attributes a lot of credit to social capital for the successful governance and economic development in North Italy compared to South Italy. Social capital brings harmony in collective actions and erodes the self-centered consciousness of individuals. It lubricates trust and brings cooperation as it induces in the minds of individuals the benefit believing other and churning the effects of collective activities rather than doing singularly. Voluntary cooperation is easier in a community that has inherited a substantial stock of social capital, in the form of norms of reciprocity and networks of civic engagement.[38]

Most forms of social capital, such as trust, are what Albert Hirschman has called 'normal resources' – that is, resources whose supply increases rather than decreases through use and which become depleted if not used.[39] Hence, level of trust and the domain of trust increases as more people develop the ability of trust to each other and utilise it for their mutual benefit.

The same also stands for social norms and networks. Coleman for this reason writes "The more extensively persons call on one-another for aid, the great will be the quantity of social capital generated.... Social relationships die out if not maintained; expectations and obligations wither over time, and norms depend on regular communication".[40]

The stock of social capital in a civil society is ordinarily a public good unlike 'capital', which is private good. Social Capital can be used by one and all for their mutual benefit, a feature, which is, absent in conventional capital. Capital benefits only the user but social capital has multiplier effect on the persons utilising it. Social capital benefits a plurality of persons unlike conventional capital, which has a singular beneficial effect.

Social trust in complex modern settings can arise from two related sources – norms of reciprocity and networks of civic engagement.[41] A norm is a standard of behavioural expectation shared by group members against which the validity of perceptions is judged and the appropriateness of feeling and behaviour is evaluted.[42] Norms are based on social values and have a moral sense. The norms are blueprints for behaviour setting, limits within which individuals may seek alternate ways to achieve their goals.[43] Norms of reciprocity, thus, means to act in a similar manner or to return the kindness bestowed upon one. This reciprocity is of two types 'balanced' and 'generalised'. The former refers to simultaneous exchange and the latter refers to a long-term exchange where there is an element of expectations and this is never broken. This latter one, i.e. generalised reciprocity, builds social capital stronger and helps to maintain cordiality and cooperative attitude among the collectivity. Communities in which this norm is followed can more efficiently restrain opportunism and resolve problems of collective action.[44] Generalised reciprocity means a greater degree of personal interaction and social networks marked simultaneously by a higher degree of trust among them.

Networks of civic engagement are also an essential form of social capital. The more we find such networks in a community, the greater the chance for citizens to cooperate for mutual benefit. Such networks, may be horizontal or vertical. In the former the members are given equivalent status and power while in the latter an asymmetric relation of hierarchy and dependence is found among the members. However, our concern here is the horizontal type viz. voluntary association, cooperatives, sports clubs, choral societies, etc., such networks strengthen the norms of reciprocity and mutual expectations through the repeated interactions and meetings. It helps in the dissemination of trustworthiness of citizens through the discussions and interactions. "As we have seen, trust and cooperation depend on reliable information about the past behaviour and present interests of potential partners, while uncertainty reinforces dilemmas of collective action. Thus, other things being equal, the greater the communication (both direct and indirect) among the participants, the greater their mutual trust and the easier they will find it to cooperate".[45]

Invariably in all societies citizens are averse to collective efforts as they are suspicious to each other and there exists a tendency to pocket the maximum benefits for themselves. This tendency erodes cooperation for mutual benefit. Voluntary cooperation depends on social capital. Norms of generalised reciprocity and networks of civic engagement encourage social trust and cooperation because they reduce incentives to defect, reduce uncertainty, and provide models for future cooperation.[46] In this circumstance we can say that social capital exists in the society and it tends to be self-reinforcing and cumulative. In a society characterized by dense networks of civic engagement, where most people abide by civic norms, it is easier to spot and punish the occasional "bad apple", so that defection is riskier and less tempting.[47]

Civic engagement also leads to better democratic governmental performance. Tocqueville assertively commended that a vigorous civil society results in strengthening, and not weakening, the democratic government. Putnam in his empirical study on civic traditions in Italy also writes better governmental performance in northern Italy compared to southern Italy for this reason.

"On the demand side, citizens in civic communities expect better government and (in part through their own efforts), they get it. They demand more effective public service, and they are prepared to act collectively to achieve their shared goals. Their counterparts in less civic regions more commonly assume the role of alienated and cynical supplicants. On the supply side, the performance of representative government is facilitated by the social infrastructure of civic communities and by the democratic values of both officials and citizens. Most fundamental to the civic community is the social ability to collaborate for shared interests. Generalised reciprocity generates high social capital and underpins collaboration.... In the civic community, associations proliferate, memberships overlap, and participation spills into multiple arenas of community life. The social contract that sustains such collaboration in the civic community is not legal but moral. The sanction for violating it is not penal, but exclusion from the network of solidarity and cooperation".[48] Putnam concludes by writing "building social capital will not be easy, but it is the key to making democracy work".[49]

Peter A. Hall while examining the trajectory of social capital in Britain writes that frequent interaction of individuals, beyond the family and market, marked by relative equality and associated for common endeavours, thereby leading to the formation of social networks "constitute an important form of 'social capital' in the sense that they increase the trust that individuals feel towards others and enhance their capacity, to join together in collective action to resolve common problems or to ensure that governments address such problems".[50] After Putnam's findings of decreasing levels of social capital in American society, Hall while making an empirical study on a similar industrialised democratic British society, concluded that aggregate levels of social capital have not declined there over the post-war years with an exception to social trust.

Hall writes that in spite of the prevalence of factors found in America, such as socio-economic factors like expression of the welfare state, sub-urbanisation, the growing participation of women in the labour force and changes in family structure marked by higher rates of divorce and more single-person households and the other factor being the impact of television viewing resulting in decline of social capital, Britain exhibits stable levels of social capital. This is because, he writes, in post-war Britain, we find (i) a radical transformation in the educational system marked by a massive expansion of both secondary and post-secondary education; (ii) a change in the overall class structure of British society, driven by economic and political developments, that has altered the distribution of occupation and life situations among the populace; and (iii) characteristically British forms of government action that have done much to encourage and sustain voluntary community involvement.[51] In his analysis of educational contribution, first of all it increased quantitatively the number of secondary or post-secondary educated persons including a significant number of women. Again, educational reform substantially altered the class composition of the student body in institutions of post-secondary education and increased the numbers of people from the working class with a post-secondary education from negligible levels in 1959 to 4 percent in 1990.[52] Higher levels of education resulted in greater community involvement and higher degree of socialisation. It is in this way that education contributed for the maintenance of the levels of social capital in Britain.

The middle-class in Britain strengthened the growth of associations and organisations. It is members of the middle class who established contact and made networks with diverse person, along with venturing new endeavours. It also participated most actively in the widest range of formal associations, joining new ones to advance more recently developed objectives. Britain witnessed an increase of middle-class occupants since 1950 which was due to "decline of an older manufacturing base, the expansion of employment in a burgeoning public sector, and the rise of the service sector. In short, in the years since the war, substantial number of people born into working-class families moved into middle-class occupations, as the number of white-collar positions expanded".[53] For this, civic involvement increased sustaining level of social capital.

Hall while commending the social policies of the British Government, writes that the Government never neglected the voluntary sector and initiated a number of policies and programmes where the involvement of the voluntary section was inevitable so as to deliver the social services. Starting from Lloyd George's budget of 1914 to the end of the Conservative Government of Mrs. Margaret Thatcher in 1997, voluntary sector received much attention and was utilised in delivering social services by the Government. "In short, not only have British Governments made substantial efforts to ensure that voluntary activity flourishes, they have also adopted an approach to social policy that makes extensive use of volunteers, along side professionals, for the delivery of social service. This commitment has been accompanied by large public expenditures, via grants and fees for services, to the kind of associations that mobilise voluntary action on the local level. All indications are that these government policies have made a major contribution to sustaining the kind of associations that augment the level of social capital in Britain".[54]

With regard to the only exception of social trust, which is declining in Britain, Hall reasons that, this might be due to two factors viz. (i) urbanisation, since those in large cities are often believed to be less familiar with their neighbours and exposed to more crime, and (ii) a 'Thatcher effect', on the grounds that the efforts, made by the conservative governments of the 1980's to break with the 'collectivist' traditions of British political culture and to promote a more 'individualistic' entrepreneurialism may have encouraged people to become more competitive and less trusting of others.[55]

The present age witnesses a phenomenal growth of market economy along with the rupturing of the state control over the economy. To a large extent market determines the global scenario. With more and more developing states adopting the principle of liberalisation and globalisation of their economy and adhering to the principle of market economy, the role of social capital assumes significant contribution for the economic development of the people. In this context, it is worth to mention Mills and Ulmer report to the US Senate Small Business Committee in 1946. "Their findings showed that the small-business cities provided a more balanced economic life than the big-business cities; that the level of socio-economic well-being was higher in the small-business cities; and that these differences were due largely to differences in the composition of the economic base, specifically to the dominance of big business on the one hand and the prevalence of small business on the other. They concluded that the general level of social welfare was appreciably higher in the small business cities".[56] In the same year, Goldschmid found that large-scale agriculture in comparison to small family farms, can have a dampening effect on community welfare. This shows that the local residents benefit for the local process and there is an ascendancy of local capitalism.

Local capitalism is organised around networks of small and medium-size firms, which always try to reinforce and sustain local socio-economic climates so as to achieve long-term vitality and welfare. According to MacKenzie, "the configuration of the local economy provides a synergistic environment in which the broad resources of the community are brought together and utilised collaboratively. Strong socio-economic relationship – specific to locale and community – are fostered on many levels, which in turn, contribute to the collective strength of the local economy, and encourage businesses to reinvest in the community".[57] Local capitalism increases the personal networks so as to reach out to the maximum number of consumers and in this process economic activity is evenly distributed within local communities.

In this context, Oldenburg gives the example of 'third places' which he defines as small-holder retail establishments like pubs, drug stores, coffee shops, barber shops, grocery etc. providing an institutional base for public life and a sort of local capitalism. A third place is open to all and does not restrain entry to any person, thereby "creating horizontal linkages in a community that increase civic engagement".[58] This civic engagement enhances participation in other voluntary associations, according to Oldenburg.

Reymond Grew extends the idea of social capital as used by Putnam and others by including the term 'cultural capital'. "By cultural capital, he means the customs of public behaviour (a part of culture in anthropological sense) and the content of shared values (as communicated through the literature and arts of high culture). Putnam measured social capital primarily in terms of voluntary organisations, on the grounds that associational life may, as Tocqueville thought it did, build habits of co-operation and trust that facilitates effective, democratic government. Thinking in the broader terms of cultural capital invites attention to less constitutionalised habits of association that may also be important, especially when governments restrict organised activity. Perhaps patterns of social connection and modes of thought constitute cultural capital that has the potential to affect collective action. Social capital is said to be greater or weaker depending on the vigor of associational life and the degree of satisfaction with government. Cultural capital is even harder to quantify. All societies have cultures; cultural capital can be deduced only from the tests that history provides".[59] Grew exploits the role of culture in Italy from a historical perspective stating from 16th and 17th centuries. The use of the enlightenment ideas formed the foundation of the growth of social capital in Italy. Further, academics and theaters in every city and town strengthened the social capital due to regular interaction. "By the eighteenth – century, Italian society had nurtured a strong public sphere of talk and festivals, cafes and theaters, academics and news papers, despite limited public politics. Nevertheless, the interest in law and in talk sustained a lively civic sense that, starting with local pride and familiar ritual, could be extended to a vision of civic education and transformed civil society".[60] The French Revolution also had its impact on Italy's social capital, no doubt it was less divisive and less violent and hence was treated as a means to bring positive changes. The networks, associations, exchanges and collective action that constitute social capital increased with the stimulus of revolutionary activity, gaining importance as more and more issues and interests became politically charged.[61] The revolutionary years strengthened forms of social capital less dependent on the state. Books, newspapers and other periodicals circulated more widely, and the habit of meeting and talking in clubs, circles, cafes and book stores – became more entrenched. This transformation of Italian associational life went further beyond intellectual elites and particular occupations than ever before, fostering important networks of opinion and interest and broadening the sets of issues that concerned them. However, governments during this period failed to visualise the presence of strong social capital among the peasantry for their face-to-face relations with city-people, their market connections and ties to land-owners. Grew ends with four points about social capital. First, particular to the context of Italy, social capital should include patterns of behaviour rooted in culture as well as in institutions. Secondly, tradition and memory do matter in the formation of social capital. Thirdly, social capital is vulnerable to power. Finally, discontinuities can seriously effect social capital. "For him, social capital is like potential energy. Its transformation into kinetic energy lies in conjunctures and events, which may reduce the value of some forms of social capital while increasing that of other".[62] In this way a balance or an equilibrium is maintained between the different forms of social capital.

According to Marjorie K McIntosh, social capital produced by human interaction "contained at least a few formal organisations that performed legal, economic, religious and / or charitable functions".[63] The non-members, transportable and convertible to other groups, contributed to the growth of the lateral and vertical ties paving the way for the emergence of a national state. Social capital is also generated by informal and loosely defined networks of friendship neighbourliness and assistance. "In the unstructured reciprocal systems, people attempted to provide some form of insurance for themselves by sharing information with their friends and neighbours, contributing their own time and labour to their needs, and giving or loaning goods or money. In doing so, they build up a pool of social (and implicitly economic) credit upon which they could draw in the future if they ran into hard times".[64] In this way the social capital so produced provides some sort of security and the dissemination of moral and ethical values among the people. The self-centred and profit motivated 'individual' helps to transform the society into an egalitarian one or from a type of 'mass society to a civil society'. The returns or the benefits that members accrue due to formal organisations like local secular courts, parish, voluntary religious organisations and private trustees, resulted in a high degree of social capital in England during the period of 1300 to 1640 A.D.

The internal returns – the benefits accruing to the participants themselves – included the creation of personal networks based upon respect, trust, and shared experiences that comprised people beyond their own families, immediate neighbours, and personal friends.[65] The external benefits include developing public mechanisms to handle disagreements, working co-operatively, promotion of shared norms and public good. It served as a bridging gap to the different communities having a distinct pattern of settlement and tradition by creating trust and sense of common identity. It also brought closer, people of different class giving rise to vertical integration. Thus, locally generated social capital contributed to the growth of an English national state in two ways; by promoting lateral interactions and common values between communities and regions, and by integrating the middle and upper strata of society vertically into a more cohesive unit with common institutions and a shared definition of themselves as a nation.[66]

Among the informal networks of the English women like networks of reciprocal social credit, mutual assistance, social interaction and social assistance, McIntosh argues a lot of social capital was generated through such networks among various class and status of women between 1300 to 1640. Women's social credit networks flourished in communities characterized by several common features: the absence of an effective governmental system that provided social security to those in need, social patterns that did not require that the extended family take care of all its members, limited opportunities for individual advancement through reinvestment of excess income, and a breakdown of older patterns that emphasized family or communal values in favour of a more individually focused and profit oriented system.[67] Such networks provided women a sort of institutionalized base and was an answer to men's organised institutions to which they (women) were denied access in those times. It served as a "problem-anchored helping network".[68] It nourished a habit of social relationships, concealing the economic aspect under a veneer of social goodwill. The social credit networks among women provided help and aid to the needy women at once without any need of approaching to the providers of such aid. Even, women belonging to high class created networks of social interaction to produce social capital. "Mc Nabb argues that, during 1530's and 1620's, even women of high rank rarely had access to the political, economic, and cultural capital through which men exercised power; they had to rely on the creation and employment of social capital. By performing a beneficial action for another, women built up social credit among friends and influential people that could then be recalled if ever the original agent was in need of assistance".[69] Informal networks gave the high-class women political and social benefits. Harris points that involvement of women in these networks of social activities was pursued deliberately and consciously "to strengthen their own networks and to perpetuate them into the next generation".[70] Such women through their networks and contacts promoted their families interest. The women of lower status and class also had an interaction for social assistance and this was done so as to enable them some sort of security in case of their husband's death or other causes of lowered income "Close contacts also produced secondary forms of social capital for women. These interactions, and a sense of reciprocal obligation among them, promoted trust and the development of cooperative skills, including how to resolve conflict at an informal level. Conversations led to shared norms, and the exchange of information could be useful in economic or social terms".[71] These interactions and informal associations had a positive impact both on the women themselves and on the social attitudes of their husbands and male relatives. According to McIntosh, social capital does not necessarily promote modernising goals like the emergence of a civil society, democratic processes or economic growth. Although works like Coleman's *Foundations of Social Theory* or Putnam's *Making Democracy Work* include examples of simple exchanges of equipment or labour between individual farmers and such weakly structured organisations as rotating credit associations, their emphasis is on how social capital contributes to wider social and political developments.[72] From this, it can well be said that the reciprocal assistance among the women of lower class does not strictly produce social capital.

McIntosh also writes about the female social networks in southern Nigeria from 1900 to 1960 A.D. among the Yoruba and Igbo societies. These women created and used networks of social credit for trading activities, social assistance, personal advancement and credit insurance. There were social restrictions and taboos for women doing market activities and neglecting their traditional gender roles. However, women to a certain extent succeeded in their endeavour and the author sees a similarity between that of the English women presented earlier.

"We must insist that historical study of social capital move beyond formal organisation, ones dominated normally by men (or occasionally women) of high local status. Structured institutions are indeed likely to have left good records, facilitating historical research, but we must be sensitive to evidence of the informal networks that flourished especially among men of lower rank and women. To ignore these social interactions and the benefits that they generated would be to slip back inadvertently into a narrower and more elitist view of what is historically important. Because the nature and effect of the social capital generated by informed networks were different, from those produced by formal organisations, we must be prepared to adjust our theoretical framework to fit the particular case".[73] Hence, the author admits the generation of social capital, both from formal and informal relations, though their degree and nature may vary and also that this social capital is beneficial to the person involved and at the same time it may not be necessarily beneficial to people at large.

Robert I Rotberg states that social capital promotes work culture, civic culture, horizontal ties, reciprocal trust, political stability, government effectiveness, greater participation of citizens and above all the making of civil society.[74] High levels of social capital contribute to the creation of a political culture that is open, pluralistic, deliberative, tolerant and democratic.[75]

Gene Brucker commenting on the civil society in Italy denies the historical inheritance of civil society as stated by Putnam that it had its roots in the past feudal communes of central and northern Italy after twelfth and through the fifteenth century. Brucker is of the view that in those days factionalism, brutality, authoritarianism, regulations and absolutism were prevalent. He sees no important distinction between the north and south Italy. Everywhere there was autocracy and not civic engagement and civic humanism and the order was vertical and not horizontal. There was negligible role of voluntary association in pre-revolutionary Italy. However, Brucker is of the view that it was only due to the nineteenth century revolution that Italy saw the emergence of civil society gradually. Associations required the permission of secular and religious authorities and these authorities were highly critical of the association as it might put challenges to them and snatch away their privileges and powers. The absence of any serious challenge to religious orthodoxy was, and long remained, a significant different to the revival of civil values and traditions.[76] If the definition of *civil society* includes as a central feature "a complex tissue of voluntary associations which occupy a public space and have a public voice", then it is difficult to find evidence for this phenomenon in pre-Revolutionary Italy.[77] Civil society came after the revolutionary period in Italy, which transformed the political, and socio economic structures of Italy. Brucker, to strengthen his arguments, cites Italian historian Jacob Burckhardt's *The Civilisation of the Renaissance in Italy* (New York, 1929) where he "stressed the progressive, innovative and 'modern' qualities of that civic world. The institutions and values fostered by those urban governments were seen as the solvent that destroyed the old feudal system, with its hierarchical social structure, its land based economy, and its fragmented political order. The towns were the dynamic engines that created a new capitalist economy; a social order based on wealth; a political system that stressed co-operation, equality and freedom, and a culture that embodied secular rather than religious values".[78] Edward Muir agrees to Putnam's findings that northern Italy has greater degree of civil society than southern Italy. In northern Italy, creating collaborative, rather than coercive, solutions to political violence owed a great deal to three characteristic forms of control that can be seen loosely as deriving from civic religion, judicial practice, and the mores of refined manners.[79] The religious life had an effective control on crucial institutions, civic cults were initiated and preached by patron-saints and the ideal of communal co-operation was repeatedly modelled and reinforced through civic rituals – mainly processions. "The juridical culture that permeated northern Italy through the ubiquitous presence of notaries brought some element of due process and regularised procedure to even the most obscure backwater villages. Furthermore, extremely influential models of personal comportment contributed to what Elias labelled the 'civilising process' in which northern Italians were decidedly precocious, if for no other reason than the fact that literate culture was more widespread there than anywhere else before modern times. These cultural forms found institutional expressions, but more important, cultural practices and institutions reinforced one another, creating ways of behaving in institutional settings that made collaboration against divisive violence possible".[80] These are the reasons given by Muir. Further he views that it is only through collective policy and self-restraint that civil society was able to eradicate the most endemic forms of political violence. "Social controls had deeply religious roots, primarily in their connection with the urban adaptation of the late medieval cult of the saints. Eventually, the juridical-notarial culture extended civil society beyond the walls of the cities by facilitating an alliance between the ruling urban elites and the bottom of the political order in the countryside. Finally, the rural aristocracy joined civil society not by accepting civic solutions but by assimilating the mores of princely courts".[81]

Jack P.Greene in his article 'Social and Cultural Capital in Colonial British America' broadens the definition of 'social capital' to include not just traditions of civil interaction but the entire range of institutions, practices, devices and learned behaviours that enable collectivities and individuals to render physical spaces productive and social and cultural spaces agreeable. In this expanded usage, *social capital* or perhaps better, *social and cultural capital*, refers to all of those elements of the larger inheritance that culture pass along to succeeding generations for later members to perpetuate, modify, discard or reconstitute in new places.[82] Greene analyses Adam Smith's 'Of Colonies' in *An Inquiry into the Nature and Causes of the Wealth of Nations* (Oxford, 1976) on the colonisation of Europe in America.

From this, Greene draws several attributes of social and cultural capital. One was transferability, which enabled social and cultural capital to combine with labour and investment capital so as to transform the society. Second was adaptability, where social and cultural capital was put to wide variety of uses in the socio-economic contexts and ecological zones. Third attribute was partibility, where the colonisers selected whatever was most suitable to their specific efforts of reconstruction in the colony. The fourth one was enhancibility, and this was done by invention, imitation or assimilation. The social and cultural capital was also transportable to other and newer settlements. He says that the human capital of particular individuals with specialised skills effectively translated into social capital and this specialised skills were injected by the colonisers.

It is acknowledged by various authors that a stimulant is required for a vibrant democracy and this stimulant is the development of civil society through the vehicle of increased civic participation. Some identify civic participation to be 'at the heart of democracy'.[83] Huntington and Nelson have made the case that people who are members of community, organisations etc. are more likely to participate in politics and this they clarify from Mexico, Chile and Peru where urban migrants who had participated in community development organisations were five times more likely to have made political demands than were non-participants.[84] Verba *et.al.* have also concluded that participation in non-political civil society organisations leads to political participation because people are open to the political stimuli by which their worldview expands.[85]

Putnam's conclusion of social capital promoting coordinated actions and enhancing the opportunities for democratic government, particularly with reference to Italy, and that participation and social capital attitudes are 'self-reinforcing and cumulative'[86] are in contrast to what Amber L.Seligson's empirical test on Putnam's thesis in Central America.[87] Seligson writes "in no country in Central America is there a significant association, between demand making and democratic attitudes. This finding suggests that Putnam's claim that civil society participation and social capital attitudes are self reinforcing, does not hold the same way in Central American Country Studies (Costa Rica, Panama, El Salvador, Guatemala, Honduras, and Nicaragua) as it supposedly does in Italy".[88] With regard to the political system, he says, apart from Honduras, in other five countries there is no significant association between people's system support and their demand making.

With regard to inter-personal trust, Seligson says, only in Costa Rica he finds significant association between inter-personal trust and demand making. In conclusion, Seligson says only participation in one form of civil society organisation, namely, Community Development Groups, consistently relates to demand making.[89] Putnam's assumption that participation in any kind of group is crucially important for making democracy work, is not upheld by the Central American empirical test. It can well be said that Putnam's thesis might well hold true for many other kinds of societies as it has shown positive outcome in two different regions i.e. Italy & Central America.

In the recent times the concept of 'social capital' has gained a phenomenal ascendancy. The World Development Report 1997 contains the concept. Harriss and de Renzio report "since 1993 ' social capital' has become one of the key terms of the development lexicon, adopted enthusiastically by international organisations, national governments and NGO's alike".[90] For any type of developmental activity, be it social, economic, cultural or political, 'social capital' is resorted by various organisations starting from world bodies to local voluntary associations and informal groups. For the World Bank itself, even though its use only seems to date back to 1994, it is already being heralded as the 'missing link' in the development.[91]

There would have no appropriate definition or theorisation of social capital other than Ben Fine's marvellous title "The Development State is Dead-Long Live Social Capital?".[92] Here, Fine considers social capital to be a substitute of state versus the market. Social capital, while not all things to all people, is many things to many people.[93] Woolcock gives seven different areas of application for social capital, viz : (dys) functional families, schooling, community life, work and organisation, democracy and governance, collective action, and intangible assets.[94]

Fukuyama is of the view that social capital has a relevance in the neo-classical perspective and for him trust begins where history ends. "The rise of the neo-classical perspective constitutes a vast improvement from earlier decades in this century, when Marxists and Keynesians held sway. We can think of neo-classical economics as being, say, eighty percent correct: it has uncovered important truths about the nature of money and markets because its fundamental model of rational, self-interested human behaviour is correct about eighty percent of the time. But there is a missing twenty percent of human behaviour which neo-classical economics can give only a poor account. As Adam Smith well understood, economic life is deeply embedded in social life, and it cannot be understood apart from the customs, morals, and habits of the society in which it occurs. In short, it cannot be divorced from Culture".[95]

Social capital is free, invisible but real, involving stakeholder participation, professional protocol, social learning, collaboration, trust, solutions to tragedies of the commons, collective responsibilities etc.[96] Social capital is a means of enforcing norms of behaviour and thus acts as a constraint as well as a resource.[97]

Gerald Gamm and Robert D. Putnam are of the view that in America, voluntary associations including women's association grew rapidly in number, relative to population, between the years 1850 to 1900 and it decelerated through 1910s. Between 1910 and 1940, the incidence of associations stagnated and even declined.[98] However labour unions, business groups and agricultural groups grew in number from 1920 to 1940. The reasons for the growth, they cite, are due to the impact of industrialisation, urbanisation and immigration on traditional communal attachments. They are also of the view that associational activity was strongest in small cities and towns compared to large cities. Other factors for the growth of associations in late 19th Century and early 20th century are religion, political, communication development through rail, road and telegraph, economic and demographic changes put forth gender-defined associational attachments, middle-class reformers stressed upon associations for betterment and social control of people, particularly the working-class men and women, and also to cope up with the new uncertainties of an industrialised age.

"Associations were buffers softening the impact of economic and social change. They were institutions created to rebuild the human attachments that had been reputed as cities grew, as families left farms and ancient villages, and as Industrial Revolution pulverised community".[99]

According to Mary P. Ryan, social capital described the beneficial associations which accumulate material and cultural resources within select groups – based on class, ethnic, religious and gender affiliations.[100] For her, social capital is not an adequate measure to gauge the vitality and extent of democratic politics in America, as it had narrower interests. At least three additional factors are necessary to encompass the democratic practices of antebellum Americans: social inclusion, genuine participation, and power to affect public realm.[101] For empowering citizens and practicing democracy, along with associations the other factors which has created a highly differentiated structure for such activity were public meetings, parties and social movements. She writes that the distinctive means of civic engagement, adapted by the persons denied of political capital of vote and economic power, are petition campaigns, public demonstrations, extensive organisational networks and strategic alliances.

From this it can be concluded that social capital alone is not enough to make democracy work. The political resources assembled in the past by mass democratic parties and radical social movements are also essential to a democratic polity, first to create it, then to expand it, and now to keep it alive.[102]

For Elisabeth S. Clemens, the operation of social capital involves a certain alchemy, transforming personal ties, trust in specific persons, and localised capacities for collective action into such macro-social outcomes as economic performance and political efficacy.[103] For her, there is a continuous process of generation and destruction of social capital in the process of political contests and collective action. She locates social capital at three levels of civic society viz: trusting relationships, changing the relations for facilitations of action and finally embeddedness in cultural categories that structured discourse about civic life. According to Clemen's expanded definition, social capital refers "either to the skills and capacities of individuals for social action or to web of ties among individuals".[104] The genius of nineteenth century voluntary associations was their development of rules that facilitated collective action and their creation of national organisations from a web of local arrays of trust. She is of the view that formal organisation transforms a network of interpersonal ties into a system of roles and routines. In addition, the establishment of formal organisations creates a new kind of social network – ties between organisations, constituted through either formal alliances or the joining membership of individuals.

Clemens' studies the Women's club in US during the second half of the nineteenth century. The involvement of women in such clubs laid the foundation of their political involvement by development and diffusing organisational skills. The clubs also transposed social capital by 'bridging social capital' through patterns of multiple membership and joint office holding. Associational life in the Nineteenth century US undergoes changes by decades. "When individual networks, formal organisations and cultural categories coincide, social arrangements are durable and present few opportunities for activists to harness social capital to struggles for social change. But where networks, organisations and categories crosscut one another, social capital generates transformation more easily".[105]

Susan Keen writing on social capital in Australia says associational activity peaked in the 1920s and again in the late 1950s and it was linked to the Australian national social policy and government funded some of these. She writes that both the left and the right were of the view that civil society and the state are mutually exclusive. "The left is concerned about the effects of deinstitutionalisation, deregulation, and devolution, advocating that non-profit organisations fill the newly created gaps resulting from government funding withdrawal. The right seems convinced that the welfare state has 'crowded out' voluntary action, and that the answer to reconstituting civil society lies in fostering a diversified associational life and dismantling the state".[106] She makes a study of the Mechanics Institutes, Friendly Societies, Women's Associations and Service Organisations and came to the conclusion that all these associations are fading away, due to varied reasons, though the degree of this is low for women's associations. The associations, in their ideal form, have the capacity to facilitate social capital, foster mutualism, and provide a training ground for participatory democracy and civic behaviour but in reality this is not happening. However, she writes that, Australian societies were always highly integrated with the state and the associations were largely purposeful-goal-directed. Directed, concreted action led like-minded people to trust and form networks of reciprocity vital to the development of social capital.[107]

Claudia Goldin & Lawrence F. Katz are of the view that "social capital was not merely the handmaiden of human capital in the past : it appears to have survived many changes in the economy and society, serving a similar function today".[108] They say that it was in small towns and cities where High School education achieved a tremendous success and this is due to high level of social capital in such small communities. Since education depends on public funding in small cities, the social capital enriched the human capital by paying taxes. Community cohesion is also a reason for this. Another potentially complementary reason is that small-town America was a locus of associations (religious, fraternal/sororal, business and political organisations) that could have played an important role in galvanising support for the provision of local publicly provided goods, including high schools.[109] In this way, social capital assisted to produce a literate populace necessary to maintain democracy.

Myron P.Gutmann and Sara M. Pullum have brilliantly summarised Putnam's work on Italy while testing it in the semi-arid American Great Plains. They write, "Putnam finds that people who form voluntary associations based on common activities or concerns experience greater levels of social integration and political involvement. He calls this civic engagement, 'social capital' because the power of the group transcends potential individual productivity. Benefits of these reciprocal networks include better community institutions; the building of neighbourhood trust, resulting in lower crime rates; and political activism to further local needs. In his work on Italy, Putnam focuses on the overtly political ramifications of social capital. He shows that as regional measures of social capital became stronger in Italy from 1970 to 1989, politicians responded by placing greater emphasis on compromise and efficiency. By pooling resources, citizens were able to alter the prevailing beliefs about government's role and its relationship to the community, which Putnam terms 'political culture'. As a result of the active application of social capital, politicians viewed regional loyalty as more important than party affiliation, and citizen satisfaction as a concrete and achievable goal".[110]

Gutmann & Pullum studied voter participation in twelve general elections between 1880 and 1988 to measure social capital. They found that participation in national elections varied according to ethnicity. The northern states, in their sample, participated more fully than the southern ones. More populous countries had lower rates of voter participation, and countries with greater proportions of older Americans had higher rates of participation. Higher education and income have a positive impact on participation. Voters belonging to Roman Catholic countries had higher percentage of voting compared to countries having Episcopalians or Baptists. In the first half of the century, the Spanish origin Hispanos of New Mexico had highest participation rates followed by Scandinavian, German and British / Irish immigrants and the lowest being African – Americans. In the second half of the century, the Germans voted most heavily.

They also examined the grazing associations, the voluntary groups of the ranchers in the Great Plains. The counties, with hardly any grazing associations, were generally poor in social capital and demonstrate low voter turnout. Their populations comprised ethnic and religious groups that tended to participate less, rather than more, in national elections. Thus levels of social capital had an impact on local rural, as well as national urban and semi-urban civic engagement.

Lucian Pye writes that every society has its own rules of *civility*, which ensures social order leading to the integration of a functioning society. According to him, "social capital builds upon the norms of civility; it is the next step up in the development of a democratic political culture".[111]

Pye considers civility, social capital and civil society to the key building blocks for democratic theory. "Civility involves the most general norms of personal interaction; social capital determines the potential for reaching community and national goals collectively; and civil society provides the critical bases for articulation and aggregation of interests essential for pluralistic democracy. The particular civility norms of a country either facilitate or impede the accumulation of social capital. The amount of social capital amassed by a society sets the state for the emergence of a healthy civil society, which in its turn provides the dynamics for democratic politics".[112] By this, Pye highlights the importance of social capital and civility in a democratic society, particularly pluralistic democracies. He equates 'social capital' with 'financial capital' saying as the later is a necessity for economic development, the former is a necessity for social progress. He cites some of the Asian countries where 'trust' is playing a major role for reciprocal relationships. Social capital, in Pye's hands, is a concept of constructive value (alongside civility) for the understanding of society, and especially for an appreciation of why certain societies embrace democratic values and others do not.[113]

Social capital, which consists of, some aspect of social structure and which refers to norms, trust and social connections helps in maintaining the social stability of a group, even though members come and go. We can very well put the norms, trust, values, etc. under the heading 'culture' of a group. "Culture includes a people's beliefs about itself and the world, values, norms of conduct, customs, and manners. Culture is tradition, the repository of that people's experience – what works, what to avoid, how to survive and prosper in the world".[114] Human groups are organic systems and therefore are 'bottom-up emergence'. It contains within itself abilities to develop and to strive for the better without loosing its autonomy. It is an interacting entity and capable of self-organising and has the prices of creativity and novelty always in operation. Human individuals interact with their environments to form groups (families, work groups etc.); groups interact with their environments to form organisations and communities; organisations and communities interact with their environments to form societies; and societies interact with their environments to form global society.[115] From this we infer how individuals interactions evolve into the formation of global societies.

Social capital, in the words of Tom Lodge, refers to those features of associational life, which generate the attitudes, habits, expectations, and relationships, which facilitate collective action directed at developmental goals.[116] From this, it can be said that social capital is a means to attain goals of development, through collective action, for the collectivity. Social capital is essentially about feelings and attitudes and the role which certain types of organisations play in generating these: the term implies a more critical or at least questioning evaluation of the part played by civil society in democracy and development and it concedes a role for the state and its institutions in helping to promote or build the relationships and values it embodies.[117] Thus social capital, as a concept, has positive ramifications on the society. According to Lodge, in the African context, the constructive relationship, which may exist between democratic practices and economic development can be cushioned with the idea of social capital. Civic associations became a major force in South African politics during the 1980s and 1990s. However, with regard to the focus of these associations, there is a difference of opinion both in academic and public forums. One school of thought, exemplified in the work of Jeremy Seekings, Mark Swilling and Tom Lodge, emphasised those concerns of these organisations which were specific to the particular communities in which they were based.[118] Hence, these organisation were essentially reformist, inspired chiefly by 'bread and butter' material preoccupation. A second 'generation' of analysts, better informed by fresh data, acknowledged the role played by civics and assigned to them in the larger political project of a nationalist movement, which during the 1980s appeared to gear to revolutionary and insurrectionary objectives.[119] A logical corollary to this is that the civics lost touch with the masses and their sentiments and thereby failed to develop a participatory political culture, representing particular groups within the community only. This view is again countered that this was inevitable due to general popular pressure and sentiment. The debate still remains fairly open-ended.

In the 1980's, civics in South Africa served simply as surrogates for the organised political life that in normal democracy would be assumed by political parties and hence would not embody significant reservoirs of social capital. But later, in 1992 when civic associations were coordinated through a national bureaucracy, the South African National Civic Organisation (SANCO) and their candidates own in the local government elections in November 1995, popular protests around environmental disputes and community issues propped up.

Greg Ruiters expresses a sort of pessimistic view at the initial stages of South African society for the presence of social capital and civil society. "Social decay, rampant crime, mass black unemployment, political demobilisation and a morally suspect black advancement ethos are among the forces wearing away accumulated horizontal solidarities and the erstwhile sense of community (social capital as understood by Putnam). All this is underpinned by a distinct hegemonic process of demobilisation of working-class identities and militant forms of social solidarity in favour of nation-building reconciliation and rain-bowism".[120]

Ruiters is of the view that Trade Unions in South Africa are a powerful source of social solidarity and social capital on a non-racial, non-ethnic basis. The civics are the second most powerful community network. Inadequate and expensive services, rising rent and transport costs, lack of housing, and illegitimate local government underpinned a broader struggle against the apartheid regime and were the primary motivating forces for the formation of civic and residence associations.

Social capital and civil society in South Africa have to resist a blurred line of division between civil society and government, primarily because of the alliance between ANC, SANCO and Cosatu Union. Again the psyche of the people that even though

ANC has a mandate and can bring changes, it is busy in appeasing the 'whites' & foreign investors.

Ruiters considers social capital to be fundamentally normative and having a strong class resonance. Social capital for one group is anti-social capital for others unless one assumes a real and sustained win-win outcome. In the new South Africa, it is the case that we cannot so easily transplant old forms of social association and old discourses into new situations. The earlier mode of social capital included violent opposition to the apartheid enemy; the new mode espoused by the ANC is meant to be one of national reconciliation and constructive social partnership between all major stakeholders to build a united nation. For this, he says, social capital to be a directional concept, which requires concretisation. If strong civil society is to be measured in terms of vibrancy of horizontal forms of associational life, norms of reciprocity and networks, then South Africa black townships and trade unions, despite recent violence and social disintegration, may still be ranked highly indeed when it comes to reservoirs of solidarity, coordination i.e. social capital.[121] In South Africa, unity and homogeneity is emphasised for the oppressed towards the oppressions. The lack of tolerance of gross inequality could be seen as social capital.

While discussing on social capital in the South African context, Kirsten Harrison distinguishes the form of social capital present in rural and urban areas. She says, in rural area the existence of social capital and its relationship to the state can best be explained through the notion of embeddedness.[122] Here both traditional authority in the form of headman and chiefs, and democratic associations such as civics, unions & political parties are simultaneously found. Division between state and civil society is not distinct. Co-operative relations in rural area mark the presence of social capital, in contrast, the urban area has a sharp distinction between civil society and the state. Social capital is often used as an informal governing tool that exists outside of and sometimes in competition to formal governing structures.[123]

According to Paul Collier,[124] social capital is 'social' – because it involves some non-market process, which nevertheless has economic effects, and is known as the externalities in economic parlance. Social capital is usually characterised by a triple involvement with 'externalities'. First, the *initiation* of social interaction always involves an externality (it makes two to tango). Secondly, the social interaction usually, though not inevitably, has some unintended, or only partly intended economic affect that is, the economic effect is external to the purpose of the *interaction*. Thirdly, this economic effect is to internalise some other externality. Putnam shows this by his example of the prevailing amateur choirs more in northern Italy than in southern Italy. Here potential members first come together and join to form the choir, their repeated social interaction generates the externality of trust and finally the internalisation of the externality inflicted by opportunism. "To summarise, social capital is social if it is a social interaction which has the effect of internalising an externality. It will be under-provided, both because the establishment of social interaction involves an externality, and because the economic benefit is likely to be unrecognised or incidental to the purpose of the interaction".[125] Collier again writes for social capital to be meaningfully capital and its economic effect must have some persistence.[126] Persistence can be intrinsic either to the social interaction, or to its effects. It is through investment in physical capital that the social interaction can have persistent effects. This he shows by giving an example of purchasing a bus or building a school by a village community. Individuals cannot do it alone but collectively they can do it and reap the benefits from it and this is the social capital of the village community. From this example we can also say that the rotating credit associations inhere in it social capital.

Social capital may not always be inherently good for the community. Sometimes it yields to negative consequences for the community as a whole, and in such circumstances it can be termed as un-social capital. Collier gives the example of the study of Gambetta (1995) on the mafia in Sicily. The Mafia have a high degree of 'trust' towards their clients and networks but in the process of their operations they destroy a lot of other social capital. This destruction of social capital requires the use of force and a monopoly of information (a by-product of which is secrecy).

Another example of social capital being dysfunctional is the relationship between ethnic diversity and civil war. It is very often said that ethnic diversity may lead to increase civil strife. Collier does not adhere to this and writes that the most ethnically diverse societies are even safer than homogenous societies. "The reason for this is that the organisation of a rebellion requires a high degree of collective action among those who are disaffected with the government. The coordination of disaffection is aided when there are two ethnic groups in society rather than one, because, if the government is disproportionately identified with one of the ethnic groups, potential rebels can more easily identify as a collectivity distinct from the government. However, as ethnic diversity increases, the disaffected become composed of many ethnic groups and so face mounting difficulties of co-ordination. In effect, for the purposes of rebellion, the (negative) value of social capital peaks when there is a moderate amount of ethnic diversity and falls as diversity increases beyond that level".[127] So, when quantitatively ethnicity in less, there is a positive social capital which then leads to disturbances and violence in the society. People become suspicious and the presence of 'trust' collapses. From the above example it can be argued that the negative consequence of social capital depends on its mobilisation. It is not the social capital, which is responsible for communal disturbance, rather, it is the misuse and abuse of social capital. Further when an ascriptive group is guided by private reason it places its interest above all other interests.

While talking of social capital, it would be of much interest to mention something about 'human capital' and 'physical capital' and to link these three concepts. If financial / physical capital is found in one's bank account and human capital inside one's head, social capital inheres in one's relations with others.[128] Human capital refers to the intellectual ability of a person. It does not necessarily depend on educational attainment or degrees/diplomas but on the capability of a person in doing his/her work and achieving success in it. Human capital includes education, skill, good health etc. all of which contribute for the promotion of good quality human life. Human capital has long been recognised by many as critical for achieving developmental goals – economic and social. Amartya Sen (1995) is of the view that it is only due to great human capital that the South-East Asian Countries could become major economic and industrial powers and also have a lot of opportunities for their citizens. However, here we are not discussing about the causes of the financial crisis, which the South-East Asian Countries had to face in 1997-98. Looking at the contribution of human capital to rapid economic growth in some countries, development in these countries can be aptly described as 'human resource led development'.

Social Capital mixed with human capital can yield to better social networks and assurances against any risk thereby providing some sort of security to the human being. "Harnessing of human capital presupposes revitalisation and effectiveness of social capital which is the key to a vibrant forward looking civil society. Social capital has a family resemblance to human capital. Human capital is the resource that resides in individuals".[129] In a way we can say that 'human capital' is individualistic while social capital is always group-oriented. Social capital inheres in the relationship between actors rather than in physical assets, like financial capital, or in personal human capital.

In the view of Portes and Senoen Brenner and Portes & Zhou, *bounded solidarity and enforceable trust* foster the development of social capital than can be used to group members. The group must have a feeling of oneness and must behave as a unity. By this way it can maintain its solidarity and cohesiveness and can develop an attitude of mutual cooperation. However, solidarity alone will not be adequate without trust among themselves. Trust is not something, which we can be very sure of its presence. For this, we require to enforce the trust among the group members so that situation like *prisoners dilemma* is eliminated to the utmost extent. Enforceable trust certainly does not mean to deliberately infuse trust among group members but to deliberately give severe punishment to anyone who breaks another person's trust. Only such sanctions and actions can foster the development of social capital in the group.

According to Bishnu N.Mohapatra, social capital, apart from its definitional value, offers new explanations concerning collective action, institutional efficacy and above all quality of democratic life in a society.[130] Greater stock of social capital facilitates citizens to undertake group activities and sustain collective practices. He writes, a rich associational life signifies a good social capital in a society and this associational life promotes the level of trust among the people. From this one can say that social capital generates a 'we' feeling among the citizens and homogenises the heterogeneous in a segmented society so as to draw benefits from the state. This we—feeling are reflected in the associational life, both formal and informal.

A community is said to have high social capital where citizens have a tendency to engage in civic affairs, form voluntary associations, which lead to collective action for the common good, and it thus creates fertile ground for political and economic development.[131] Such type of community is called by Putnam *et.al.* as 'civic community'. By civic community they refer to a literate, informed community of citizens participating in a vibrant associational life that is based on horizontal bonds of mutual solidarity and that upholds liberal, modern values within the frame of common good.[132] Civic community by all means reflects an egalitarian society. It is only in a civic community we find the existence of social capital, which leads to better democratic performance. This is what Putnam concludes in his study of Italy where northern Italy due to the presence of civic community has superior institutional performance than southern Italy.

The notion of civil society came to prominence with the Eastern European uprisings of the late 1980s. These events were taken as signaling a paradigmatic shift, from a state-centered to a society-centered perspective, from a strategy of armed struggle that seeks to capture state power to one of an unarmed civil struggle that seeks to create a self-limiting power.[133] It is only in the late 1980s that the terminology of civil society began to gain wide currency in academic discussions and the self-characterizations of democratic movements around the globe. In this context, 'civil society' is used to highlight the role of associational life – interest groups, social movements, grass roots organisations and so on--in occupying or creating social spaces beyond the full control of the state apparatus.[134] This 'self – organising' or 'autonomous' quality of 'civil society' is said to allow associational life to act as both a staging ground for opposition to the (always potentially, if not actually, authoritarian or predatory) state and the basis for mobilising plural, popular agencies as an alternative site of politics in an evolving democratic society. Or, to highlight a different emphasis, civil society is associated with the cultivation or a set of social and political virtues described as 'civility': trust, tolerance of different life-style, respect for rule of law and common standards of public behaviour and commitment to collective goals.[135] We can say that in a civil society, citizens apart from their engagement for sustenance of their life and livelihood, also spend their leisure time in doing volunteer work, join voluntary or civil association, attend churches, participate in fraternal organisations and philanthropy activities and contribute for charity and fund raising activities. When we engage in these activities, we occupy civic space and (whether we know it or not) help define citizenship as membership in civil society rather than just as voting.[136]

Different authors and scholars of the present day define civil society in a wide variety of definitions but the core meaning of all these definitions is more over the same. Thus Gellner's definition of civil society is "that set of diverse non-governmental institutions which is strong enough to counter balance the state and whilst not preventing the state from fulfilling its role of keeper of the peace and arbitrator between major interests, can nevertheless prevent the state from dominating and atomising the rest of society".[137] For Robertson, civil society is "the organised society over which the state rule".[138] For Roberts and Edwards it consists of "those relations which are a part neither purely of the private sphere of the family, nor purely of the public sphere of the state".[139] Scruton typifies it as forms of association which are "spontaneous, customary and in general not dependent on law".[140] Urry has it as "the individualising sphere of the circuit of capital's path to expanded reproduction".[141] Tester defines civil society as "an imagination which attempted to identify, represent and legislate some basic unity in the experience of being human".[142] If we make an analytic understanding of these definitions we will see that civil society occupies a place between the individual / citizen and the overarching state, disturbing neither of the two but facilitating both of them and smoothening the processes of both for a better and happier life and a longevity for the state, or to be more particular for the political party governing the state and people. Though an active associational life may check or reform the state in certain respects, civil society itself often calls forth an expansion of the state apparatus as an agent of social reform, regulating uses of social power, checking inequalities and mediating conflicts generated by and within society.

Larry Diamond, writing on civil society, "conceives it as the realm of organised social life that is voluntary, self generating (largely), self-supporting, autonomous from the state, and bound by a legal order or set of shared rules. It is distinct from 'society' in general in that it involves citizens acting collectively in a public sphere to express their interests, passions and ideas, exchange information achieve mutual goals, make demands on the state and hold state officials accountable".[143] From this one can infer that civil society is some sort of space or platform which provides the citizens a chance for solidarity and put forth their voice in a legitimate way to achieve just desired goals. Diamond lists the democratic functions of civil society: checking government power, developing participatory skills and practices as well as democratic values, recruiting and training leaders, disseminating information and providing channels for the expression of interests. However, these functions can be performed if the civil society(ies) have certain features. First is compromising and having democratic goals and methods. Second, it should have high organisational institutionalisation. Third, civil society should be pluralistic to the optimum without fragmentation. Pluralism helps groups in civil society survive, and encourages them to learn to cooperate and negotiate with one another.[144] Finally, it should be dense and provide maximum opportunity to people to involve themselves in the multiple associations and informal networks. The more associations there are in civil society, the more likely it is that they will develop specialised agenda and purposes that do not seek to swallow the lives of their members in one all-encompassing organisational framework.[145] The associational life of civil society may also turn its attention to the further democratisation of formal political institutions or of civil society internally.

Civil society needs, for its survival and existence, certain rights, rule of law and citizenship, which should be juridically guaranteed and enforced. This enables the civil society to counteract the state whenever needed. Civil society has, therefore, been privileged by democratic theory as a vital precondition for the existence of democracy.[146] However, civil society, itself needs to be democratic to carry out this programme. A democratic state in effect, requires a democratic civil society.[147] The concept of civil society includes within it the whole lot of assumptions, values and institutions, like political, social and civil rights, the rule of law, representative institutions, a public sphere and above all a plurality of associations, which cannot be dispensed as the preconditions for democracy. The classical political theory located the emancipatory potential of civil society in the fact that it is here that individuals come to recognize themselves as social beings.[148] Individuals gained the idea that, cooperative efforts among them can yield better results of their private ends. Hegel writes, "through working with others, the individual's particularity is mediated; he ceases to be a mere unit and eventually becomes so socially conscious, as a result of the educative force of the institutions of civil society, that he wills his ends only in willing universal ends".[149] This process helps in the socialisation of the individual. To Hegel, civil society is an intermediary stage between the unreflective emotions of the family and the universal logic of the state. Civil society in Hegel, says Shlomo Avineri, "is nothing else than the market mechanism".[150] As articulated in the *Philosophy of Right* (Hegel, 1820), 'civil society' encompasses not only the 'system of needs' that had been the particular concern of political economists, but also the system of civil law that makes exchange relationships possible, and the public and private agencies that carry out the supervisory and welfare functions a market society requires. Civil society is, for Hegel, a creature of the modern world, presenting a 'spectacle of extravagance and want' that is historically unprecedented. The individual, who driven onward in a relentless pursuit of self-interest, brings into existence a social order that transcends the intentions of any given individual.

Civil society for Hegel, is a curious mixture or "the historical product of a two-dimensional process".[151] Hegel's idea of civil society reflected the concrete conflicts of the universalism of modern thought by employing the earlier critical core of formalism and empiricism.[152] It is rooted in the market but cannot be reduced to it. It includes political and legal functions that were split off from the subsequent discussion of the state. Hegel stated that civil society represents the state "as understanding envisions it"[153], it is on account of the state that grasped only the 'external' attributes of political life and, hence, reduced the state to a set of contractual relations between individuals who view their own ends as absolute and see interactions with others – and with the state itself – as a way of achieving these ends.[154] This contractual relations was henceforth regulated by civil law. Bounded by law, the modern state recognised the rights of citizens. The rule of law meant law-governed behaviour was the rule. It is in this sense that civil society was understood as civilised society.[155] The sphere of civil society, for Hegel, contains not just economic but social and civic institutions. It includes not just the market, the system of production and exchange for the satisfaction of needs, but also classes and corporations concerned with social, religious, professional and recreational life.[156] As Pleczynski says, civil society in this sense is an arena in which modern man legitimately gratifies his self-interest and develops his individuality, but also learns the value of group action, social solidarity and the dependence of his welfare on others, which educate him for citizenship and prepare him for participation in the political arena of the state.[157] As a meeting ground of contradictory interests, civil society in Hegel comprises two related moments, the first explosive, the second integrative; the first in the arena of the market, the second of public opinion.[158] In Hegel, civil society came to designate the sphere of economic production and exchange and the legal and social institutions that made such activities possible. When Hegel and others coined the term 'civil society' (*burgerliche Gesellschaft*) they were pointing to the growth of a web of private autonomous associations that they believed were necessary to consolidate the nation state in an organic unity.

Karl Marx distinguished civil society, 'as a sphere of economic activity unlimited by political considerations', from 'the bourgeoisie as a social class'. Marx transformed Hegel's distinction between the state and civil society by denying the universality of the state and insisting that the state expressed the particularities of 'civil society' and its class relations, a discovery that compelled him to devote his life's work to exploring the anatomy of 'civil society' in the form of a critique of political economy. Civil Society to Marx is the totality of relations submerged in the market and the bourgeoisie is the authority that describes its quality.

Marx in *The German Ideology* writes about 'civil society' in dual ways and simultaneously both having a relation between them. "Civil society embraces the whole material intercourse of individuals within a definite stage of the development of productive forces. It embraces the whole commercial and industrial life of a given stage, and in so far, transcends the state and the nation, though, on the other hand, it must assert itself in its external relations as a nationality and internally must organise itself as state. The term 'civil society' emerged in the eighteenth century, when property relationships had already extricated themselves from the ancient and the medieval communal society. Civil society as such only develops with the bourgeoisie : the social organisation evolving directly out of production and commerce, which in all ages forms the basis of the state and of the rest of the idealistic superstructure, has, however, always been designated by the same name".[159] Marx thus considered civil society was 'bourgeois society', a particular historical phase of the process of material production. In his base and superstructure model, Max dissolved the social structures of civil society in the economic base; and then enlarged the economic perspective of the society upto the extent it was co-terminus with the society itself. This resulted in the dichotomy of 'society-state'. The State – the political order - is the subordinate, and civil society – the realm of economic relations – the decisive element.[160]

Marx was of the view that class divisions are not found in every society but it appeared only when a surplus is generated, such that it becomes possible for a class of non-producers to live off the productive activity of others. Those who controlled the means of production became the dominant or ruling class and then the exploitative character inherent in it evolved. This capitalist phase produced the civil society, which remained autonomous of the state and was ostensibly depoliticised. The apolitical civil societies necessarily tend to produce bureaucratic authoritarian forms of state. The state became enmeshed in civil society and looked after the interests of the bourgoisie. The citizen, when he gives his vote establishes his universal characteristic. Apart from this, the citizen, as a member of what Marx called *burgerliche Gesellschaft*, civil society, is imprisoned in his particularities; he is not connected to the collectivity as a whole. Civil society imprisons all individuals in their particularities and consequently prevents them from realising their vocation of universality.[161]

Marx, therefore considers that individuals of the proletariat class should come out of this particularity and be universal. The worker, who has only his wage to live on, who places his labour power on the market in exchange for a wage, bears no resemblance to the citizen who every four or five years elects his representatives and, directly or indirectly, his leaders. Thus individuals at work would have to be able to participate in universality as citizens do by means of the voting. This can be done by abolishing the private property system and enabling to establish the communal property system or in other words in ending the capitalist system where profit is the sole motive.

Civil society in Gramsci is antagonistic to the economy. It was a weapon against capitalism, not an accommodation to it. Gramsci appropriated the concept of civil society to mark out the terrain of a new kind of struggle, which would take the battle against capitalism not only to its economic foundations but also to its cultural and ideological roots in everyday life.[162] In *Prison Notebooks,* Gramsci says "between the economic structure and the state with its legislation and its coercion stands civil society".[163] As it is in between the economy and the state, it draws from both. Like Marx, Gramsci does not associate civil society on purely economy. Civil society in Gramsci does not belong to the structural sphere (i.e the 'base'), but to the superstructural sphere.[164] The formula most commonly found in Gramsci is the State = political society plus civil society. Political society is the arena of coercion and domination; civil society that of consent and direction (or 'leadership').

Gramsci showed us how the state seeks the conditions of its reproduction by hegemonizing civil society. He thus sometimes narrowly equates the state with political society, the system of direct coercive rule, leaving to civil society the main work of organising hegemony. Gramsci says, it is precisely in civil society that intellectuals operate especially and perform their key function of supplying legitimacy and creating consensus on behalf of the ruling groups.[165]

"Force and consent; coercion and persuasion; State and Church; political society and civil society; politics and morality; law and freedom; order and self-discipline 'or again; force and consent, authority and hegemony, violence and civilisation, the individual moment and the universal moment ("Church" and "State")".[166] These antinomies are widely found in Gramsci's writings, and make clearer than any elaborate discussion just how and where we are supposed to see civil society. For Gramsci, 'civil society' referred to a heterogeneous political and ideological arena, united mainly in so far as it corresponded to a modification of the bourgeoisie's form of political and ideological representation from one, which was direct and concentrated to one which was indirect and diffuse.[167]

While concluding on Gramsci we can write that the capitalist state builds up its hegemony through the civil society and hence the latter is dependent on the former. For Gramsci, civil society provides the buffer for the state. He differentiates the civil society from the state, the economy and society. The realm of civil society is not the market but public opinion and culture. Its agents are intellectuals, who figure prominently in the building of hegemony. Its hallmarks are voluntary association and free publicity, the basis of an autonomous organisational and expressive life. Although autonomous of the state. This life cannot be independent of it, for the guarantor of this autonomy of civil society can be none other than the state.

Alexis de Tocqueville was a liberal theorist and in his view civil society was the arena, which was basically meant to protect the individuals against the overarching state. Liberal theory insists on the need to create and sustain a sphere of individual and social interaction free of state intervention. Civil Society, in a way, provides a space, which is relatively free of state interference. Indeed, the presence of a vibrant and active civil society has come to be seen as a vital and indispensable precondition for democracy.[168]

Tocqueville distinguishes between Political Society (*Societe politique*) as relations between the Federal and State Governments and (between) the citizen of the union and of each state; Civil Society (*Societe civile*) as relations of the citizens among themselves and Religious Society (*Societe religieuse*) as relations between God and the members of society, and of the religious sects among themselves.[169] While religious society and political society involves relation between superior and inferior, civil society involves relations among individuals joining together, free from the control of either the state or the Church. Civil society for Tocqueville, is essentially the arena of private interest and economic activity, and which corresponds more or less directly to the capitalist economy that Marx also identifies with civil society.[170] Tocqueville perhaps considered civil society to be a complementary to democracy.

In Tocqueville's conception for the first time, civil society and democracy were viewed as inherently linked together, and not antagonistic and disconnected. Tocqueville was perhaps the first major theorist to present civil society as the indispensable counterpart to a stable and vital democracy, rather than as an alternative to it. For him, civil society is a compound of two elements : "the whole sum of social and associational elements and those that comprised the active political (republican) community".[171] Civil Society, in him, was concerned to the needs of daily life and aimed at the preservation of 'civilisation' itself which otherwise would have been eroded to barbarism.

Most writers of civil society agree however, that civil society has an institutional core constituted by voluntary associations outside the sphere of the state and the economy. Habermas says, such associations range from, for example, churches, cultural associations, sports clubs and debating societies to independent media, academics, groups of concerned citizens, grass-roots initiatives and organisations of gender, race and sexuality, all the way to occupational associations, political parties and labour unions.[172]

In his *Philosophical Discourse of Modernity*, Habermas develops his inter subjective approach to modernity using the concept of 'communicative rationality'. The communicative rationality recalls older ideas of logos, in as much as it brings along with it the connotations of a non-coercively unifying, consensus-building force of a discourse in which the participants overcome their subjectively based views in favour of a rationally motivated agreement.[173] Communicative reason is directly implicated in social life processes in so far as acts of mutual understanding take on the role of a mechanism for coordinating action.[174] The generalisation we draw from this is that human social life is based upon processes for establishing reciprocal understandings.

Habermas draws five key processual requirements of discourse ethics for the participants so as to reach to the validity and truth of a certain argument. He calls this principle of validity as 'the universalisation principle of discourse ethics'.[175] These are "(1) no party affected by what is being discussed should be excluded from the discourse (the requirement of generality); (2) all participants should have equal possibility to present and criticize validity claims in the process of discourse (autonomy); (3) participants must be willing and able to empathize with each other's validity claims (ideal role taking); (4) existing power differences between participants must be neutralised such that these differences have no effect on the creation of consensus (power neutrality); and (5) participants must openly explain their goals and intentions and in this connection desist from strategic action (transparence)".[176] In a society following this model, citizenship would be defined in terms of taking part in public debate. Society exhibiting these preconditions reflect that individuals have respect for others view, they give a patient hearing to them and reposing trust on them and above all it reflects the benevolent character of the society.

Harbermas in the name of 'enlightenment project' distinguished between post-traditional and traditional notions of civil society, reserving legitimacy only for the former. The traditional civil society was some sort of historical depth, in which communities, interpersonal bonds, public institutions and national cultures are created over long periods of time and become resistant to even the most oppressive political authorities. It was lacking a normative force even if it may have its validity to natural communities. With the political and economic modernity, he modified the civil society. Civil society in his post-traditional sense indicates an arena of association where emphasis is put on choosing those with whom one wants to associate and choosing the terms on which associations are formed.[177] It is meant to indicate a mature form of critical reflection, which marks the transition from a 'conventional' orientation to fixed rules, unreflective duty and respect for authority, to a 'post-conventional' critical attitude towards identity construction.[178] For Habermas, identity formation is a matter for the private sphere, it is prior to the participation of national and critical debate of the individual in the public sphere.

Habermas with respect to civil society spoke about 'public sphere' and this he followed from the Gramscian notion of civil society as public opinion and culture. The public sphere was the space where private individuals met and discussed issues of public interest. The public sphere aroused the consciousness and nationalisation of citizens and made the state of the seventeenth and eighteenth centuries in England and France accountable to its subjects. In this way it led to the birth of political public. The *publicum* developed into the public, the *subjectum* into the (reasoning) subject, the receiver of regulations from above into the ruling authorities adversary.[179] Habermas accents both structural processes and strategic initiatives in explaining the historical formation of civil society. "In the context of a structural change 'embedded in the transformation of state and economy', the strategic initiatives of an embryonic bourgeois class shaped 'an associational life' along voluntary and democratic principles. At first, this 'public sphere' was largely apolitical, revolving 'around literary and art criticism'. The French Revolution, however, 'triggered a movement' leading to its 'politicisation' thereby underlining its democratic significance".[180] In his account of what he calls the 'structural transformation of the public sphere', Habermas views civil society as the arena in which pluralistic public opinion makes itself felt as an independent source of power. But of course some voices express themselves more loudly than others in the arena of public opinion, and not all the opinions expressed in an unconstrained public arena will be equally 'civil'. For strengthening the civil society, he is of the view of writing the constitutions and institutional development. For him the constitution is the main device for uniting citizens in a pluralist society. Written constitutions and institutional developments can yield to change in government through democratic process by means of discourse ethics and the theory of communicative rationality. Habermas thus theorises within a perspective of law and sovereignty. Habermas' approach is oriented toward universals, context independence and control via constitution writing and institutional development.[181] The concept of civil society embraces an entire range of assumptions, values and institutions, such as political, social and civil rights, the rule of law, representative institutions, a public sphere and above all a plurality of associations, which are indispensable as the preconditions for democracy. The idea of civil society entered political theory, when theorists began to insist that a social community is capable of organising itself independent of the specific direction of state power. Civil society is essentially a concept, which belongs to the tradition of political modernity founded on individualism and defense of human rights. Civil society indicates the arena of implicit freedom and it advocates the self-management of this arena through the conscious creation of dense networks of associations, self help bodies and social movements. It makes a resurgence to the classical liberal tradition that a democratic state is one which is limited not only by constitutions and institutions such as parliaments, political parties and organised modes of politics belonging to the political sphere, but by associational life that occurs in the space beyond the purview of the state.[182] Civil society is accordingly conceptualized as a space where people can pursue self-defined ends in an associational area of common concerns. For this, Jean Cohen conceptualises civil society as involving a classically liberal stabilisation of societal institutions on the basis of rights.[183] Arato described civil society as a complex of institutions that endorse the rule of law and the guarantee of civil rights, a free public sphere and a plurality of independent associations.[184] Both Cohen and Arato believe civil society to a sphere of social interaction between economy and state, composed above all of the intimate sphere (especially the family), the sphere of associations (especially voluntary associations), social movements, and forms of public communication.[185] For them the goals of civil society are self-limiting (i.e. not assuming the power of state or transforming it), aiming to cultivate from below a highly articulated, organised, autonomous and mobilizable civil society.

Civil society is generally intended to identify an arena of (atleast potential) freedom outside the state, a space for autonomy, voluntary association and plurality or even conflict, guaranteed by the democratic process. Civil society in contemporary theory is being treated as a residual category, as a veritable collection of everything that is not the state.[186] Civil society retains a distinctive character to the extent that it is made up of areas of social life – the domestic world, the economic sphere, cultural activities and political interaction – which are organised by private or voluntary arrangements between individuals and groups outside the direct control of the state.[187] Civil society is the domain that can potentially mediate between the state and private sectors and for women and men a space for activity that is simultaneously voluntary and public; a space that unites the virtue of the private sector – liberty – with the virtue of the public sector – concern for the general good. It shares with the private sector the gift of liberty, it is voluntary and is constituted by freely associated individuals and groups. However differing from private sector, it focuses on common ground and consensual, integrative, and collaborative action. Civil society, in a certain way is public without being coercive, voluntary without being private.

Giddens writing on the un-wielding nature of big government and giving instances of Burke, American Conservatism and Thatcherism shows the distaste of state. He views civil society as "a self generating mechanism of social solidarity"[188] vis-à-vis the thesis of a minimal state. Elsewhere,

Giddens writes the very notion of the 'state' as separable from civil 'society', is a modern one, because it is only in the post-medieval period that the sphere of interests in civil society, especially economic interests, have become part of the 'private rights' of the individual, and as such separable from the 'public' sphere of politics.[189] The little platoons of civil society must be allowed to flourish, and will do so if unhampered by state intervention. The virtues of civil society, if left to its own devices, are said to include good character, honesty, duty, self-sacrifice, honour, service, self-discipline, toleration, respect, justice, self-improvement, trust, civility, fortitude, courage, integrity, diligence, patriotism, consideration for others, thrift and reverence.[190] Giddens glorifies the role of the civil society and enumerates the virtues of it in comparison to the state and also in particular to the economic interests of the individuals i.e. the market.

Coming to the Indian usage of the term 'civil society', quite a large number of scholars and authors depict it as the upsurge of popular movements against the state. Kohili describes this upsurge as the 'crisis of governability'. Decadence in the governance due to the emergence of personalised rule, ineffective government and violence and corruption in public life has given rise to such a crisis. Kohili sees the crisis of governance and the decay in public life, as the result of the weakening of a normative commitment of the leaders to 'institutional constraints on personal power' as well as the result of the increasing demands from a variety of politicised social groups.[191] Rudolph and Rudolph, in a like manner, write that the crisis of governability is because of the 'demand polity', the groups, which demand and impose pressure upon the governments for benefits and concessions.

Civil society in India is seen by most theorists as a fluid association of social groupings which are based on caste and kinship linkages, or on religious mobilisation as much as on voluntary social associations. The problem associated with situation is that it is unable to recognise the distinction between counter-civil society movements such as religious fundamentalism, from associational life based on voluntary and revocable membership. Society, in this perspective, is collapsed into civil society.[192]

Some other scholars view civil society as a conglomeration of protest movements, which challenge the unjust and inequitable Indian state. Gail Omvedt writes, "by the late 1980s, the predominant feature of Indian politics had become the 'new social movements' of women, *dalits* and low castes, peasants, farmers, and tribals as well as ethnicity – based struggles for autonomy or independence on the periphery.... The hegemony of the Congress party has been decisively broken; 'Nehruvian' models of development are discredited".[193] Civil society here assumes the role of Tocquevillian model and represents "a non-state domain of protest and challenge".[194] It is pertinent to mention Manor (1989) who writes that to counter the centralising tendencies of the Indian State, the civil society was conceived as a plural sphere of social and political forms helping the nourishment of democracy. Again civil society was conceived as a series of cultural practices accepting diversity, dialogue and respect for each other and thereby cultivating the soil for tolerance to counter the fascist tendencies of communalism. In this context Rajni Kothari writes, "with us the creation of civil society becomes the task facing leaders of diverse social and cultural entities – in co-operation and communion with each other, drawing upon available and still surviving traditions of togetherness, mutuality and resolution of differences and conflict – in short, traditions of a democratic collective that are our own and on which we need to build in a changed historical context. This is the basic political task facing Indians – the creation of a civil society that is rooted in diversity yet cohering and holding together".[195] This reflects our social traditions and factual realities and the oft-commented 'Unity in diversity' in Indian society. Our ancient culture and heritage preaches Indian society to be *'Vasudeva Kutumbakum'* i.e. all are united and there is natural equality to all.

In India, civil society argument gains importance because the consensual model of democracy represented by the

Nehruvian state has exhausted itself and in this situation it is only a politically conscious civil society which will be able to solve India's political, social and cultural problems.

Neera Chandhoke argues that "civil society as a site which connects society and state is absolutely indispensable for democracy. It is not, however, merely the presence of a site, but the fact that this site has been historically connected with democratic values of participation, accountability and the construction of a public discourse through associational life, which makes civil society so indispensable".[196]

The strengthening of civil society is an important part of any political and theoretical agenda to build democracy and safeguard it, but before this can be done, the nature of civil society, the space it occupies in the social formation, and its relationship to the state needs to be grasped.

In an address to the Pretoria Rotary Club on January 15th 1998, James, A. Joseph defined social capital as "the vast array of ideas, ideals, institutions, and social arrangements through which people find their voice and mobilise private energies for a public good". He stresses on voluntary activities and associations as components using social capital to bring social development in three areas (1) providing help to the poor and marginalised, (2) promoting healing for a fragmenting world and (3) providing hope for those who do not yet enjoy the benefits of new democracies. Voluntary involvement brings unison to the problems faced not only by the affected persons but also to the volunteer and thereby leads to social integration and formation of new allegiances. The voluntary contribution and assistance also provide the hope that the marginalised need to believe that they can improve their situation.

Social capital comprises the endowment of mutually respecting and trusting relationships, which enable a group to pursue their shared goals more effectively than would otherwise be possible. Social capital therefore concerns the quality of the set of relationship of a social group. It can never be the possession or attribute of an individual. It concerns the communicative capacities of a group—something shared in a common and in which all participate. A fundamental point is that the relationship must be of a form that entails the active and willing (uncoerced) participation of all members in their shared activity or goal, on a basis of formal equality and mutual respect, "... social capital ... is embodied in the relations among persons ... a group whose members manifest trust worthiness and place extensive trust in one another will be able to accomplish more than a comparable group lacking that trust worthiness and trust".[197] Social capital refers to a set of respectful and trusting relationship which represent a generalised norm of goodwill and mutual confidence among the participating members of a social group. Such a norm enables multilateral dialogue and information - sharing to occur among the widest variety of individuals in the most efficient manner. Merely the numerous existence of voluntary associations in a society does not entail a high social capital. It is only where participation in the activities of such associations and groups is undertaken on conditions of mutual respect, trust and equality, both in relations with other members of the organisation in question and in the disposition of the association towards all others in society, that there is the capacity for true social capital to be generated. Here, two key qualities, which are required for voluntary associations, are apt to mention – (1) that they entail active participation on a basis of formal equality and (2) they do not contribute to forms of social exclusion and closure of lines of communication and fellow-feeling with other citizens. Hence, the principle of 'communicative equality' is emphasised upon by Putnam in his 'horizontal' contacts of association between equals, rather than 'vertical' networks (which imply inequalities of power or authority).

Any type of voluntary participation and creating and maintaining networks among persons requires a strong amount of trust between them. The presence of trust eliminates situations like we have in *Prisoner's Dilemma*. On the role of 'trust' in the creation of social capital with particular attention to economic development, Fukuyama in his book *Trust: The*

Social Virtues and the Creation of Prosperity (1995) writes about high trust and low trust societies and cultures. High trust societies tend to develop greater social capital, and consequently enjoy greater economic growth, particularly in the transition to a post-industrial economy. Likewise, high trust groups and cultures accumulate greater social capital. Fukuyama sees social capital as the glue that holds the otherwise centrifugal structures of the market together. He argues that the most successful nations in the new free-market world will be those with religious and cultural underpinnings that promote voluntary associations and help prepare people to work cooperatively in large organisation.[198] It is voluntary association in corporations that promises to promote economic growth.

Indian society is predominantly, an agrarian and it lives in villages. Villages can be viewed as little autonomous republics. It is rich with potential social capital. It is not the poverty of social capital rather poverty of human capital that apparently project social capital differently in a segmented manner.

REFERENCES

1. Putnam, Robert (1993), *Making Democracy Work*, Princeton University Press, p. 167.
2. Putnam, Robert D. (1995), 'Tuning in and Tuning Out: The Strange Disappearance of Social Capital in America', *Political Science and Politics*, Vol. XXVIII, No. 4, pp. 664-65.
3. Coleman, James S. (1990), *Foundations of Social Theory*, Harvard University Press, p. 300.
4. *ibid*, p. 302.
5. *ibid*, p. 300; Loury, Glenn (1997), 'A Dynamic Theory of Racial Income Differences' in Wallace, P.A & LcMund, A. (eds.), *Women, Minorities and Employment Discrimination*, Lexington Books.
6. Coleman, James (1988), "Social Capital in the Creation of Human Capital", *American Journal of Sociology*, 94 (Supplement), p. 97.

7. Putnam (1993), *op. cit.*, p. 167.
8. Newton, Kenneth (1997), 'Social Capital and Democracy', *American Behavioural Scientist*, Vol. 40, No. 5, p. 576.
9. Olle Tornquist (1999), *Politics and Development*, Sage Publications, London, p. 95.
10. Hadenius, Axel & Uggla, Fredrik (1996), 'Making Civil Society Work, Promoting Democratic Development: What can States and Donors Do !', *World Development*, Vol. 24, No. 10, p. 1621.
11. *ibid*, p. 1622.
12. Kornhouser, William (1960), *The Politics of Mass Society*, Routledge & Kegan Paul, London.
13. Hadenius, Axel & Uggla Fredrik, *op. cit.*, p. 1623.
14. *ibid*, p. 1628.
15. Foley, Michael W. & Edwards, Bob (1996), 'The Paradox of Civil Society', p. 38.
16. *ibid.*, p. 39.
17. Olson, Mancur (1982), *The Rise and Decline of Nations: Growth, Stagflation, and Social Rigidities*, Yale University Press, New Haven, p. 23.
18. Putnam, Robert (1993), *op. cit.*, pp. 173-6.
19. Putnam, Robert (1995), 'Bowling Alone', *Journal of Democracy*, January, p. 143.
20. Foley, Michael, W. & Edwards, Bob (1996), 'The Paradox of Civil Society', p. 41.
21. Bellah, R., et al. (1985), *Habits of the Heart: Individualism and Commitment in American Life*, Harper & Row, New York, p. 61.
22. Putnam, Robert (1993), *op. cit.*, pp. 167-75.
23. Coleman, J.S. (1988), 'Social Capital in the Creation of Human Capital', *Amercian Journal of Sociology*, 94, p. 98.
24. Greeley, Andrew (1997), 'Coleman Revisited - Religious Structure as a Source of Social Capital', *American Behavioural Scientist*, Vol. 40, No. 5, pp. 388-9.
25. *ibid*, p. 389.

26. Minkoff, Debra C. (1997), 'Producing Social Capital - National Social Movements and Civil Society', *American Behavioural Scientist*, Vol. 40, No. 5, pp. 606-19.

27. *ibid*, p. 607.

28. *ibid*.

29. *ibid*, pp. 610-11.

30. *ibid*, p. 611.

31. Foley, Michael W. & Edwards, Bob (1997), 'Escape from Politics? Social Theory and the Social Capital Debate', *American Behavioural Scientist*, Vol.-40, No. 5, p. 552.

32. Das, Gurucharan (1997), 'Revive the Republic – Concentrate on Civic Engagement', *Times of India*, 16.2.97.

33. Aron, Raymon (1991), *Main Currents in Sociological Thought*, Vol. I, Penguin Books, London, p. 197.

34. *ibid*.

35. Kenworthy, Lane (1997), 'Civic Engagement, Social Capital and Economic Cooperation', *American Behavioural Scientist*, Vol. 40, No. 5, p. 647.

36. *ibid*, p. 649.

37. *ibid*, p. 651.

38. Putnam, Robert (1993), *op. cit*., p. 167.

39. Hirschman, A.O. (1984), 'Against Parsimony: Three Easy ways of Complicating some Categories of Economic Discourse', *American Economic Review Proceedings*, 74 (93), as cited in Partha Dasgupta, 'Trust as a Commodity', in Gambetta., (ed.), *Trust*, p. 56.

40 Coleman, J. (1990), *op. cit*., p. 321.

41. Putnam, Robert (1993), *op. cit*., p. 171.

42. Secord & Buckman (1964), *Social Psychology*, McGraw Hill Book Company, New York, p. 323.

43. Broom, L. & Selznick, P. (1958), *Sociology*, Row, Peterson & Company, New York, p. 52.

44. Elinor Ostrom (1994), *Governing the Commons: The Evolution of*

Institutions for Collectivce Action, Combridge Uriversity Press, New York, pp. 200-11.

45. Knoke, David (1990), *Political Networks: The Structural Perspective*, Cambridge University Press, New York, pp. 68-9.

46. Putnam, Robert (1993), *op. cit.*, p. 177.

47. *ibid*, p. 178.

48. *ibid*, pp. 182-3.

49. *ibid*, p. 185.

50. Hall, Peter A. (1999), 'Social Capital in Britain', *British Journal of Political Science*, 29, p. 418.

51. *ibid*, p. 434.

52. *ibid*, p. 436.

53. *ibid*, pp. 439-40.

54. *ibid*, p. 443.

55. *ibid*.

56. Tolbert, Charles M., et al. (1998), 'Local Capitalism, Civic Engagement and Socio-economic Wellbeing', *Social Forces*, Vol. 77 (2), p. 403.

57. MacKenzie, Lynn Ryan (1995), 'Capitalism, Power and Community Well-Being: Developing a model for understanding the effect of local economic configuration on cities and their citizens', *Ph.D Diss.*, Cornell University.

58. Tolbert, Charles M., *op. cit.*, p. 407.

59. Grew, Raymond (1999), 'Finding Social Capital: The French Revolution in Italy', *Journal of Interdisciplinary History*, XXIX : 3 (winter), pp. 407-8.

60. *ibid.*, p. 417.

61. *ibid.*, p. 426.

62. *ibid.*, p. 433.

63. McIntosh, Marjorie K. (1999), 'The Diversity of Social Capital in English Communities: 1300-1640', *Journal of Interdiciplinary History*, XXIX : 3 (Winter), p. 459.

64. *ibid.*, p. 460.

65. *ibid.*, p. 466.

66. McIntosh, M.K. (1998), Response in the symposium about 'Controlling Misbehaviour in England: 1370-1600', *Journal of British Studies*, XXXVII, pp. 291-305.

67. *ibid.*, pp. 468-9.

68. *ibid.*, p. 468.

69. McNabb, Jennifer (1997), 'The Use of Social Capital by Women of the Upper Ranks of Early Modern England', paper presented at the *Western Conference on British Studies*, Fort Worth, Tex., October.

70. Harris, Barbara (1990), 'Women and Politics in Early Tudor England', *Historical Journal*, XXXIII, pp. 259-81.

71. McIntosh, *op. cit.*, pp. 477-8.

72. McIntosh., *op. cit.*, p. 479.

73. McIntosh., *op. cit.*, p. 490.

74. Rotberg, Robert I., (1999), 'Social Captial and Political Culture in Africa, America, Australasia & Europe', *Journal of Interdisciplinary History*, XXIX : 3 (Winter), pp. 339-356.

75. *ibid.*, p. 340.

76. Brucker, Gene (1999), 'Civic Traditions in Pre-modern Italy', *Journal of Interdisciplinary History*, XXIX : 3 (winter), p. 376.

77. *ibid.*, p. 377.

78. *ibid.*, p. 358.

79. Muir, Edward (1999), 'The Sources of Civil Society in Italy', *Journal of Interdisciplinary History*, XXIX : 3 (winter), p. 382.

80. *ibid.*, p. 382; Nobert Elias (trns. Edmund Jephcott), *The History of Manners. I. The Civilising Process*, New York, 1978.

81. *ibid*, p. 405.

82. Greene, Jack P. (1998), 'Social and Cultural Capital in Colonial America', *Journal of Interdisciplinary History*, XXIX: 3 (Winter), p. 492.

83. Verba, Sidney, Schoolman, Kay Lehman, & Brady (1995), *Voice and Equality: Civic Voluntarism in American Politics*, Harvard University Press,Cambridge, p. 1.

84. Huntington, Samuel P. & Nelson, Joan M. (1976), *No Easy Choice: Political Participation in Developing Countries*, Harvard University Press, Cambridge, p. 85.

85. Verba, Nie & Kim (1978), *Participation and Political Equality: A Seven Nation Comparison*, Cambridge University Press, pp. 81-92.

86. Putnam, Robert, *et al.* (1993), *op. cit.*, p. 177.

87. Seligson, Amber L. (1999), 'Civic Association and Democratic Participation in Central America – A Test of the Putnam Thesis', *Comparative Political Studies*, 32(3), pp. 342-62.

88. *ibid.*, p. 355.

89. *ibid.*, p. 357.

90. Harris, J. & P.de Renzio (1999), ' "Missing Link" or Analytically Missing?: The concept of social capital, An Introductory Bibliographic Essay', *Journal of International Development*, 9(7), p. 920.

91. Fine, Ben, (1999) , 'The Developmental State is Dead – Long Live Social Capital', *Development and Change*, Vol. 30, p. 4.

92. *ibid.*, pp. 1-19.

93. Narayan, D. & L. Pritchett (1996), 'Cents and Sociability: Household Income & Social Capital in Rural Tanzania', Draft Paper, *World Bank Environment Dept. & Policy Research Dept.*

94. Woolcock, M. (1998), 'Social Capital and Economic Development: Toward a Theoretical Synthesis and Policy Framework', *Theory & Society*, 27(2), pp. 193-6.

95. Fukuyama, F. (1996), *Trust: The Social Virtues and the Creation of Prosperity*, Penguin, London, p. 13.

96. Wilson, P. (1997), 'Building Social Capital: A Learning Agenda for the Twenty First Century', *Urban Studies*, 34(5-6), pp. 745-60.

97. Walker, G., B. Kogut & W. Shan (1997), 'Social Capital, Structural Holes and the Formation of an Industry Network', *Organisation Science*, 8(2), p. 111.

98. Gamm, Gerald & Putnam, Robert D. (1999), 'The Growth of Voluntary Associations in America, 1840-1940', *Journal of Interdisciplinary History*, XXIX: 4 (Spring), pp. 511-557.

99. *ibid.*, p. 548.

100. Ryan, Mary P. (1999), 'Civil Society as Democratic Practice: North American Cities During Nineteenth Century', *Journal of Interdisciplinary History*, XXIX: 4,(Spring), pp. 559-84.

101. *ibid.*, p. 569.

102. *ibid*, p. 569

103. Clemens, Elizabeth S. (1999), 'Securing Political Returns to Social Capital: Women's Associations in the US, 1880s – 1920s', *Journal of Interdisciplinry History*, XXIX: 4 (Spring), p. 614.

104. *ibid.*, p. 615.

105. *ibid.*, p. 584.

106. Keen, Susan, (1999), 'Associations in Australian History: Their Contribution to Social Capital', *Journal of Interdisciplinary History*, XXIX: 4, (Spring), p. 641.

107. *ibid.*, p. 658.

108. Goldin, Claudia & Katz, Lawrence F. (1999), 'Human Capital and Social Capital: The Rise of Secondary Schooling in America, 1910-1940', *Journal of Interdisciplinary History*, XXIX: 4 (Spring), p. 685.

109. *ibid.*, p. 707.

110. Gutmann, Myron P. & Pullum, Sara M. (1999), 'From Local to National Political Cultures: Social Capital and Civil Organisations in the Great Plains', *Journal of Interdisciplinary History*, XXIX:4 (Spring), p. 725.

111. Pye, Lucian W. (1999), 'Civility, Social Capital and Civil Society in Asia', *Journal of Interdisciplinary History*, XXIX: 4, (Spring).

112. *ibid.*, p. 764.

113. Rothberg, Robert I. (1999) , 'Social Capital & Political Culture', *JIH*, XXIX, 3, (Winter), p. 343.

114. Bishop, Peter (1998), 'Social Change of Futures Practice', *American Behavioural Scientist*, Vol. 42, No. 3, Nov./Dec., pp. 407-764.

115. *ibid.*, p. 409.

116. Lodge, Tom (1999), 'A Research Agenda for Investigating Social Capital & Development in South Africa', *Agora Project*, p. 45.

117. *ibid.*, p. 46.

118. *ibid.*

119. *ibid.*

120. Ruiters, Greg (1996), 'Contesting Social Capital in South Africa', *Agora Project*, p. 122.

121. *ibid.*, p. 128.

122. Harrison, Kristen (1999), 'Pinning down social capital in South Africa', *Social Capital Conference Paper*, (Unpublished), p. 5.

123. *ibid.*, p. 8.

124. Collier, Paul (1998), 'Social Capital & Poverty', *World Bank Working Paper*, April, p. 2.

125. *ibid.*, p. 4.

126. *ibid.*,p. 4.

127. *ibid.*, p. 18

128. Das, Gurcharan (1997), "The Search for a Civic India", *Times of India*, New Delhi, 24.10.97.

129. Satapathy, Brahmananda (1997), 'Literacy and Social Capital: An Interface,' *Research Paper* (Unpublished), South Africa, 1997.

130. Mohapatra, Bishnu, N. (1999), 'Social Connectedness, Civility & Democracy' unpublished conference paper, Uppsala University, Swden.

131. Das, Gurucharan, *op. cit*.

132. Bhattacharyya, Dwaipayan (1997), 'Social Capital and Political Society', *Unpublished Workshop Paper on Social Capital*, South Africa.

133. Mamdani, Mahmood (1997), *Citizen and Subject – Dencentralised Despotism and the Legacy of Late Colonialism*, OUP, New Delhi, p. 14.

134. Keane, John (1988), *Civil Society and the State*, Verso, New York,

p. 1; Cohen, Jean L. (1988), 'Discourse Ethics and Civil Society', *Philosophy and Social Criticism*, 14 : 325.

135. Pasha, Mustapha K., & Blancy, David (1998), 'Elusive Paradise: The Promise and Peril of Global Civil Society', *Alternatives*, 23, p. 420.

136. Barber, Benjamin R. (1996), 'Three Challenges to Reinventing Democracy' in Hirst, Paul & Khilnani, Sunil (Ed.) *Reinventing Democracy*, Blackwell Publishers, UK, p. 149.

137. Gellner, E. (1995), 'The Importance of Being Modular' in John A. Hall (ed.) *Civil Society: Theory, History, Comparison*, Polity, London, p. 32.

138. Robertson, *The Penguin Dictionary of Politics*, p. 44.

139. Roberts, G. & Edwards, A. (eds.), (1991), *A New Dictionary of Political Analysis*, Arnold, London, p. 133.

140. Scruton, R. (1982), *A Dictionary of Political Thought*, Pan, London, p. 66.

141. Urry (1983), *The Anatomy of Capitalist Societies*, Routledge, London, p. 12.

142. Tester, Keith (1992), *Civil Society*, Routledge, London, p. 124.

143. Diamond, Larry (1994), 'Toward Democratic Consolidation', *Journal of Democracy*, 5(3). Reprinted as 'Third World Civil Society can promote democracy' in Jonathan S. Petrikin (ed.) (1995). *The Third World, Opposing View Points*, San Deigo, Greenhaven, pp. 151-9.

144. *ibid.*

145. *ibid.*

146. Chandhoke, Neera (1995), *State & Civil Society*, Sage Publications, New Delhi, p. 9.

147. *ibid.*, p. 12.

148. *ibid.*, pp. 33-4.

149. Hegl, G.W.F., (1942), *Philosophy of Right*, translated by T.M. Knox, OUP, Oxford, pp. 353-4.

150. Avineri, Shlono (1972), *Hegel's Theory of the Modern State*, Cambridge Univ. Press, Cambridge, p. 12.

151. Mamdani, Mahmood (1997), *Citizen and Subject*, OUP, Delhi, p. 14.

152. Loannidou, Anastasia (1997), 'The Politics of the Division of Labour: Smith & Hegel on Civil Society', in Fine, Robert & Rai, Shirin, (eds.), *Civil Society*, Frank Cass, London, p. 58.

153. Schmidt, James (1995), 'Civil Society & Social Things', *Social Research* , Vol. 62, No. 4, (Winter), p. 910.

154. Steinberger, Peter J. (1998), *Logic and Politics: Hegel's Philosophy of Right*, Yale Univ. Press, New Haven, pp. 202-205.

155. Mamdani, M., *op. cit.*, p. 14.

156. Kumar, Krishna (1993), 'Civil Society', *British Journal of Sociology*, Vol. 44, No. 3, Sept., p. 379.

157. Pleczynski, Z.Z. (1988), 'Solidarity & the Rebirth of Civil Society' in Keane (ed.) *Democracy & Civil Society*, Verso, London, 1988, p. 364. See also Pleczynski (ed.), 1984), *The State & Civil Society: Studies in Hegel's Political Philosophy*, Cambridge Univ. Press.

158. Mamdani, M., *op. cit.*, p. 14.

159. Marx, Karl & Engels, F. (1975), *Collected Works*, International Publishers, New York, p. 89.

160. Engels, F. (1996), 'Ludwig, Feuerbach & the End of German Classical Philosophy' in Marx & Engels, *Selected Works*, Vol. 2, Foreign Languages Publishing House, Moscow, pp. 394-5.

161. Aron, Raymond (1991) , *Main Currents in Sociological Thought*, Vol. I, Penguin Books, England, p. 145.

162. Wood, Ellen, Meiksins (1995), *Democracy against Capitalism: Renewing Historical Materialism*, Cambridge Univ. Press, Cambridge, p. 241.

163. Gramsci, A. (1997), *Selection from the Prison Notebooks of Antonio Gramsci*, edited & translated by Quintin Hoare & Geoffrey N. Smith, Lawrence & Wishart, London, pp. 208-9.

164. Bobbio (1998), 'Gramsci and the concept of Civil Society', in Keane, John (ed.) *Civil Society and the State: New European Perspective*, Verso, London, p. 82.

165. Gramsci, A. (1971), *op. cit.*, p. 56.

166. *ibid.*, p. 170.

167. Gibbon, Peter (1998), 'Some Reflections on 'Civil Society' & Political Change' in Rudebeck, lars, Tornquist, Olle & Rajas, Virgilic (eds.), *Democratisation in the Third World – Concrete Cases in Comparative & Theoretical Perspective*, Macmillan, London, p. 26.

168. Chandhoke, Neera (1995), *State and Civil Society*, Sage Publication, New Delhi, p. 193.

169. Schleifer, James T. (1980), *The Making of Tocqueville's Democracy in America*, University of North Carolina Press, p. 7.

170. Kumar, Krishnan, *op. cit.*, p. 381.

171. Grzegorz, Ekiert (1991), 'Democratisation Processes in East Central Europe: A Theoretical Reconsideration, *British Journal of Political Science*, Vol. 21, Part-I, p. 300.

172. Habermas, J. (1992), 'Further Reflections on the Public Sphere' in Calhoun (ed.), *Habermas and the Public Sphere*, MIT Press, Cambridge, p. 453.

173. Habermas, J. (1987), *The Philosophical Discourse of Modernity*, MIT Press, Cambridge, pp. 294, 315.

174. Habermas, J. (1983), *The Theory of Communicative Action*, Vol. J, MIT Press, Cambridge, p. 316.

175. Habermas, J. (1990), *Moral Consciousness and Communicative Action*, MIT Press, Cambridge, pp. 120-1.

176. Habermas, J. (1993), *Justification and Application: Remarks on Discourse Ethics*, MIT Press, Cambridge, p. 31 and Habermas J., (1990), *op. cit.*, pp. 65-6.

175. Wagner, Peter (1994), *A Sociology of Modernity: Liberty and Discipline*, Routledge, London, 1994, p. 186.

178. Fine, Robert (1997), 'Civil Society Theory, Enlightenment and Critique', in Fine, Robert & Rai, Shrin., (eds.), *Civil Society: Democratic Perspectives*, Frank Cass, London, p. 12.

179. Habermas, J. (1989), *The Structural Transformation of the Public Sphere*, translated by L Burger, Polity Press, Cambridge, p. 26.

180. Mamdani, M., *op. cit.*, p. 15.

181. Flyvbkerg, Bemt (1998) 'Habermas & Foucault: Thinkers for civil society?', *British Journal of Sociology*, Vol. 49, p. 227.

182. Chandhoke, Neera, *op. cit.*, p. 31.

183. Cohen, Jean (1988), 'Discourse Ethics and Civil Society', *Philosophy & Social Criticism*, No. 14, p. 325.

184. Arato, A. (1981), 'Civiil Society Vs. the State', *Telos*, No. 47, p. 23.

185. Cohen, J., & Arato, A. (1992), *Civil Society and Political Theory*, MIT Press, Cambridge, p. ix.

186. Chandhoke, N., *op. cit.*, p. 37.

187. Held, David (1989), *Political Theory & the Modern State I*, Polity & Basil Blackwell, Cambridge, pp. 180-81.

188. Giddens, A. (1998), *The Third Way – The Renewal of Social Democracy*, Polity Press and Blackwell, Cambridge, p. 11.

189. Giddens, A. (1971), *Capitalism and Modern Social Theory*, Cambridge University Press, p. 6.

190. Green, David (1993), 'Reinventing Civil Society', *Institute of Economic Affairs*, London, p. viii.

191. Chandhoke, N., *op. cit.*, p. 28, & Kohli, Atul (ed.), (1988), *Indian Democracy: An Analysis of Changing State—Society Relations*, Princeton University Press, p. 305.

192. Chandhoke, N., *op. cit.*, p. 28.

193. Omvedt, G., (1993), *Reinventing Revolution*, M.E. Sharpe, New York, p. xii.

194. Chandhoke, N., *op. cit.*, p. 29.

195. Kothari, Rajni (1991), 'Human Rights: A moment in Search of a Theory', in S. Kothari & H. Sethi (eds.), *Human Rights: Challenges for Theory and Action*, New Horizons Press, New York, pp. 19-30.

196. Chandhoke, N., *op. cit.*, p. 40.

197. Coleman, J. (1990), *Foundations of Social Theory*, Harvard Univ. Press, Harvard, p. 304.

198. Portes, Alejandra & Landolt, Patricia (1996), 'The Downside of Social Capital', *American Prospect*, Vol. 26.

3

SOCIAL CAPITAL AND PUBLIC POLICY

In the previous chapter we have dealt the nature, meaning and various interpretations of social capital. Social Capital is always socially useful and beneficial to the individuals. The individuals come to believe about the utility of the norms of solidarity, trust, networks which leads to better understanding and cohesiveness of the people ignoring whatever inequalities that may be prevalent. In the process, social capital helps in the integration and unity of the society, which then contributes, to nation-building and the democratization process. Much concern is expressed to the deceleration of the democratisation process in some of the third world countries. These third world countries are also marked for its segmented and plural society and very often this breeds into hostility and antagonizes the social groups against each other. In this situation it is ultimately the society i.e. the individuals in the micro-analysis, who are the worst sufferers. A society lacking the virtues of social capital is not identified as a civil society but is referred to be a 'mass society'.

The State has an immense role to play in the welfare and development of its citizens. Here we are not concerned about whether it is a democratic or authoritarian/totalitarian state. Every form of government has a certain degree of responsibility towards its citizens but when we are talking about a democratic state it means a great thing. Such a form of government gives utmost respect to the wishes and needs of its citizens and it governs in such a manner which is conducive to both itself and its citizens. The demands of the citizens are articulated and aggregated by various agencies in the state and communicated to the government so as to be suitably considered and necessary actions are taken.

The presence of a high level of social capital in the civil society can effectively conduct the business of the welfare of the citizens by themselves. High level of trust and networks among the citizens bring them into close contact and they begin to discuss the pros and cons of a certain thing. This discussion very often lays the foundation of associational life and associations begin to emerge from it. Such associations do not exist in vacuum but have the backing and support of the citizens, so they are quite legitimate as an organisation. After a thread bare discussion of the needs and requirements, the association, or to be more appropriate, the voluntary associations as it is voluntarilly formed by the participating citizens for the welfare of common good, articulates the needs into demands and places it before the government for its redressal.

The Government after a detailed study and examining the validity of such demands and after analyzing the feasibility of granting of conceding the demands draws up policy and programmes to meet it.

A policy is more a general notion than a decision. It includes in it a bundle of decisions. It involves a general predisposition to respond in a particular way. It emerges when it is put into practice. It will be modified in the field and have effects beyond those envisaged by its original designers. A policy may be the result of deliberate action. In the words to Terry, "a policy is verbal, written or implied basic guide to action that is adopted and followed by a manager".[1] Dimmock defines policies as "the consciously acknowledged rules of conduct that guide administrative decisions".[2] Policy should be distinguished from the goal or the objective, on the one hand, and the operative steps, on the other. Thus, making every person in the country educated is an objective, compulsory primary education is a policy designed to realise the goal; and the opening of the schools and training of teachers, etc. are the steps necessary to carryout the policy.

Robert Eyestone terms Public Policy as the relationship of government units to it environments. He is however ambiguous to the term 'environment' and has not elaborated it. Environment contains within itself a whole lot of things.

Thomans R. Dye says that public policy is whatever the government chooses to do or not to do. Richard Rose says that public policy is not a decision, it is a course or pattern of activity. The public policy process requires a thoroughly close knit relation and interaction between the important governmental agencies and the non-governmental agencies. Carl J. Friedrich says "public policy is a proposed course of action of a person, group or government within a given environment providing opportunities and obstacles which the policy is proposed to utilise and overcome in an effort to reach a goal or realise as objective or purpose". This definition is an exhaustive one and leaves no doubt in the mind of the reader. It encompasses within itself a whole gamut of things.

We can draw a general outline of the characteristics/natures/features of public policy by studying some of the above mentioned definitions.

1. Public policies are goal-oriented. They aim at general public welfare and are so formulated and designed by the Government.
2. Public policy is a pattern or course of activity of the governmental and non-governmental officials and actors collectively, rather than being termed as their discrete and segregated decision.
3. Public policy is what the government actually decides or chooses to do and is the relationship of the government units to the specific field of political environment in a given administrative systems.

4. Public policy is positive in the sense that it depicts the concern of the government and involves its action to a particular problem on which the policy is made. Negatively, it involves a decision by governmental actors not to take any action on a particular issue.

5. Public policy, in its positive form has the sanction of law and authority behind it.

6. Public policy stems from a well-defined procedure wherein the power, control, bargaining and gaming concepts play a significant role.

Stated most simply, public policy is the sum of the activities of governments, whether acting directly or through agents, as its has an influence on the lives of citizens.[3] Governments very often implements the policies itself and sometimes it seeks the cooperation and coordination of other agencies like non-governmental bodies, private individuals who may be directly or indirectly, involved or associated with such policy. In developed countries, here comes the role of civil society. Observing this phenomenon the third world countries are now gradually adopting this phenomenon for public welfare.

Public policy is never an one-sided phenomenon i.e. it is not only the government's responsibility. It has at least three levels. At the first level we have policy choices, decisions made by politicians, civil servants or others and directed toward using public power to affect the lives of citizens. In this policy choices, demands, agitation's and protests are sometimes conducted by group of citizens or more appropriately called 'civil society' for the initiation of certain policies beneficial to the citizens at large. At the second level, we can speak of policy outputs - policy choices being put into action. At this level the government is doing things : spending money, hiring people, or promulgating regulations that will affect the economy and society. Outputs may be virtually synonymous with the term "program" commonly used in government. Finally at the third level we have policy impacts – the effects of policy choices and policy outcomes on citizens. Here it is the evaluation process, which is conducted, and accordingly modifications, if required, are made in the policies.

There are certain political and socio-economic environment, which influence the nature of policies adopted and their effects on citizens. Policy is the result of the interaction of the background factors with desires and decisions of those who make policies. Citizen participation is one of such background factor in shaping public policy. A corollary to democratic politics, citizen participation has much value. The cry of "no taxation without representation" in United States was essentially a demand for the right to participate. Governments of various states not only welcome citizen participation but also initiate community action programmes for maximum feasible participation of the communities. In 1952 the Government of India initiated the Community Development Programme in the rural community for positive transformation. It was conceived as a total programme involving the people and the government. The people were associated with the formulation of the schemes, with arranging resources for these, and with their execution. The government provided the technique and the administrative support for the programme. This combination of the people and the government at the community level was accepted as the real step forward. The programme was comprehensive and included among other things improvement of communication, education, health, sanitation, housing, rural employment, welfare of women and children. Similarly in United States in 1964 community action programmes were authorised by law.

The policy making process in a democratic form of Government like India gives due respect and weightage to the 'collective conscience' i.e. the majority view without ignoring the minorities opinion. Choosing a policy implies that you possess both normative standards and empirical judgements.[4] For when we choose a policy, we are trying to move towards some goal that we believe is desirable and we are therefore compelled to make judgements about the possible ways of reaching that goal and how easy or difficult each might be. The policy must be a combination of desirable best and resources available to pursue it. Before the adoption of particular policy, the ground realities must be thoroughly examined so as to suit the needs of people. Policies have the power to make or break an elected government.

Public policy is an instrument of transformation of a given environment into a preferred environment. Problems arise out of the environment—political, social, economic and technological but it also has the resources needed to provide solutions. It is the function of a policy to precisely identify the problems, prioritises then, formulate alternative approaches and solutions to make a choice among these alternatives on the basis of comprehensive analysis of benefits and costs, to articulate the choice in terms of goals expressed in quantitative terms, to provide organisation, personnel and resources to ensure an effective implementation of the policy, and to lay down a mechanism for a continuous monitoring of the policy and finally for its evaluation so that after a period of time the policy could be reformulated. Public policy, therefore, is the visible structure which provides the foundational framework within which all the identified national goals, plans and programme together with the appropriate workable measures established for the fulfillment of set goals and objectives are to be soundly activated.[5] The main focus of public policy is to serve and develop an individual and to establish a conducive environment for his compatibility. Public policy may be expressed in a variety of forms, including laws, local ordinances, court decisions, executive orders, decisions of administrators, or even unwritten understanding of what is to be done. It is formulated by the government authorities sometimes with the help of non-governmental agencies and actors. Policies provide the standard guides, which facilitate planning, and acting in line with legal requirements to realise the predetermined goals and objectives.

The Input-Output model given by Gabrial A. Almond describes the process of policy-making and the role civil society plays. Inputs, in a political system, result in demands upon and support for the system, which converts them into outputs in the form of authoritative policies and also implementing actions. The inputs are classified as political socialisation and recruitment, interest articulation, interest aggregation and political communication. Output activities are those, which are carried on by a political system in response to demands or stresses placed upon the system in the form of inputs. Outputs usually take the form of governmental policies, programmes, decisions and implementing actions. It has been categorised as rule making, rule-application and rule-adjudication.

1. Political Socialisation & Recruitment — Demand — 1.Rule Making
2. Interest Articulation — 2. Rule Appilcation
3. Interest Aggregation — 3.Rule Adjudication
4. Political Communication — Support

Input-Output Model

The above figure reveals that the outputs, i.e. the policies, are made on the basis of the input by the various governmental and non-governmental actors having the promises of the input factors of the masses. The demands on the basis of the factors in the input category have been supported in the process by the governmental actors and agencies ultimately, resulting in the outputs in the shape of certain policies.

Modern policy analysis is informed by two general models of decision-making— the rational or synoptic model, associated with H. Simon (1983) and the incremental model, associated with Lindbloom (1979).[6]

The Synoptic model requires decision-makers to examine a problem in a comprehensive way. Specifically policy-makers have to (a) rank all their values, (b) formulate clear options, (c) calculate all the results of choosing option, and (d) select the alternative which achieve most values. However, this model has its own demerits. It was not practically feasible to foresee the unforeseeable and measure the unmeasurable. So the advocates of synoptic model offer the notion of 'bounded rationality'. In this, the policy makers focus on a few 'good looking' options and look only for a satisfactory rather than the best solution. This model is adopted mostly by second-world countries.

The incremental model, on the other hand, is change by small steps. Its central feature is that a policy is simultaneously made and implemented making necessary adjustments to suit the needs. Hence it is an on-going process. Here consensus is not based on a 'holistic' basis but on what should be the next step. Here, the drawback is that long term cumulative consequences are ignored. As Lindbloom himself points out, incremental decision making is based on dealing with existing problems rather than avoiding future ones.[7] Public policy is seen as remedial rather than innovative. The first world countries mostly adopt this model.

The rational model holds that decision-makers should try to consider all the consequences of all options for all values before reaching a verdict. The incremental model maintains that policy-makers make small adjustments to patch up defects. There also exists a mid-way between these two models and it is called the 'mixed scanning model'. The mixed scanning model advocates careful scrutiny of key problems and routine monitoring elsewhere. Here focus is given to problems which require immediate attention and policies are framed in a like manner and in other normal situations a long-term strategy is applied. Hence, it involves both the uses of *tactics* and *strategy* in the formulation of public policies. While analysing public policy it is widely believed that policy process is a cyclical process starting from 'realisation of problems, and moving to 'finding a solution' implementing the solution, 'reviewing the impact' and finally moving back to an 'assessment of the problem'.[8] This belief, which is shared by most scholars of policy analysis, is based on a number of assumptions. Firstly, if there is a policy, there must have been a problem in the past. Secondly, if there is a policy, it must be a product of some process involving a search for alternative solutions and an agreement as to which solution is the optimum one. Thirdly, if there is a policy, it must be followed by implementation. And last, if there is a policy, there must still be a problem present, which may arise in the process of its implementation.

Stages of the policy process - There are four stages of the policy process, (1) Initiation—the 'decision to make a decision' in a particular area; otherwise known as agenda-setting, (2) Formulation—the detailed development of a policy into concrete proposals, (3) Implementation—putting policy into practice, and (4) Evaluation—appraising the consequences and success of the policy.

Initiation: It is at this stage that the idea of certain policy arises in the minds of the policy-makers due to the collective effort of number of players i.e. the policy - community and not only the public opinion. In any complex society the agenda cannot be controlled by a single group; it is the product of debate between a variety of competing though often-unequal forces.[9] The policy-community is the network of interest in a particular policy area. It is this policy-community that draws up the feasible conditions required for the formulation of a certain desired policy. Here the civil society has an immense role to play in influencing the policy-makers and creating public opinion in favour of initiation of such policy. They prepare the groundwork as they are well versed with the ground realities of the society. In a way, this approach is a bottom-up approach and not a top-down imposition.

Formulation: This is the second stage in the policy process and it involves the core political craft so as to formulate a certain policy through legislation or administrative proposals and then enacting it. It should be done in a proper manner so as to achieve the goals for which a said policy is formulated. Three steps are required at this stage - (a) knowing when to proceed the question of identifying the right moment; (b) knowing what to propose—the question of understanding the problem so that the proposals will (apparently) ameliorate it and (c) knowing how to proceed - the question of building a political consensus around the proposals.

Implementation: This is the most important stage in the policy process. It is the applicative aspect of a particular policy. How well a certain policy is implemented; depends on the capability and adaptability of the government. It is only through proper implementation that the government can expect to yield better results. A number of steps are taken for this purpose. First, there must be sufficient time and resources, both overall and at particular 'bottlenecks' in the execution of policy. Secondly, there should ideally be few 'stations' where the policy has to sit, awaiting clearance from a variety of different groups, each with its own interests. Thirdly, those in authority must be able to achieve compliance from subordinates.

At its execution stage, a policy must have flexibility over its application and also in its content. A policy emerges from interaction between local bureaucrats and groups (civil society) affected by the policy. The objectives of policy can often be better achieved by adapting its contents to local conditions. The civil society plays the role of connecting chord between the bureaucrats and the general people. The presence of social capital in a society smoothens this process and interaction between people and bureaucrats helps in designing suitable policies.

Again at the implementation stage, sometimes the government requires the involvement or association of the civil society for an effective implementation of a certain policy. For example in the national policy of Total Literacy Campaign (TLC) the role of voluntary associations is sought for better results. The government alone cannot undertake on its own the herculean task of bringing literacy in the country. Here social capital plays an immense role in the implementation of the TLC policy. Not only voluntary associations involve themselves in assisting the government at the implementation stage, but also informal associations of people, networks among people (literate or illiterate) and trust reposed on the government functionaries by the illiterate persons for improving their life conditions do have a vital role to play.

Generation and articulation of interest towards a policy by the people is also brought out by the voluntary associations and/or social capital. First of all the awareness about a certain policy is made to the people and they are explained about the benefits of such a policy. People may not be knowing about a policy but this is to a great extent ameliorated if there is a greater social capital. Social capital enables them to maintain networks and have contact with each other thereby promoting an associational life. It is during their course of discussions about governmental functioning that polices are discussed and it is disseminated among the unaware persons thereby generating interest among them.

Evaluation: The job of policy evaluation is to work out whether a policy has achieved its goals. The government must know whether a policy is benefiting the people for whom it is meant. It is just like a reflection of the work one does. Policy evaluation must distinguish outputs (what government does) from outcomes (the effects, including the unintended consequences, of government activity). The connection between the two is often tenuous especially when governments spend money with the supposed purpose of reducing inequalities. It is often alleged that benevolent policies benefits the better off more than the poor, even when the purpose is just the reverse. Whether or not this allegation is true, it is clear that outputs and outcomes are two different things and that policy evaluation is therefore an important task, which should become a routine part of the policy process.

Policy Implementation

It is the most vital aspect of public policy. If the implementation is good than one can expect better results to accrue due to the policy. Policy implementation, defined as the process of carrying out authoritative public policy directives, is neither easy nor automatic. As recently as 1975 Donald Van

Meter and Carl Van Horn observed at present what we know relatively little about the process of policy implementation.[10] Edwin C. Hargrove labelled the policy implementation as "the missing link" in the study of social policy.[11] According to More and Allison, "in designing and advocating policies, we must be able to anticipate the actual performance of the government in adopting and implementing the proposed policy. This anticipating in turn requires analytic procedures that enables us to: (1) outline the main features of the political and the bureaucratic settings within which specific policy proposals will be considered, and (2) make reliable judgements about whether the setting is hospitable or inimical to the proposed policy."[12]

Pressman and Wildavsky,[13] defining implementation as to carry out, accomplish, fulfil, produce, complete - conclude their analysis with a series of following observations and warnings: (1) implementation should not be divorced from policy, (2) designers of policy must consider direct means for achieving their ends, (3) consider carefully the theory that underlines their action, (4) should have continuity of leadership for successful implementation and (5) adopt simplicity in policies list that run the peril of breakdown. They thus suggest integration of policy design and implementation.

In public policy implementation, we have a framework of rules set by policy makers, under which the implementation process occurs. Implementors can also formulate their own policy goals and marshal sufficient power to convince the formal policy makers to adopt these goals. They can also negotiate with policy makers to secure the means necessary to achieve their own policy goals. There may be situations in which implementors may possess a considerable degree of independent judgement in order to influence and shape the policy process. They may also use discretionary power.

Bureaucracy plays an increasing role in making policy decisions and policy implementation through interaction between the needs of the community and the expertise of bureaucrats. Thus, in designing the implementation process, we have to maintain both effectiveness and responsiveness. On close inspection, we may find an executive agency far from being uniform in its attitude and behaviour.

Implementing a public policy is a process of discovering what works and what does not work. Implementation should not be taken as a routine activity. It is only when policy becomes operational, some of its trivial aspects become routinised. During the implementation phase, the policy organisation is always concerned with finding out how best the goals of the policy could be achieved. Implementation always makes and changes policy in some degree. The policy makers also know that they cannot write a law that can cover all aspects, contingencies, and all possible cases. In short, the administrators design large elements of the policy at the implementation stage. The function of the implementation is the largest of government, whether measured by the number of people employed and engaged or by the funds spend on it.

Richard Elmore has identified four distinct institutional models, which describe alternative approaches of implementation process:[14]

1. The "System management model" views implementation as an ordered and goal directed activity;
2. The "Bureaucratic process model" views implementation as a mere routine process of continually controlling direction;
3. The "Organisation development model" views implementation as a participatory process in which implementors shape policies and claim them as their own; and
4. The "Conflicting and bargaining model" views implementation as a conflict and bargaining process. This model is based on the principle of circularity.

The policy implementation process depends on number of factors, important among them are (a) internal procedures,

(b) allocation of resources, (c) bureaucratic norms, and (d) motivations and working conditions. Apart from the executive who executes the policies, it is also seen that the legislature, judiciary, political executive and non-governmental organisations also contribute towards the execution of policies.

In a Parliamentary democracy, the legislature exercises control over the executive through parliamentary questions, adjournment motions, no-confidence motions etc. Hence, the legislative control over administration is of three types (a) control over policy (b) control over implementation and the day-to-day working of the ministry/department and (c) control over finances. The legislature in democratic political systems exercises control over administration by reviewing, scrutinizing and evaluating the actions of the administration.

The judiciary plays the role of a 'watch-dog' in policy implementation and sees that everything is carried in accordance of law or procedure established by law. The judiciary safeguards the citizens right in case of misuse of power by the authority.

The executive, in order to cope with the quantum of exercise workload, encourages various non-governmental organisations and voluntary agencies to take up some of its tasks. However, the executive retains the over all control of the policy execution.

The non-governmental organisations and voluntary agencies sometimes play a vital role in policy implementation. The first five-year plan in India emphasized the importance of voluntary organisations in the implementation of public programmes. However, only in seventh plan document, there is a detailed discussion about the role of voluntary agencies in rural development.

The role mentioned are: [15]

To supplement government programmes—to provide choices and alternative to the rural poor to enable them to improve the quality of their life;

- To serve as eyes and ears of the villagers;
- To devise simple, innovative, flexible and inexpensive strategies and projects of participate types;
- To actuate and improve responsiveness of the delivery system to meet the felt needs of the poorest of the poor;
- To disseminate information about on-going and proposed welfare and development programmes of the government;
- To stimulate local communities to adopt a self reliant attitude of mind;
- To demonstrate a more effective utilisation of local resources, material and humans, to the local people;
- To demystify and simplify technology and make it available to the rural poor;
- To motivate communities to mobilize local resources for a self-reliant development process; and
- To create social awareness among the poor to demand a better performance of service from the concerned public sector agencies and also to impose local accountability on their performance.

Off late, NGO's and voluntary associations have been actively involved in contemporary social issues, like environment protection, legal aid to poor, consumer protection, human rights protection, scheduled caste and tribal development, adult education and literacy, etc. The expansion of the scope and nature of activities of NGO's, through social awareness, public interest litigation provision in judiciary, etc. indicates their importance in the socio-economic transformation of society.

The individuals as citizens also have a role in the policy

implementation. The Indian people practice all known democratic principles in effecting the execution of public policies, while the governmental actors, like the pressure groups and opposition political parties are indirectly engaged in influencing the successful execution of public policies.[16]

Policy implementation assumes the main role in the success or failure of a particular public policy. The administrative officials have a major role in implementing the policies but it is observed that in India there are certain constraints or problems, which hamper the proper implementation of public policies. One of the constraints is the inadequacy of official staff. Sometimes the absence of competent personnel handicaps the well-planned out policies. Secondly, there is also the non-availability of matching financial and infrastructural resources required for a particular policy. Another factor which also hampers the policy implementation is the bossism of higher authorities towards the lower officials. At every stage, the lower rung of officials, who are directly involved at the implementation stage, require the permission of their higher authorities and they lack independence. This causes delay and timely action. These are some of the constraints.

The overall performance of public administration for development in any political system can be measured only in relation to the implementation of the policies. This phase of the policy process is of crucial as well as of critical importance to governmental success. Through implementation, a bridge is formed whereby the policy aims and objectives are achieved in the form of governmental activities. Though there are a number of governmental and non-governmental agencies and actors involved in implementation of the policies, yet the major role is played by administrators. The policy implementation process is action-oriented with stress on issuing sound, clear, consistent and properly planned policy directives, developing the existing organisational structures and also creating new units whereever required to cope with quantum of task; training and retraining of the staff and equipping them with required knowledge and authority for properly administering the policies, coordinating human and financial resources to give maximum benefits to the target groups and areas concerned being covered by the policy and having proper monitoring, evaluation and timely feedback for the officials concerned.[17]

Social capital in the form of associations and groups appeared in political theory as social pluralism. Pluralists from Locke to Cole recognised the reality of groups against the classical liberal notion of a state of individuals held together by the sovereign power of the state.[18] The group was conceived of as a mediator between individuals and the state. Thus pluralism was both a statement of political and social reality and an ideology that sought to divide the monolithic power of the state. Pluralism can be said to be a doctrine, which visualizes a decentralized state. Pluralism leads to the revivification of local life. Local problems can be effectively solved through local action. Central control in all matters kills local initiative, which is highly dangerous for democracy. "Most observers agree that vocational groups are taking an increasing part, or at least an increasingly obvious part, in determining the action of formal governing bodies. This appears in the lobbying activities of associations of labourers, professional men, farmers, manufacturers, traders, banker's etc. Governments, indeed, often take the initiative in securing the cooperation of these associations in formulating policies of legislation or administration. The operation of systems of compulsory arbitration of industrial disputes, for example, is largely dependent upon the activities of workers and employers in the respective associations. In various other ways the state recognises the value of dealing with economic problems through agencies representing the organised groups immediately concerned".[19] The main purpose of groups and associations is to contribute to the happiness and enrichment of human life and this can be achieved by gainfully cooperating and coordinating with the functions of the State. Society represents a multitude of groups and associations which compete for the loyalty of the individuals and according to

Laski, the state is no more than one of these associations which works in cooperation with them for the progress and happiness of the members of society.

Apart from the pluralists, the group theorists subscribe to the idea that political process can best be understood by examining the political structures called 'groups' which play a significant role in political and governmental decision-making. Particular sets of individuals seek specific policy goals suited to their social or economic interests and engaged in various kinds of activities to generate pressure, which will influence decisions in their favour. Graham Wooton express this idea through the formulation PA = T.G. which means that private actors (other than political parties) seek to influence governmental targets to secure certain goals.[20] David Truman describing a 'group' in a broad sense refers it to any collection of individuals who have some characteristics in common. But in the policy process these groups have no value as it does not produce uniformities of behaviour. It can be called groups only when it interacts with some frequency on the basis of their shared characteristics. As Truman says, 'it is the interaction that is crucial, not the shared characteristics for being designated a group'.[21] Here Truman shows the importance of interaction among individual members and that too in an evenly pattern. So that 'group' can have influence on the government. These 'group' can be attributed as voluntary associations and in modern parlance as the 'civil society'. The forms and methods of government depends upon the character of the groups and the purpose it serves. Hence group determine the forms and method of government and not vice-versa. Truman's theory that at any given moment in time, society consists of a number of groups which are always in a state of equilibrium is crucial as it provides a cushioning effect in case of conflict between the groups itself.

Groups and network approaches stress the importance of interactions between the participants in the policy process. Groups formulate policy and set the agenda; they try to influence the legislative and executive decisions, they usually participate in the decisions about implementation; and they often implement policies themselves.[22] Government and bureaucracies need groups because they are sources of policy ideas. Groups are repositories of expertise, they can help make a policy legitimate; and their cooperation can ensure the successful implementation of a policy. Whereas governments can come into office with grand ideas and proposals for change, and legislatures and bureaucracies can swiftly enact policy measures, formal office holders need groups to formulate and implement those policies in a manner, which reflects the complexity of the real world.

Networks between group representatives, bureaucrats, politicians and other participants in decision-making account for the various ways in which political systems process policy. The networks establish the relationship between different actors and it is this, which matters. Participants put some effort into networking so as to build relationships for mutual advantage. Due to the complexity of policy-making, "networks need to be 'open' responsive, opportunity laden and permeable to wide-ranging demands from Congress"[23] if they are to work. Networks is essentially co-ordinative device whose permeability enables the policy domain to respond to change and to resist or co-opt destabilizing demands.

It is a matter of concern to know how strong is the 'network' establishing relationships. The idea is that the relationship within a network can be measured by finding out how dense it is (to what extent are the actors linked to each other), where is the centre of the network (who is the person, people contact in order to reach each other), what is the structural equivalence of the network (how close are the actors to each other in terms of the structure of their relationship) and how many cliques are there (clusters of relationship). These findings can reflect the strength and effectiveness of a network in influencing public policy.

Jean Dreze and Amartya Sen have suggested that public pressure may be vital in shaping government policy and in enhancing a government's political will' to engage in sound development management.[24] Public pressure works to effectively yield developmental and welfare goals from the government of developing countries and it also forms as a guideline for the government and to gauge the needs of the public and in formulating policies aiming at providing social security to them. Greater incidence and severity of deprivation, a low degree of development of formal social-security systems, limited or inappropriate coverage of public support, resource constraints, low levels of institutional development for social security provision and the relative powerlessness of the poor and vulnerable are all factors which combine to make the problems of social security in developing countries both important and difficult.[25] The public can exert pressure on the government to provide social security. One can regard this pressure both as a normative justification for social security (if, for example, it embodies a majority) or as a positive exploration of why governments do in fact provide social security.[26] The survival of a government or the political party's chances of governing again very well depends on protective policies upto a large extent. Even those not directly affected by deprivation or adversity may have motivations which go beyond their own well being and hence they may rally in support of the deprived. Here, comes the involvement of the civil society for the promotion of general welfare. Pressure from individuals, communities, and social or political organisations may provide one of the strongest (positive) reasons for government provision of social security.

From the perspective of both preventing temporary adversity and removing chronic deprivation it then becomes critical that the needy or threatened have access to institutions on channels of influence by which dissent can be expressed and action instigated. The nature and influence of the institutions which exist in a given country, whether they be political (such as opposition parties), social (grass-root organisations, voluntary associations) or legal (e.g. labour unions) are critical in determining whether the pressure for provision of social security, in form of welfare policies, is effective. The empowerment of the poor and their participation in the process of development appear to be instrumental for formulation and implementation of policies, which are required. This empowerment and participation can be possible through associations constituting group of men having common social interest. Group organising has been one of the crucial means of empowering the vulnerable sections—the poor, the low caste, the women—not only the better to enforce their legal entitlements within the community and family, but also to expand the scope of these legal entitlements through agitating for changes in the laws themselves.

Considering the immense task of public welfare and its difficulties and shortcomings on the part of the government, the role of 'grass-roots' organisations acquires much importance. Such organisations, which generally arise from local initiatives, are often oriented towards helping the poor and needy. They also carry the advantage of being able to draw on local information by directly involving the poor, and are often large enough to deal to an extent with covariant risk. Social and political organisations which provide support somewhere between the community level and the government level would appear to be important both in providing a voice for the poor and vulnerable as well as in serving as an effective alternative source of support which does not depend on the whims or machinations of state bureaucracy.[27]

Social Capital enables the public to play the political role of pressuring the government. Dreze and Sen write that there is considerable evidence, for instance, that early action in preventing famines has often been precipitated by newspaper reports of early cases of starvation and by pressure from political and social organisations demanding action. Public involvement and activism may have the role both of drawing the attention of the government to problems that may otherwise be neglected and of forcing the hands of the government by making it politically impossible - at least unwise for it to ignore impending threats.[28]

In another instance Prindle studied village community's response in Nepal during the drought in 1971 and found that local pressure from below has much value and does a lot in ameliorating the sufferings by various means. He describes how the combined pressure of the less well-off brahmins and *bhujels* (hereditary ploughmen for the richer brahmins) succeeded in (1) preventing surplus farmers from selling their grain outside the village at a profit and making it available instead to villagers on interest free credit; (2) preventing wealthy brahmins from reducing their daily wages for agricultural work; (3) persuading the wealthiest and most influential brahmin village patron to secure a loan of Rs. 15,000/- from shopkeepers in the market centre in the nearby town and relend it to almost every villagers, thus enabling the villagers to buy grains at lower rates than those prevailing later when the drought worsened; (4) getting this patron to secure government credit assistance for them, as well as obtain cloth on credit from cloth merchants in the town and provide the cloth to the villagers on credit; and (5) getting the rich to maintain the system of sponsoring festival feasts at which poorer brahmins and *bhujels* were fed.[29] In this cooperative pressure, the fact that many of the brahmins were also poor, appears to have helped create a tie of solidarity between them and the *bhujels;* at the same time the poorer brahmins could draw upon their caste connections to persuade the wealthy brahmins to cede to the demands that benefited not only them but also the *bhujels*. This experience reflects the effectiveness of group pressure from the poorer families in the village in getting credit and grain not only from the government but also from men of riches.

The notion of 'enfranchisement' has also its relevance to public policy with regard to social capital. Appadurai (1984) introduces 'enfranchisement' and defines as the degree to which an individual or group can legitimately participate in decisions of given society about entitlements".[30] This focuses on accountability and participation within a democratic political framework in increasing public capacity to achieve their goals. People are not passive actors in this process, reliant on provision from governmental and non-governmental organisations; instead this is an active process in which people must have certain resources and facilities at their disposal that enable to act to maintain their human needs. These pre-conditions include channels for the public to voice their needs, to influence policy making and to ensure that those charged with implementing policy remain accountable to those whose livelihoods and future they will affect.

In recent studies on public policy, much thrust is given to 'good governance' or 'democratic governance' for promotion of social and economic development. The World Bank in *Governance and Development* defines governance to be "the manner in which power is exercised in the management of a country's economic and social resources for development. Apart from other requisites, good governance requires' a dynamic and informed citizenry, which can provide feedback through voice, channels, on policy performance.[32] Good governance is also dependent on the presence of governmental and non-governmental 'service providers' which are responsive to the demands and needs of the people. The civil society advocates for the needed reforms in the administrative system.

Rhodes suggests that the term 'governance' implies a changing process of governing based in self organising, inter-organisational networks, characterised by interdependence, resource exchange - and significant autonomy from the state.[33] Hence the policy process is shaped by 'partnership' between elected and non-elected agencies, or by 'policy networks' structured by through an 'organisational interdependence between public organisations and private interests' that have become a pervasive feature of service delivery.[34] None of these structures, Rhodes argue, are intrinsically 'good' or 'bad' the choice is not necessary or inevitably a matter of ideological conviction, but rather one of practically a question of finding the conditions under which each governing structure works most effectively.[35]

Government at certain times try to maintain a balance

between needs and expectations of the people and its capacity to provide those needs. Kooiman is of the view that in the new governance model there is a change in the balance between government and society, characterised by a shift in the balance from government sector to private sector and by efforts to encourage stronger co-operation between elected and non-elected agencies. This has featured an enhanced division of labour and division of knowledge between governmental and non-governmental agencies, recognising that no single actor has on its own, the necessary knowledge and capacity to manage the varied and complex problems involved in 'modern governance'.[36] Kooiman argues that, through these new forms of partnership, the process of governing has shifted from a 'top-down' focus, in which government makes policy and society experiences it effects, towards a 'two-way traffic model' in which policy is shaped more by inputs and needs coming from both governmental and non-governmental spheres.[37] Hence, Kooiman rather than using the notion of bottom-up approach in plan and policies, prefers the 'two way traffic model' and thereby brings equivalence in governmental and non-governmental organisations/civil society.

Dreze and Sen's public action model state that the Government, which is responsible for relief and welfare administration, alone cannot accomplish the whole thing on their own. In their study on India, this work commonly operates through a wider network of actors, including government departments (with inputs from elected representatives and appointed civil servants), non-governmental and private agencies—a sharing of responsibilities made necessary by constraints on availability of resources and suitably qualified personnel, the need for access to 'local knowledge' and connections with local notables, and the need to overcome logistical constraints posed by administering welfare support over large areas, often served by poorly developed communications network[38]. In short elected & non-elected agencies need to co-operate in policy-making and its implementation, as both do not possess the necessary skills, resources, knowledge and contacts to get the jobs on their own.

This, to an extent, shows that public policies cannot yield effective results if implemented by the government alone and it cannot meet the demands/needs of people if the government alone is concerned in its formulation. The active involvement of the civil society strengthens the efforts of government in public policies in all its stages.

Public policies, in a welfare state and more particularly in Indian context, are mainly concerned with the welfare of people at large and revolve around development in all aspects and respects. For this, the core issue of the VIII plan of India recognised 'human development' as the first priority. The concept of 'development centered in man' is now increasingly used for the promotion of democracy and welfare of people. In this process emphasis is given on individual self-determination and participation of the individual in decision-making in cultural, economic and political and legal matters in the state and in co-operation with the government. Here, it is very necessary to differentiate between 'state' and 'government'. The state is, in many ways, a broader concept, which includes the government, but also the legislature that votes on public rules, the political system that regulates elections, the role that is given to opposition parties, and the basic political rights that are upheld by the judiciary.[39] Development cannot be construed of alienating the individuals. They need to participate in this development process which is brought forward by public policies and their participation can be possible only through presence of social capital.

The Cocoyoc Declaration regards the satisfaction of the basic needs of the poorest sections of the world's population as a main concern of development, but does not limit to that: Development is also freedom of opinion and its dissemination, including the right to give and receive ideas and propositions.[40] For better implementation of development policies, not only the social and political consciousness of the people needs to be improved but it also requires the willingness of active participation on the part of the people affected in the development process and also depends on group's collective initiatives and networks. In the present era, development is understood as "development from the bottom up" in which "participation and democratic governance have been widely recognised in theory as the basic pattern of development as the preconditions for its practical implementation, at least in terms of fundamental efforts".[41] It is in this context that the phenomenon of "participatory development" on the basis of a true partnership between government and people is increasingly stressed on. The local people's participation brings indigenous efforts and methods in the implementation of development public policies.

Konard Ginther while bringing in the concept of civil society into the development discourse and the promotion of popular participation in the African process of development and democratization refers to the African Charter for Popular Participation in Development and Transformation (Arusha Charter) adopted in February 1990.[42] This conference was attended by over five hundred representatives from African NGO's grass-roots, peasant's, women's and youth organisations, representatives of African governments and donor countries, institutions within the UN system and some non-African NGOs. The conference evolved a model of interaction of the actors ideally to be involved in the development process, in which non-state sector institutions (usually referred to as 'civil society') has a function which is critical for development. Among other things the charter stated that it is decisive for transformation that the population take the initiative via non-governmental institutions, grassroots organisations and the like, which draw support from the society or the people, are based on voluntary membership are democratically organised and are rooted in African tradition and culture, and in this way can guarantee independent development from the bottom-up. The charter gave the civil society, a *prima facie* constitutional right to participation in the development policies.

The non-governmental organisations (NGOs) are private, non-profit, professional organisations, with a distinctive legal character, concerned with public welfare goals. In the developing world, NGOs include philanthropic foundations, church development agencies, academic think tanks and other organisations focussing on issues such as human rights, gender, health, agricultural development, social welfare, the environment, and other indigenous peoples. In contemporary NGO literature, NGOs are distinguished from People's Organisations (POs), local, non-profit membership based associations that organise and mobilise their constituents in support of collective welfare goals.[43] POs include local community associations and cooperatives as well as peasant associations and trade unions, but exclude other professional or business associations and it is usually regarded as a sub category of NGO.

Basing on their ideological commitments; Korten distinguishes between three generations of NGOs the first committed to relief and welfare activities, the second to the small scale, local development projects, and the third to community organisation, mobilisation and coalition building.[44] It is the third generation NGOs which work with network of People's Organisations (POs) "to replicate and multiply the local successes of 'second generation' strategies and organise NGO-PO coalitions that underpin issue based social movements".[45] This coalition brings social movements, which place demands before the government. The second and third generation NGOs, like the interest or pressure groups in liberal democracies, exerts significant influence over legislation and public policy. In India and Bangladesh, for instance, NGOs influence legislation in areas such as minimum wages, feudalism and bonded labour.[46] Apart from these areas there are a number of other areas where the NGOs are actively involved in shaping the dignity of the individual and facilitating the role of government in governance.

In the developing world, counter-mobilisation in response to shortcomings in state performance in promoting economic development and in mobilising broadly based popular support represents the most significant aspect of NGO action. In a majority of the developing world, however, the "duality of state strength, to use Migdal's phrase, where states seem able to penetrate society extensively yet are unable to implement goal oriented change",[47] increases their strategic significance. Further, this counter-mobilisation role by NGOs gains importance due to less percentage of membership in political parties and trade unions in developing countries. NGOs play a vital role in facilitating political participation through their involvement in issue - based social movements and through their support to People's Organisations.

The World Bank in 1991 reported, "NGOs have become an important force in the development process, mitigating the costs of developing countries' institutions weaknesses and bilateral and multilateral donors pressured governments to forge links with NGOs".[48] The Indian Government's Seventh Five -Year Plan (1985-90) sought to channel Rs.2 billion (US $ 150 million) through NGOs and gave NGOs three main roles in promoting rural development: Linking government programmes and beneficiary communities, mobilising local resources, and organisng local communities to ensure the accountability of village - level officials.[49] Again, in 1986, the Government of India tried to co-opt NGOs through the establishment of Council for the Advancement of People's Action and Rural Technology (CAPART).[50] As the Asian Development Bank notes "the government, recognising on the one hand the positive reputation of NGOs and on the other, the problem of local vested interests and the limitations of its own bureaucracy, has called upon NGOs to help create a 'countervailing force' amongst the poor via the organisation of beneficiary groups".[51] This reflects how much importance or relevance social capital/civil society has in the operation of public policies aiming at welfare of the people. The Government of India having fully aware of its limitations and not yielding significant achievements in welfare and development in the past, resorts to the cooperation of the NGOs and people's voluntary organisation in assisting their efforts. In present times we observe a changing character of interest articulation due to the heterogeneous nature of social structures arising out of economic change and diversified political interests. In this perspective the government alone is adequate to effectively and judiciously meet and solve people's expectations, desires and demands. In fact, the new vision of management required to seek continuous mobilisation and participation of the public in government projects, planning, problem-solving and innovation to cope with unpredictable environmental circumstances became central aspects of the emerging model even without explicit enunciation of the concept 'development'.[52] Modernisation and economic growth are no longer the only goals of the government. In addition to it, issues of quality of life, satisfaction of basic needs and improvements of the human conditions are emerging as new areas, which needs immediate attention.

The present day administration believes in action and goal-orientation and emphasizes on a series of teleological conditions such as responsiveness, participation, equity, choice and responsibility. Weidner has pointed out, "environmental factors, in general, and cultural factors, in particular, are important to those who attempt to bring about major change in a society. Such factors condition the outcome of any governmental programme or other innovation. Therefore, changes in man's culture and environment are among the goals of highest priority in the countries most committed to change".[53] Within any society, it is maintained, political, economic and socio-cultural developments interact with the administrative system, as all social systems (including the government) "enter into transactions with their environment influencing and being influenced by them".[54] Participation is one of the most important aspects of political development. It has been defined as "the pressure from groups in the society for having a part in the decision making of the system".[55] By participating in the decision making process, the individuals get an opportunity to express their feelings and needs to the concerned authorities and as we have mentioned earlier, it becomes a two-way process.

In a segmented society like that of India we find divisions based on caste, class, religion, ethnicity, language, etc. The state has to govern without being biased to any one group and maintaining a balance among these division. For this the state has to be a unified whole representing all the sections of people and hence is regarded as a "Social Union of social Unions, where intensity, commitment and the most satisfying forms of common work are realised in the plural social unions, which the singular state support and facilitate".[56] The communities and associations, representing civil society, are now increasingly relied on by the people to solve the problems like poverty, unemployment, exclusion and others—which are supposed to be solved by the state but it is unable to solve it. The plural social unions are called to the rescue of the singular social union: the members of civil society must do what the citizens of the State can not do even though these are the same people.[57] It does not imply that the civil society will takeover the state or it will parallel to the functioning of the state but it means that the civil society will be complementary to the state and will fill the void wherever the state is unable to perform.

It is often remarked by scholars and authors that public policies, which particularly aim to the community as a whole, can yield definite results by the involvement and association of the civil society. Government can act in partnership with agencies in civil society to foster community renewal and development, writes Giddens.[58] We are now observing an expansion of the public sphere and this is because of transparency and openness system adopted by many governments in their drive to end corruption. One of the biggest changes affecting the political sphere is that governments and citizens increasingly now live in a single information environment.[59]

Greater interaction and contacts with citizens can be established by a government through, "experiments with democracy—local direct democracy, electronic referenda, citizens, juries and other possibilities".[60] Giddens cites an example of citizen involvement in policy formulation in Sweden in 1968. Here, the government draws the public directly into the formulation of energy policy. The government, unions, parties and education agencies set up day long courses on energy. Anyone who took such a course could make formal recommendations to the government. Seventy thousand people participated in an exercise that decisively shaped policy. Here we see how the government first tries to educate its citizens on a particular issue on which it requires their recommendations. The citizens, after being fully aware, and knowing its pros and cons, give their opinion and thus accordingly the particular public policy is framed.

Giddens further writes "State and Civil Society should act in partnership, each to facilitate, but also to act as a control upon, the other. The theme of community is fundamental to the new politics, but not just as an abstract slogan. The advance of globalisation makes a community focus both necessary and possible, because of the downward pressure it exerts. 'Community' does not imply trying to recapture lost forms of local solidarity, it refers to practical means of furthering the social and material refurbishment of neighbourhoods, towns and larger local areas. There are no permanent boundaries between government and civil society. Depending on context, government needs sometimes to be drawn further into the civil arena, sometimes to retreat. Where government withdraws from direct involvement, its resources might still be necessary to support activities that local groups take over to introduce - above all in poorer areas. Yet it is particularly in poorer communities that the fostering of local initiative and involvement can generate the highest return".[61]

The role of civil society cooperating with the government is found not only in developed countries like US or European nations but also in less developed countries. To prove his point, Gidden cites the example of Ceara in northeastern Brazil.[62] The reforms in the area were initiated by a group of young business leaders, working in sectors such as television, retail marketing and services. The traditional elites in Ceara exported agricultural products abroad, and were interested more in keeping the wages down than in local development. The reformers in their bid to bring in general welfare, joined with government agencies, using participatory planning techniques and meeting community organisation. In order to promote indigenous development, schemes were set up to introduce new enterprises into the area. Families with the greatest need were allocated one minimum - wage job per household. Day - care centres were set up, run not by the government but by volunteers. Neighbourhood groups and community organisations were given resources to lend on a small - scale: for example, lending a woman money to buy a sewing machine so she can earn a living on her own. Between 1987 and 1994 Ceara's economy grew at a rate of 4 percent, compared with 1.4 percent for Brazil as a whole. From this one can easily visualise the immense role of civil society at the implementation stage of different public welfare policies and how their involvement gives significant success to the government which otherwise would not have been possible.

By proper implementation of public policies with the involvement of associations, both the state and the civil society are mutually benefited. Developmental theorists have found many cases in which active governments and mobilised communities enhanced each other's development efforts. Scholars use such words as "synergy" and "co-production" to describe how civic engagement strengthens state institutions and effective state institutions create an environment in which civic engagement is more likely to thrive.[63] Embedded autonomy is regarded as the key characteristic of the developmental state.[64] Elaborating on embedded autonomy Peter Evans in *Embedded Autonomy: States and Industrial Transformation,* writes, "states tend to be most successful in achieving economic transformation when they exhibit the characteristic of embedded autonomy, i.e. states having a strong Weberian bureaucracy and not being corrupt by those seeking undue benefits, and state elites are enmeshed in social networks that put them in close contact with private actors in civil society". Evans is of the view that both embededness and autonomy are indispensable conditions for successful economic transformation. A State that was only autonomous would lack both sources of intelligence and the ability to rely on decentralised private implementation. Dense connecting networks without a robust internal structure would leave the state incapable of resolving collective action problems of transcending the individual interests of its private counterparts.[65] The combination of these two characteristics enables the state to define and seek long term developmental goals and to acquire information and cooperation from society, while social forces constrain it so that its policies do not simply follow state elites' own interests.[66]

Evans contrasts the economic development of Korean state with that of India and Brazil and say it is only because of this embedded autonomy that the private industrial capital was enable to strengthen the economy while the state played the role of a facilitator. This was not the case with the other two countries. The state's infrastructural power is not simply held over society, but actually relies on cooperation and coordination from plural groups of civil society. In Evans' words, "a robust and coherent state apparatus facilitates the organisation of industrial capital; an organised class of industrialists facilitates a joint project of industrialisation, which in turn legitimates both the state and industrialists".[67]

In the case of the poor, marginalised and powerless groups, embedded autonomy also pays dividends. Evans in his book cites to the agrarian communism in the state of Kerala, India, "where a relatively well developed autonomous bureaucracy embedded in dense networks with highly mobilized powerless groups successfully accomplished a transformative project aimed at increased levels of trust".[68]

Strong and robust civil associations play an active role in helping the state to reinvigorate its public institutions. From a study of sub-Saharan Africa by Naomi Chazan, it is clear that either development of strong civil society facilitates the process of state building or newly emerging corporatist style civil associations play a positive role in helping the state to overcome the serious problem of local protectionism and patron - client fuctionalism. Naomi Chazen in *State Power and Social Forces*[69] argues that 'the development of civil society in Africa has paralleled processes of state formation on the continent'.[70] She says, the two key stages of state construction in recent Africa's history (during decolonisation and since the crisis of the 1980s) have also been periods of most vibrant and autonomous associational activity, indicating that social organisations not only react to government measures but also adapt to circumstances and therefore, play a major role in the construction and allocation of power in particular settings. These institutions not only contributed to what was described as veritable explosion of associational life in Africa, "they also injected an explicitly political dimension into the associational arena, pressing for guarantees for basic human rights and advocating sweeping democratic Reforms".[71] Further she writes, 'involvement in associational activities afforded opportunities for social mobilisation, communication of new ideas, leadership training, participation in the state arena, and progressively, opposition to the colonial order. In many respects, these organisations constituted pre-political networks that used the colonial state as their frame of reference. Virtually every nationalist leader received his political education in these settings and drew on the political support they proffered. Civil associations were the foundation upon which anti-colonial movements were constructed in the immediate postwar period. From this perspective, decolonisation may be viewed as the process of the empowerment of civil society, which developed in tandem with the colonial state".[72] From this one can deduce that the civil society had a major role in the process of decolonisation of African State and also in the building of the state process. Civil Society became a sort of training ground for the citizens so as to shoulder the responsibilities of nation-building in the future. This instance is not a process of co-operating with the state in policy implementation but in creating a viable state structure itself.

Chazen, in her study, noted a significant resurgence of African civil society since the second half of 1980s which consequently resulted in enhancing both the autonomy and capacity of the states in the continent. She writes, "the diversity of associational orientations and structures has been reflected in the growing repertoire of strategies they employ. Many local organisations, especially those geographically remote from the capital cities, have continued to resort to techniques of self-enclosure, local retrenchment, or evasion, Grassroots associations in both rural and urban areas have also employed more subtle methods to express their positions, including impassivity, indifference, mimicry and ridicule. Many have engaged in illicit activities, and some have used overt tactics, such as vigils, demonstrations and petitions. Depending on their specific purpose, group strategies have been designed to support, collaborate with, exploit, evade, defy, confront or take over official institutions".[73] These are some of the methods of influencing the authorities so as to reap the desired outcomes. Civil society in Africa adopts a number of tactics to reach their needs and requirements.

Let us now turn to the outcomes of influence of civil society in African States. How does the State react to their requirements and demands and is the civil society achieving success in their endeavours? The interplay of voluntary groups with government institutions at this juncture has taken place at all levels of interchange, and has consisted not only of struggles for domination but, equally as significantly, of negotiations and bargains over various forms of accommodation.[74] The informal sector was heavily depended upon. Economic activities in this sphere included the development of micro-industries and small manufacturing cooperatives, the revival of local markets, shifts in patterns of agricultural production and the creation of new distribution networks. The economic activity, with the passage of time, was concentrated in the informal sector. Concurrently, certain social programmes were taken over by welfare and service organisations, including sanitation, housing, local policing and major aspects of health and education.[75]

When the institutions of civil society are robust, the capacities of the state may also expand. Civil society has tremendously helped the African states to strengthen the State's beneficial programmes and in the process has proved its efficiency and its mutual necessity for the State. Chazen for this reason while concluding writes. "In very important respects, the strengthening of civil society has also had the effect of enhancing both the autonomy and the capacity of the state. Structurally, developments at both social and state levels were mutually reinforcing".[76]

Robert Putnam in *Making Democracy Work* argues that public institutions usually work well in a community that has inherited a substantial stock of social capital, in the form of norms of reciprocity and networks of civic engagement. These two forms of social capital encourage social trust and cooperation because they reduce incentives to defect, reduce uncertainty and provide models for future cooperation. Vigorous civil associations nurture effective and responsible government and such a government in turn further fosters civic engagement. "On the demand side, citizens in civic communities expect better government and (in part through their own efforts), they get it. They demand more effective public service and they are prepared to act collectively to achieve their shared goals. Their counterparts in less civic regions more commonly assume the role of alienated and cynical supplicants. On the supply side, the performance of representative government is facilitated by the social infrastructure of civic communities and by the democratic values of both officials and citizens. Most fundamental to the civic community is the social ability to collaborate for shared interests. Generalised reciprocity generates high social capital and underpins collaboration".[77] Tocqueville, in this sense very correctly remarked that democratic government is strengthened, not weakened when it faces a vigorous civil society. The civil society transforms the government into a 'good' government which not only tenders public services according to the demands of the citizens (i.e. responsive) but it also acts efficaciously upon these demands (i.e. is effective).

Machiavelli and scholars of his time, who witnessed unstable history of republic institutions in ancient as well as in renaissance Italy, are of the view that the determinant of successful or unsuccessful free institutions rests on the character of the citizens, or their civic virtue.

Putnam says citizenship in a civic community in marked, first of all by active participation in public affairs. To Walzer, interest in public issues and devotion to public causes are the key signs of civic virtue.[78] Participation in civic organisation inculcates skills of cooperation as well as a sense of shared responsibility for collective endeavours. Honesty, trust and law abidingness are prominent in most philosophical accounts of civic virtue. Citizens in the civic community, it is said, deal fairly with one another and expect fair dealing in return. They expect their government to follow high standards, and they willingly obey the rules that they have imposed on themselves. In such a community, Benjamin Barber writes, citizens do not and cannot ride for free, because they understand that their freedom is a consequence of their participation in the making and acting out of common decisions.[79] Citizens in the civic regions expressed greater social trust and greater confidence in the law abidingness of their fellow citizens than did citizens in the least civic regions.

Kothari, while analysing and reflecting L.C. Jain's book *Grass without Roots*[80], writes that "the kind of development we have had so far has led to a lot of grass being grown all over the place - grass that has no roots. Moving from grass without roots to grassroots is the fundamental task before those interest in making development a truly democratic process with its roots in society".[81] Without citizen involvement on a continuous basis, Kothari says, development by itself will become autocratic and will lead to an authoritarian and fascist orientation.[82] To prevent this non-party voluntary organisations' role of transforming the political process cannot be overlooked. However, Kothari holds the view that it will be an error to think of voluntary organisations and their work in a non-political sense, because their key contribution lies in making and giving to politics a new orientation, to reconceptualize the political process. To make politics an inhibition for the voluntary organisations would mean limiting the role, concerns and activities of the voluntary sector, says Kothari.

The Constitution of India in Part-IV, containing provisions of Directive Principles of State Policy, elaborates principles of general welfare of the people thereby making India a 'Welfare State'. In the 30's and 40's the concept of welfare state arose to counter the totalitarian and authoritarian forms of state. In welfarism the model of the state assumed a primary role in all areas of development. The state was seen as an instrument of liberation from the inhibiting shakles of tradition as well an instrument of egalitarianism in areas like the economy, education and even the social structure, all of which were arenas of growing inequality and injustice.[83] However, with the passage of time, the role of the state in welfare and development activities is not encouraging. There is a growing concern that the state has not been able to function as an instrument of liberation and enfranchisement of the poor and the deprived of the excluded and the various peripheralised minorities. Secondly, the model of centrally planned economic development as the catalyst of both growth and justice and relying on the belief of trickle down theory did not yield good results. "Development was to be, in the vocabulary we were using, for 'target groups' viz; the poor, the rural folk, the backward classes. Development was conceived as something in which people were to be treated as objects rather than subjects".[84]

With the realisation of the iniquitous nature of the state and the inability of government programmes to benefit the deprived sections, there emerged another sector known as the civil society i.e. voluntary associations. New groups and associations were formed which were ready to struggle on behalf of the poor, the landless, *the Dalits* (Backward Castes), the tribals, the bonded labourers, and many other who were deprived of state's welfare policies and discriminated by the dominant interests in the social structure. These voluntary organisations are operating in a variety of areas, particularly in the periphery of society and are increasingly taking on new issues and problems as they come up and affect the mass of the people. "These include the problems of ethnic or religious minorities, of the forest people affected by environmental degradation, of people in the north east and lately, of various 'nationalities' asking for regional autonomy. There are others who concentrate on important aspects of bonded labour, child labour, women's labour, migrant labour, and the labour of those displaced from their homelands by various development projects (dams, thermal plants, 'social forestry' projects) all this being the result of fast changing national and international division of labour. Such struggle oriented work among these sections of society often takes legal forms, working not only to establish the rights of the people according to the law of the land, but also to uphold rights that are being constantly violated".[85] It is the voluntary sector of the struggle-oriented groups among the disadvantaged sections that show signs of hope and strength.

The independent and voluntary associations and people's organisations ventilate grievances and perform watchdog functions. They present the various interests of the diversified castes and classes keeping the Government at the focal point.

According to Kothari, "it is necessary to reduce the overall size of the bureaucratic establishment and indeed also the scope and canvass of government which seems to encroach upon territories that are best left to the workings of civil society. A much greater role that hitherto needs to be played by local groups, voluntary organisations, political parties and periodic movements on behalf of deprived groups and classes. A decentralised polity is not just a description of the spread and distribution of the governmental apparatus. It also assumes (a) a plural structure of socio-political organisation and (b) a widespread of voluntary groups, political associations for a intellectual debate, independent media, vigilance groups and mass movements of various kinds'.[86] In spite of all odds, like corruption criminalisation of the polity, decline of institutions and of accountability in public life, deliberate marginalisation of certain segments of population in the democratic process, etc. there still exists some signs of hope and strength among the disadvantage sections and this is due to the voluntary sector of these struggle oriented groups and alternative development oriented groups.

When India became a politically free country, there were two models to be emulated. One was the 'liberal' model making for the gradual evolution of a society in which the state, the market and civil society were autonomous but interdependent. In contrast to this was the 'socialist' society in which the state not only occupied the central position but the autonomy of the market and civil society was substantially curbed. India chose a mid-way and attempted to combine the two by adopting planned economic development from the later and multiparty democracy from the former. Therefore, the state in India became the active actor to bring in economic development and distributive justice. But neither of these goals has been achieved upto a considerable unit.

Rudolph and Rudolph[87] are of the opinion of decline of state autonomy, which encompasses both authoritarian and democratic regimes, in India. This is, according to them, associated with two phenomena; (a) a long term increase in social mobilisation as measured by indicators of demand politics; and (b) deinstitutionalization - i.e. a secular decline in the authority and capacity of state agencies and political parties to articulate a public philosophy and to respond to and broker political demands within the framework of that philosophy. It is in this context that they spoke of 'demand polity' and 'command polity'. In a demand polity, extractive and allocative decisions are governed by voter sovereignty expressed through elections and through the demands of organised interests and classes, political parties, social movements and agitational politics. In a command polity, extractive and allocative decisions are governed by state sovereignty expressed through state policies.

The demand polity is oriented towards short-term goals, competitive processes for determining policies and the public interest and the provision of private goods. In demand polity, the civil society has a prominent role to play and it enjoys its autonomy. It is not inhibited by the state in performing public welfare functions. Demand polity provides ample scope and opportunity to the citizens to articulate their demands and place before the state for the redressal of their problems and grievances.

Rudolph and Rudolph, periodise from 1958-80 by alternating periods of types of regimes and politics. Accordingly they classify.

1.	1956-57 to 1965-66	:	democratic regime/ command politics.
2.	1966-67 to 1974-65	:	democratic regime/ demand politics.
3.	1975-76 to 1976-77	:	authoritarian regime/command politics.
4.	1977-78 to 1979-80	:	democratic regime/ demand politics.

1. **1956-57 to 1965-66**

   This was the Nehru era and the dominant Congress party. Nehru led Congress Government were able to invest in the future because they could rely on his persuasive leadership, the effectiveness of the Congress party's organisational wing at the centre and in the states, and autonomous and authoritative state institutions quantitative indicators of demand politics (such as voter turn-out, strikes, agitations) remained low.

2. **1966-67 to 1974-75**

   This period saw many important incidents. These are shocks caused by security, political and economic events military failures in wars with China (1962) and Pakistan (1965); the deaths of two prime-ministers (Nehru in May

1964 and Shastri in January 1966); and the worst weather on record in 1965-6 when food production plummeted and prices soared.

"Quantitative and historical evidence for the rise of demand politics after 1965 includes increases in electoral participation (turn-out), riots, strikes, student 'in-discipline' and again unrest.... Between April and August 1966, when food shortages were acute, there were widespread *bandhs* (suspension of business) and demonstrations demanding food rationing and protesting price rises tax increases, hoarding and profiteering".[88] Many workdays in industries were lost due to strike and electoral participation in the 1967 election increased by 11.7% over the 49.6% average of the first three general elections.

This period also saw Jaya Prakash Narain (JP's) efforts of mobilising students' participation in electoral politics and which eventually culminated in proclamation of emergency in 1975 and JP's anti-congress movement for 'total revolution' (i.e. fundamental transformation of Indian Society).

3. **1975-76 to 1976-77**

Mrs. Gandhi's authoritarian and corporatist version of command politics ended the 1965-75 period of demand politics by banning strikes and demonstrations, arresting opposition leaders, censoring the press and depriving citizens of their civil and political rights. The declared purpose of the emergency regime was to restore civil order and economic discipline. Reported incidents of student indiscipline declined dramatically in 1976 as did the number of workdays lost due to strikes.

4. **1977-78 to 1976-80**

1977 saw for the first time a non-Congress party government of the centre. This government of the Janata, Party restored constitutional government, a liberal state and democratic political processes, quantitative and qualitative evidence indicate a resurgence of demand politics. The rate of student indiscipline and the number of workdays lost surpassed those of the sixties. The Home Ministry reported serious law and order problems for 1978-9 and 1979-80. It specially noted the appearance in 1980-81 of 'farmers' agitation's for remunerative prices, a development that signaled the emergence of a new constituency for demand politics.

These are the periodisation made by Rudolph and Rudolph classifying the regime and the politics.

T.K. Oommen reflecting a similar view writes, "the state in India wanted to retain its centrality not only in initiating planned economic development but also in launching and sustaining civil society. Although one - party dominance persisted for most of the time in independent India, India did not become a one-party state or usurp the space of civil society. Therefore, it is no surprise that by the 1970s one witnessed a proliferation of organisations, which started integrating the state, when it tended to become authoritarian. While some of these organisations are not explicitly anti-state, quite a few are. Further, some are neither anti-nor pro-state but object to the consequences of state-initiated 'destructive development' leading to the ravaging of ecology and the environment. The prominent new collective actors are women, *Dalits, Adivasis,* religious minorities, the rural poor, urban slum dwellers, environmentalists and so on. They heralded a new beginning and manifested a new strings—an emerging vibrant civil society. However, it would not be correct to say that civil society emerged in India only a quarter of a century after it attained political freedom. In fact, the Indian 'national' State and India's Civil Society are twins, if by the later one denotes a separate space of activity independent of the former".[89]

The idea of people's action is rooted deep in India's history. Indian communities have for centuries found ways of joining at the local level to address shared concerns. Such traditional institutions have included village Panchayats which oversaw local self-government, tribal councils, craft guilds, associations built around festivals, agricultural operations or sacred observances, customs of caste observance and decision making. Voluntary action in contemporary India draws sustenance from this past, and from the introspection and resurgence caused by colonial rule. It draws most of all on India's freedom movement which Mahatma Gandhi predicted on personal and community empowerment. The Societies Registration Act of 1860, which has regulated NGO activity ever since, reflected the emergence of citizens' institutions in India.

There is now a phenomenal growth of voluntary associations. Previously voluntary associations were generally accepting the state as regulator and prime mover in every sector of development, and its virtual monopoly on development resources. But now there is indication of the frequency with which NGOs are called in for consultation on official policies and programmes. Those, once regarded as passive participants, are now expected to function increasingly as managers.

With regard to the NGO interaction with the Government, Ashoke Chatterjee says "the capacity to influence such public policy is relatively rare in the NGO community. Its past interactions have usually been restricted to contact with decision makers, rather than organised as lobbying by interest groups. Strengthening this capacity can however draw on significant NGO achievements. The National Campaign for Housing Rights has impacted on policy change. Awareness created by the Centre for Science and Environment has been internationally acknowledged. The Voluntary Health Association of India has influenced drug policy through a network of some 3000 health institutions linked to VHAI chapters in 17 states. There is also growing experience in public interest litigation. It has been used towards protection of communities such as bonded labour and minority groups, regions such as the Doon in the Himalayan foot hills and Silent Valley in Kerala State, neglected monuments countrywide and of those affected by the AIDS Virus. A landmark campaign by the Mazdoor Kisan Shakti Sangathan in Rajasthan has established the right of rural communities to information of local development expenditures, challenging provisions of the Official Secrets Act imposed during British rule".[90]

Implementation of government programmes ultimately depends less on authority and control than on mobilising policy stakeholders, including policy recipients. The less the social capital, the more difficult such mobilisation becomes.

At the extreme, in a society with very low social capital, administrator are much more apt to find reliance on authority and control necessary, with resulting low governmental effectiveness. At the other extreme, in a society with very high social capital, many problems are taken care of by social networking outside of Government and when remaining problems arc addressed through governmental intervention, administrators find a rich array of implementation allies. The issue of public discussion and social participation is thus central to the making of policy in a democratic framework.[91]

Table 1

Types of Voluntary Associations in the area selected

Associations	*Rural*	*Urban*
Voluntary Association	04	08
Youth Association	03	04
Caste Association	02	02
Religious Association	02	01
Cultural Association	02	06
Women's Association	00	05
Peasant's Association	01	00
Professional Association	01	03
Sports Association	01	01
Political Party	02	04

Source : Field Study.

Table 1 shows the different types of association existing in the areas selected for the study. As the provisions of the Government, an association in order to have legal entity and status has to be registered under the Societies Registration Act, 1860. Nearly all types of associations are existing in both the rural and urban areas of Cuttack district, however the frequency of occurrence is high in urban area in comparison to the rural area. We also find that in rural area the caste association and professional association somewhat overlap each other. This is because people of a particular caste are engaged in a particular hereditary occupation or profession for their livelihood as is seen in occupations of the fishermen, washermen, carpenters etc. Again some of the associations in the rural area are of informal type, i.e. it is not registered and does not have any written records. Their association work is mostly done verbally but they do maintain a high degree of trust among themselves and the networking among them is very strong.

Table 2

How often do the associations meet

Area	*Daily*	*Weekly*	*Fortnightly*	*Monthly*	*Quarterly*
Rural	00	06	08	01	08
Urban	00	22	28	10	07

Source: Field Study.

Table 2 shows how often the members of the association meet. None of the associations in urban area meet daily but some of the members of the informal and grass-root associations in rural area meet every day and discuss among themselves on various subjects. Most of the associations usually meet on a monthly basis and some meet quarterly. The meeting place of the associations is usually held in the residence of one of the members of the association as very few associations and that too in urban area, have their own office. In the rural area sometimes the meetings are held at an open space where usually the villagers at their free time sit and gossip. Utmost cordiality

Table 3

Types of discussions held in the meetings of Voluntary Association

Area	*Local*	*State*	*Nati-onal*	*Inter-national*	*Social*	*Poli-tical*	*Eco-nomic*	*Cultural*	*Relig-ious*	*Sports*	*Dev.*	*Assoc-iation matter*
Rural	100	100	54	23	98	92	73	73	37	18	100	100
Urban	100	100	100	91	100	61	84	89	34	54	100	100

Source: Field Study.

is maintained in these meetings and the host i.e the member in whose house the meeting is held, serves snacks and tea to the other members.

Table 3 depicts the type of discussions held in the meetings at the association members. In both rural and urban areas the discussion issue mainly revolves on association works, local issue, state issue, social issue and developmental issue. In rural area, association also discuss on political issues relating to their locality in particular and to the State in general; the economic issues discussed are those which affect their day to day life like increase in the price of fertilisers, reduction in subsidy and price-rise of essential items; religious and sports issues are very seldom discussed in the meetings. However, in urban area, discussion in international and national issues are regularly held but on political issue it is comparatively low; economic issues discussed is not only limited to day-to-day life but is also held on the national and international events and its impact on Indian economy; religious issues here in also not a favoured topic but on sports issue the members after discuss. From the nature of discussions we infer that whereas in rural area it tends to be narrow and limited but in urban area it is much broader and holistic.

Table 4

Means of establishing contact with the members

Area	*Face-to Face*	*Letters*	*Net-works*	*Media/ News-papers*	*Assn meeting room*	*Tele-phone*
Rural	93	43	89	--	100	34
Urban	69	94	87	39	100	100

Source: Field Study.

Table 4 depicts the means of establishing contact with the members so as to communicate with each other. In both rural and urban areas, the association meetings are best means to contact each other. Apart from it, in rural area, face-to-face communication and networks are also means to establish contact and to communicate. The use of letters and telephones are not utilised for this purpose. This is because very few members have a telephone connection and the use of letters will incur an additional expenditure. However, in urban area these two means are often utilised to establish contact. Networking and fact-to-face contacts are also held. Some of the associations also publish in the local newspapers about their activities and their meetings. This provides them a scope to reach a larger number of people and to strengthen their activities.

Table 5

How can a new person be a member

	Rural	*Urban*
Has to attend 3 meetings consecutively	--	89
Has to be introduced by a member	100	100
Has to give membership fee	--	78
By invitation from the association	100	100
Suo-motto by virtue of his ascribed status	100	100

Source: Field Study.

Table 5 shows how a person can be a member of the association and work for common welfare. In both the rural and urban areas the method is same but in case of urban area some of the associations have their own rules and norms, for which it becomes essential for a person to attend three meetings consecutively and also sometimes to give joining membership fee which is quite reasonable.

Table 6 shows the processes which are adopted by the voluntary association members so as to initiate for the formulation/alteration of an appropriate public policy. Both in rural and urban areas, the associations discuss about it in their meetings and act according to their decision. They arrange local meetings with the general public in order to aware them about it and also try to convince the opinion leaders of a locality, who in turn can be able to convince the local people. They also meet the local MLA and some of the members of the rural area also meet the local MP and tell them about it and try to convince them about its utility. They also give representations to the local Government authorities/bureaucrats explaining about the utility of the formulation/alteration of a particular public policy. Many of the members of both the areas also give representation to the Chief Minister/concerned Minister. The association members also take the help of the media in order to reach a large mass of people and also the Governmental authorities. However, in rural area, the association members conduct protests and agitation for the implementation of a particular policy. The protests and agitation held are block development office *gherao*, road blockage if at that time some minister goes in their locality road. In urban area, the association members sometimes also petition before an appropriate judiciary forum in order to obtain a judicial direction to the Government.

Table 6

How does the associations initiate a process for alteration of an implemented policy

Process	*Rural*	*Urban*		
		V.A	*W.A.*	*Total*
Decide in association meetings and make it public	100	80	20	100
Publish in newspapers	79	66	18	84
Arrange local meetings and convince opinion – leaders	100	76	14	90
Meet local MLA	100	80	20	100
Meet local MP	56	74	14	88
Discussion with local Government Authorities	100	80	20	100
Representation to Chief Minister / Concerned Minister	81	71	09	80
Petition before Judiciary-through PIL	12	39	08	47
Protests & Agitations	72	29	02	31

Source: Field Study.

At the time of the field study in the rural area, some of members were conducting a protest meeting in front of the block office and demanding for drought relief measures in some of the villages affected. They had also given representation to the local governmental authorities and had also met their MLA and appraised him about it. Later it was also published in a local newspaper. After a few days we came to know that appropriate steps were taken to meet the demands of the people.

Table 7
How are the associations aware of the policies implemented by Government

Process	*Rural*	*Urban*		
		V.A	*W.A.*	*Total*
Through their members	71	56	10	66
Through Newspapers / media	81	78	13	91
Through local bureaucracy	07	67	11	78
Through Gram Panchayat/ Municipality Members	94	45	26	61
Through local people networks	97	53	08	61

Source: Field Study.

Table 7 shows how does the voluntary associations come to know about the policies and programmes implemented by the Government. In the rural area, the voluntary associations come to know about the policies and programmes of the Government through nearly all the means mentioned in the table, but in urban area, excepting one variable i.e. through the members of the Municipal Corporation all other means mentioned have a high degree of positive contribution. In the rural area in comparison to the urban area, the networks among people helps in the dissemination of a policy. Most of the members of voluntary associations in urban area attribute the media for the awareness of the policies and programmes.

Table 8
Association involved in the various programmes & policies of the Government

Programmes & Policies	*Rural*	*Urban*		
		V.A	*W.A.*	*Total*
Adult Literacy	76	80	20	100
Primary Education	81	80	20	100
Social Forestry & Plantation	94	70	12	82
Land Consolidation & Settlement	92	--	--	--
Health & Hygiene Programmes (Polio immunisation, Cataract, Hepatitis B, AIDS, etc.)	100	80	20	100
Agriculture (Farming) improvement (loans for tractor, free seeds, fertilisers, etc.)	100	30	04	34
Housing (Indira Awas Yojana & Kalinga Kutir)	100	--	--	--
Identification of people living below the poverty line (BPL)	100	72	06	78
Waiving of taxes, education fees & cess cess during national calamity	100	80	20	100
Legal-aid & human rights violation	81	80	20	100
Area Development	100	80	20	100
Animal Welfare	21	24	08	32

Source: Field Study.

Table 8 shows the involvement of the voluntary associations in the policies and programmes implemented by the Government. All the members of the voluntary associations in the urban area were engaged in the adult literacy programme of the Government; whereas in the rural area three-fourth of the members interviewed were engaged in it. The details of this particular programme are being discussed in the subsequent chapters. Apart from this in other programmes and policies of the Government, the voluntary associations also assist for the facilitation of such policies. In the rural area the programmes and policies are social forestry and plantation, land consolidation and settlement, health programmes, agriculture improvement, housing, identification of people living below the poverty line, waiving of taxes and cess during natural calamities and local area development. In the urban area, the programmes and policies are primary education, health programmes, waiving of taxes during natural calamities, legal aid and human rights violations, and local area development. Health programmes and policies are immunisation programme against polio, hepatitis B, TB, cholera, cataract operations, diabetes check-up and blood test, AIDS awareness and its prevention, distribution of disinfectants, etc. Agricultural improvement includes arrangement of Government loans for purchase of tractors and power-tillers, free and subsidised seeds and fertilisers, availability of water by means of canals, lift irrigation during drought, pest control, etc. Housing schemes are provided by the Government for the economically disadvantaged sections of the people and the voluntary association help the poor people so as to get a house. Two housing schemes viz: Indira Awas Yojana (Central Government sponsored) and Kalinga Kutir Yojana (State Government sponsored) are being implemented. Identification of people living below the poverty line is a major task for the Government and the voluntary association assist the former so that real poor people are identified and they get the benefits of the welfare schemes and programmes of the Government. Natural calamity like drought, flood, super-cyclone make the life of the people miserable and their resources gets exhausted. In these circumstances, it becomes very difficult for them to pay the various taxes and cess like water-tax, agricultural tax, house-tax, education fees etc. and the voluntary associations play a major role for the waiving of such taxes by the Government. Local area development includes within it all the developmental activities of the area concerned and voluntary association members contribute to this also.

Table 9
How does the associations assist the Government in the policies implemented?

Assistance	*Rural*	*Urban*		
		V.A.	*W.A.*	*Total*
Aware people about the policy	93	59	15	74
Aware the Opinion Leaders of the locality	100	80	20	100
Arrange road-side & market corner meetings	88	10	02	12
Visit local areas to communicate it to the people	100	80	20	100
Involve themselves with the Government at the implementation stage	100	80	20	100
Give feedbacks about the ground realities (local conditions) to the authorities	100	80	20	100
Render service to people so as to enable them to get the benefits	100	80	20	100

Source: Field Study.

Table 9 shows how the members of voluntary associations assist the Government in the implementation of different policies and programmes. As soon as the members come to know about the benefits of a particular policy, they in turn communicate it to the people for whom the policies and programmes are meant. For example, the policy of social assistance to the elderly people living below the poverty line or the policy of giving maternity relief to women living below the poverty line. These schemes need to be spread among the mass and the Government alone cannot undertake it without the support and assistance of voluntary associations. The associations assist the Government by various means so that the target groups reap the benefits of the welfare policies and schemes. Excepting one parameter i.e. arranging roadside meetings and market-corner meetings, there is no discrepancy seen in the rural and urban voluntary associations. Some of the policies require the direct involvement of the voluntary associations at the implementation stage while other policies require the assistance of voluntary associations only for its dissemination and awareness among people.

REFERENCES

1. Terry, G.R. (1954), *Principles of Management*, p. 171.
2. Dimmock, M.E., & Dimmock, G.O. (1936), *Public Administration*, Rinchart & Co., New York, p. 82.
3. Peters, B. Guy (1988), *American Public Policy – Promise and Performance*, Affiliated East-West Press, New Delhi, p. 4.
4. Dahl, Robert A., (1991), *Modern Political Analysis*, Prentice India, New Delhi, p. 136.
5. Tandau, Alfred C. (1996), *Policy Implementation in India*, Vikas Publishing House, New Delhi, p. 43.
6. Hague, Rod, et al., (1993), *Comparative Government and Politics*, Macmillan, London, p. 398.
7. *ibid*., p. 400.
8. Khator, Renu (1987), 'Determinants of Policy Performance – An Empirical Examination of the Impact of Environmental Bureaucracy in India', *Indian Journal of Public Administration*, Vol. XXXIII, No. 1, p. 418.
9. Hague, Rod, *et al*., *op. cit*., p. 403.
10. Vanmeter, Donald. D Vonltorn, Carl (1975), 'The Policy Implementation Process: A Conceptual Framework', *Administration & Society*, Vol. 6, No. 4, p. 449.
11. Hargrove, Edwin C., (1975), *The Missing Link*, Urban Institute, Washington D.C., p. 9.
12. Moore, Mark, H., & Allison, G.T. (eds.), (1978), *Public Policy*, Harvard University, Cambridge, p.
13. Pressman, Jeffrey & Wildavsky A. (1973), *Implementation*, University of California Press, Berkeley, p. 37-38.

14. Elmore, Richard F. (1979), 'Organisational Models of social Program Implementation, *Public Policy*, No. 2, (Spring), pp. 186-228.
15. Tandau, Alfred.C., *op. cit.*, pp. 118-9.
16. *ibid*, p. 121.
17. *ibid.*, p. 144.
18. Ashraf, Ali & Sharma, L.N. (1983), *Political Sociology: A New Grammar of Politics*, University Press, Madras, p. 76.
19. Coker, F.W. (1934), *Recent Political Thought*, p. 510.
20. Bentley, Arthur F. (1908), *The Process of Government: A Study of Social Pressures*, The Principia Press, Bloomington, pp. 208-9.
21. Truman, David B. (1957), *The Governmental Process*, Alfred A. Knopf, New York, p. 27.
22. *ibid.*, p. 32.
23. John, Peter (1998), *Analysing Public Policy*, Pinter, London p. 66.
24. Curie, Bob (1998), 'Public action and its limits', *Third World Quarterly*, Vol. 19, No. 5, pp. 873-893, p. 873.
25. Burgess, Robin & Stern, Nicholas (1999), 'Social Security in Developing Countries' in Ahmed, Ehtisham *et al*. (Ed.), *Social Security in Developing Countries*, OUP, New Delhi, p. 42.
26. *ibid.*, p. 57.
27. *ibid.*, p. 60.
28. Dreze & Sen (1999), 'Action for Social Security', in Ahmed et al. (Ed.) *Social Security in Developing Countries*, OUP, New Delhi, p. 29.
29. Aggarwal, Bina (1999), 'Social Security and the Family' in Ahmed et al. (Ed.), *Social Security in Developing Countries*, OUP, New Delhi, p. 208.
30. Appadurai, A. (1984), 'How moral in South Asia's Economy? A review article', *Journal of Asian Studies*, SXIII (3), pp. 481-497.
31. Curie, Bob, *op. cit.*, p. 874.
32. *ibid.*, p. 1-875.

33. Raw Rhodes (1997), *Understanding Government: Policy Networks,* Government Reflexivity and Accountability,' Open University Press, Buckingham, p. 15.

34. *ibid.,* pp. 11-12

35. Rhodes (1996), 'The New Governance: Governing without Government', *Political Studies,* XLIV, pp. 652-67, p. 653.

36. Curie, Bod, *op. cit.,* p. 876.

37. Kooiman, Jan (ed.), (1993), *Modern Governance: New Government–Society Interactions,* Sage, London, pp. 2-5.

38. Curie, Bob, *op. cit.,* p. 876.

39. Dreze & Sen, *op. cit.,* p. 17.

40. Ginther, Konard (1998), 'Civil Society and Development', *Law & State,* Vol. 58, pp. 82-106.

41. *ibid.,* p. 85.

42. *ibid.,* p. 95.

43. Carroll, T.F. (1992), *Intermediary NGOs: the supporting link in Grassroots Development,* West Hartford, Kumarian, pp. 9-11, Korten, D.C., (1990), *Getting to the 21st Century: Voluntary Action and the Global Agenda,* West Hartford, Kumarian, 1990, p. 2.

44. Korten, *op. cit.,* pp. 115-27.

45. Clarke, Gerard (1998), 'NGOs and Politics in the Developing World,' *Political Studies,* Vol. XLVI, pp. 36-52, p. 42.

46. Clarke, J. (991), *Democratising Development: The Role of Voluntary Organisations,* Earthscan, London, p. 5.

47. Migdal, J. (1998), *Strong Societies and Weak States: State-Society Relations & State Capabilities in the Third World,* Princeton Univ. Press, Princeton, pp. 8-9.

48. *World Development Report 1991: The Challenge of Development,* (1991), The World Bank, Washington D.C & OUP, Oxford, p. 135.

49. *Cooperation with NGOs* (1992), Asian Development Bank, Vol. 1, p. 57, Brosch (1990), 'The Discourse on NGOs and the Political Economy of Development in India,' *M.A Thesis,* University of London, p. 16.

50. *Council for Advancement of People's Action and Rural Technology* aims at encouraging, promoting and assisting voluntary action for enhancement of rural prosperity. It was registered under the Societies Registration Act, 1860 on 1st Septemeber, 1986.

51. *Cooperation with NGOs* (1992), ADB, Vol. 2, p. 30.

52. Singh, Birkeshwar Prasad (1980), 'Development Administration in India', *A working paper at All India Political Science Conference*, Dec. 27-29.

53. Quoted in Arora, Ramesh K. (1992), *Comparative Public Administration*, Associated Publishing House, New Delhi , p. 152.

54. Riggs, I.W. (1970), 'The Idea of Development Administration', in Edward W. Weidner (ed.), *Development Administration in Asia*, Duke Univ. Press, Durham, p. 34.

55. Almond & Powell (1992), *Comparative Politics: A Developmental Approach*, Amerind Publishing Co., New Delhi., p. 35.

56. Walzer, Michael (1999), 'Rescuing Civil Society', *Dissent*, Winter, p. 62.

57. *ibid.*, p. 63.

58. Giddens, A. (1998) *The Third Way: The Renewal of Social Democracy*, Polity Press, Malden, USA, p. 69.

59. *ibid.*, p. 73.

60. *ibid.*, p. 75.

61. *ibid.*, pp. 79-80.

62. *ibid.*, p. 82 and Judith Tendler (1997), *Good Government in the Tropics*, Johns Hopkins Univ. Press, Baltimore, p. 72.

63. Evans, Peter (Ed.), (1997), *State-Society Synergy: Government and Social Capital in Development*, University of California, Berkeley, 1997, p. 132.

64. Evans, Peter (1995), *Embedded Autonomy: States and Industrial Transformatory*, Princeton Univ. Press, Princeton, p. 10.

65. *ibid.*, p. 52.

66. Wang, Xu (1999) 'Mutual Empowerment of State and Society,' *Comparative Politics*, January, 1999, p. 237.

67. Evars, Peter, 1995, *op. cit.*, p. 228.

68. Wang, Xu, *op. cit.*, p. 238.

69. Chazen, Naomi (1994), 'Engaging the State: associational life in sub-Saharan Africa' in Migdal, Votili & Saue (Eds.), *State Power and Social Forces*, Cambridge Univ. Press, pp. 255-289.

70. *ibid.*, p. 258.

71. Diamond, Larry and Oyediran, Oyeleye (1990), 'Military Authoritarianism and Democratic trasition in Nigeria', *Paper presented at the American Political Science Association*, San Francisco, Sept., p. 31.

72. Chazen, Naomi, *op. cit.*, p. 262.

73. *ibid.*, p. 273.

74. Rothchild, Donald & Foley, Michael (1988), 'African States and the Politics of Inclusive Coalitions' in Rothchild & Chazen, *The Precarious Balance*, Westview Press, Boulder, Colo, pp. 223-264.

75. Van Dijk, Peter (1987), 'Collaboration between Government and NGOs', *Development*, 4, pp. 117-121.

76. Chazen, Naomi, *op. cit.*, p. 275.

77. Putnam, Robert (1993), *Making Democracy Work*, Princeton Univ. Press, 1993, pp. 182-3.

78. Walzer, M. (1980), 'Civility & Civic Virtue', in his *Radical Principles*, Basic Books, New York, p. 64.

79. Barber, Benjamin (1984), *Strong Democracy: Participatory Politics for a New Age*, California Univ. Press, Berkeley, p. 179.

80. Jain, L.C. (1985), *Grass without Roots*, Sage Publications, New Delhi, p. 61.

81. Kothari, Rajni (1990), *Politics & the People, Vol. II*, Aspect Publications, London & Ajunta Publications, New Delhi, pp. 427-8.

82. *ibid.*

83. *ibid.*, p. 414.

84. *ibid.*, p. 415.

85. *ibid.*, p. 420.

86. *ibid.*, pp. 290-1.

87. Rudolph, L.I. & Rudolph, S.H. (1997), Regime Types: An Economic Performance' in Sudipta Kaviraj (ed.), *Politics in India*, OUP, Delhi, pp. 177 – 86.

88. *ibid.*, p. 182.

89. Oommen, T.K. (1998), 'Society: Tradition & Autonomy', in H. Karlekar (ed.), *Independent India: The First Fifty Years*, ICCR & OUP, New Delhi, p. 239.

90. Chatterjee, Ashoke (1998), 'NGOs: An Alternative Democracy' in H.Karlekar (Ed.), *Independent India: The First Fifty Years*, ICCR & OUP, New Delhi, p. 287.

91. Sen, Amartya (2000), *Development as Freedom*, OUP, Delhi, p. 110.

4

VOLUNTARY ASSOCIATIONS AND LITERACY POLICY

Social Capital is a qualitative term. Among its varied manifestations, voluntary associations, both formal and informal, contribute in making social capital an operational concept. There is a need to study voluntary association, including its functioning, facilitating coordinated action. As already mentioned in earlier chapters, social capital refers to features of social organisation, such as trust, norms and networks, that can improve the efficiency of society, by facilitating coordinated action. Voluntary associations are structurally horizontal and it inheres features of social capital within it. Tendency of social capital is that which facilitates coordinated action or collective action and present chapter makes an attempt to examine whether these features are present in voluntary association, thereby facilitating implementation of public policy.

The basic purpose of the present study is to investigate and analyse the role and functioning of Voluntary Associations in Cuttack Urban and Rural areas in the implementation of the national policy of Total Literacy Campaign (TLC) so as to achieve the goal of a total literate population in India. It is widely acknowledged that literacy has tremendous contribution to the welfare of people thereby leading to the socio-economic development of a nation and in strengthening the democratic principles. India is a vast country with myriad diversities and it had an experience of colonial rule in the past.

In the later part of the colonial rule, educational development, both in English and vernacular medium, did take place but it was inadequate. Supplementing to it, the dominance of Hindu religion with its emphasis on the caste system further contributed a lot to the deterioration of the educational development in general and achievement of literacy in particular. The 1951 census, the first after India became independent, shows the all India literacy to be at 16.6% and that of males and female at 24.9% and 7.9% respectively. The corresponding figures for Orissa and Cuttack district are 12.57% (Male 20.62%, Female 4.55%) and 23.31% (Male 38.6%, Female 7.99%) respectively. The 1991 census shows the literacy rate of Orissa and Cuttack district at 49.09% (Males 63.09%, Females 34.68%) and 53.36% (Males 63.7%, Females 42.63%) respectively. The 1991 census shows an improvement of this census but achievement of total literacy is yet a distant dream in India. Hence achievement of a literate population became a major objective for the Government and it initiated policies and programmes for literacy promotion and educational development in India. The Constitution of India also contains provisions for educational development viz. Article 45 which states "The State shall endeavour to provide, within a period of ten years from the commencement of this Constitution, for free and compulsory education for all children until they complete the age of fourteen years" and under Article 41 it provides "The State within the limits of its economic capacity and development, make effective provision for securing the right to work, to education".[1] However, these Constitutional provisions are included in the Part IV Directive Principles of State Policy (DPSP) which cannot be enforced by the Judiciary, if the State failed to implement the provisions. These two articles and other provisions relating to socio-economic development form the constitutional base of the various educational policies including the literacy policy in India.

Our ancient scriptures define education as that which liberates—i.e., provides the instruments for liberation from ignorance and oppression. In the modern world, it would naturally include the ability to read and write, since that is the main instrument of learning. Hence the crucial importance of adult education including adult literacy. Literacy in simple terms mean the ability to read and write 'with understanding' in any language. This simple ability on the part of individuals has a tremendous contribution to the growth of civil society and strengthening the democratic performance. The contributive aspect of literacy is its better communicative ability between people thereby helping to maintain the networks among people throughout the world. The advancement of Information Technology has made it possible to maintain contacts beyond the physical barriers. Again, the democratic doctrine of equality provides each person with equal opportunity. And this equal opportunity could best be utilized with the possession of some knowledge, which can be acquired by becoming literate. Literacy among individuals enhances the horizon of knowledge in them and sharpens the intellectual ability by reading, qualitative discussions and exchange of ideas. A person becoming literate tends to read a newspaper or a book, gets a chance to examine the validity of a certain thing on which he has doubts. He gets an opportunity to be aware of the remedies to his problems and like wise, many other things. It enhances political consciousness and equips individual with better understanding of the political process and the value of his vote. It helps exploring the economic opportunities available to him of which he was previously unaware. Literacy has other 'spill-over' effects which contributes to social development on the whole. Hence literacy acts as process of empowerment. "Lenin, for instance, not only noted that the non-literate person stands outside of politics, he also made clear his perception that the strength of the State lies in the awareness of the mass; a State is strong only when the masses are well informed, can pass judgements on any issue, and can make their own decisions".[2] Similarly Sen and Dreze lament the slow growth of local democracy and local participatory politics due to low levels of literacy and basic education in India. They write, "literacy obviously helps people to understand the functioning of the system, to deal with the government bureaucracy, to be aware of their rights, to understand and tackle new problems, and to achieve other abilities that are important for an effective role in local politics. Also, the possibility of decentralizing particular functions of the government depends on adequate expertise being available at the local level".[3] Thus literacy in this way can strengthen what Rudolph and Rudolph said 'demand polity'. The Indian Constitution's 73rd and 74th Amendment Acts establishing Panchayati Raj bodies in rural area and Urban Local Bodies respectively are means of local political participation for better effective governance. But this can happen if there is a high level of literacy and universalisation of elementary education. As A.K. Shivkumar writes "after all, the quality of decision making, and to demand transparency and public accountability, will be contingent open how well people understand and act, and ultimately upon the levels of educational attainment" .[4]

Sen and Dreze again point out that illiteracy breeds inequality. According to them, "the sections of the population that are most affected by the absence of literacy are typically much worse off than the groups that benefits from higher education".[5] According to them "literacy is not a requirement of effective participation in the political process, but it is certainly a useful tool of active involvement".[6] This they exemplify by contrasting south Indian State Kerala with the north India. Kerala has high literacy rate which has "helped to empower the public to demand extensive state involvement in the provision of health care, public distribution, social security, and, of course, education itself"[7]. Where as in the educationally backward states of north India this features are conspicuously absent. Here the privileged castes and classes have an upper hand and the illiterate masses have a chance only at the time of elections. Also we see in the states of north India a greater incidence of criminalisation of politics.

Yogendra Singh in his paper on 'Contemporary Social Crisis and its Dimensions'[8] writes "removal of illiteracy has been one major area where we witness monumental failure. Non-accomplishment in tackling the problem of illiteracy and universalisation of education bear organic relationship with failures in the domains of population and health policies. Control of population holds key to most problems that have reached the dimensions of crisis in India such as the social structural issues of distributive justice, unemployment, pressure on infrastructures and other related developmental goals: The rate of population growth is lower in states where standards of education and organised voluntary efforts in implementing state programs are higher, but this rate (of population growth) is much higher in the less literate states like Uttar Pradesh, Madhya Pradesh, Rajasthan, and Bihar which together account for the bulk of the country's population. Interestingly, these are also the states which rate poorly on most indicators of development having high degree of poverty, lower productivity in agriculture, high rate of illiteracy, poor indigenous mobilisation of voluntary bodies for development and endemic problems of social unrest and violence. This pattern of what Gunnar Myrdal called 'cumulative causation' in the process of underdevelopment has to be reoriented through planned investment in crucial sectors, such as the economy, education and infrastructures".

Jayati Ghosh in her paper 'Development Strategy in India'[9] says there is an uneven decline of rate of poverty in India, it has become increasingly concentrated in the central and eastern regions of India, and still remains primarily a rural phenomenon, indicating lack of adequate rural development. This central and eastern region of India contains the bulk of the illiterate population. The state of Orissa is situated on the eastern region of India. The illiterates, due to their lack of knowledge and awareness remain perpetually poor. They are unable to utilise the welfare and developmental policies implemented by the Government for their benefit and further these benefits are misappropriated. Hence, Government papers and facts present success but in reality things are not so. Many of the rural illiterate labcurers, take loans from local moneylenders instead of going to Banks, they put their thumb impression on contract papers without knowing its contents. They then become indentured labourers of the moneylenders and are exploited. This hampers an equitable development in India.

There is now a growing debate in India to make elementary education a Fundamental Right so that every child gets an opportunity to be literate and educated incurring no extra costs. If we are able to control illiteracy at the very beginning stage i.e. at early years of a child then there is every possibility that illiteracy can be removed within a decade or two combined with the allied TLC policy focussing on elders. A bill to make elementary education a Fundamental Right has been introduced in the Rajya Sabha (the Upper House of Indian Parliament) in the form of 87th amendment to the Indian Constitution in July 1997 but it is yet to be passed.

Literacy has got an important role to play in the economic front of a nation. Jagdish Bhagabati in 'The Design of Indian Development'[10] opines that the productivity of the imported equipment for production would be greater with a workforce that is literate and would be further enhanced if many had even secondary education. Consequent upon this the economy will grow leading to the growth of export-promotion strategy and ultimately demand for educated workforce. Growth of exports will have a pull-up effect upon the workforce. According to him primary education and literacy plays an enhancing, rather than initiating, role in export promotion strategy-led East Asian drama. One of the reasons he cited for the success of East Asia in contrast to India's failure is the raising of production due to the presence of a literate workforce. Literacy enhances the capability of man thereby strengthening 'human capital'. "The crucial role of human capital makes it all the more essential to pay attention to the close relation between sensible public action and economic progress, since public policy has much to contribute to the expansion of education and the promotion of skill formation".[11] Sen and Dreze commenting on the success of East Asian nations write that these nations have high rates of adult literacy, which is one of the factors for their success. They say an essential goal of public policy has been to ensure that the bulk of the young population had the capability to read, write, communicate and interact in a way that is quite essential for modern industrial production. They cite the comparative adult literacy rates of India with selected Asian countries.

Adult Literacy Rates in Selected Asian Countries

Country	*1960*	*1980*	*1992*
India	28	36	50
South Korea	71	93	97
Hong Kong	70	90	100
Thailand	68	86	94
China	N.A	69	80

Source: Sen & Dreze, India – Economic Development & Social Opportunities, 1998, p. 37.

Literacy and education also contribute to food security in the long run by contributing productive employment and adequate income to all. Kirit S. Parikh in his paper on 'Food Security: Individual and Nation'[12] writes that we must invest generously in education for our people so as to create employability and skills among them and to be employed. He states even for long-term food security it is important that we now make elementary (primary plus middle school) education compulsory and effective. He advises to increase the outlay on education to 6 percent of GDP from its current level of 3 per cent and even this increase will be below the level of expenditure, both as a percentage of GDP and in per capita terms, in the East Asian economies. He writes "studies in many countries, including India, have shown that female literacy results in decline in fertility, infant mortality and better nutritional status for children. A reduction in the growth rate of population means a quicker increase in per capita income. Hence he argues for functional education and massive literacy which can enable food security in India."

Post-Independent India inherited a system of education which was characterised by large scale inter- and intra-regional imbalances. The system educated a select few, leaving a wide gap between the educated and the illiterate. The country's literacy rate in 1947 was only 14 per cent and female literacy was abysmally low at 8 per cent. Only one child out of three had an opportunity for enrolment in primary schools. Educational inequality was aggravated by economic inequality, gender disparity and rigid social stratifications.

Eradication of illiteracy has been one of the major national concerns of the Government of India since Independence. The need for a literate population and universal education for all children in the age group 6-14 years was recognised as a crucial input for nation building and was given due consideration in the Constitution as well as in the successive five year plans. A number of significant programmes have been taken up since Independence to eradicate illiteracy among adults. Some of the important programmes have included:

i) ***Social Education***

The main elements were literacy, extension, general education, leadership training and social consciousness. The programme was implemented in the First Five-Year Plan (1951-56).

ii) ***Gram Shikshan Mohim***

Movement for literacy in the rural areas was started in 1959 in Satara district of Maharashtra, and was later extended to other parts of the state. The programme aimed at imparting basic literacy skills within a period of about four months and by 1963, it spread to all the districts of the state. The programme, however, suffered from a lack of systematic follow-up and consequently, relapse to illiteracy was massive.

iii) ***Farmers' Functional Literacy Project***

Started in 1967-68 as an inter-ministerial project for farmers' training and functional literacy, the project aimed at popularisation of high yielding varieties of seeds through the process of adult education. The programme was confined to 144 districts of the country where nearly 8,640 classes was organised for about 2.6 lakh adults.

iv) *Non-formal Education*

In the beginning of the Fifth Plan, a programme of non-formal education for 15-25 age-group was launched. Although the scope, content and objective of the non-formal project was clearly spelt out, its understanding in the field was very limited and the programmes actually organised indistinguishable from the conventional literacy programmes.

v) *Polyvalent Adult Education Centres*

Workers' Social Education Institutes and Polyvalent Adult Education Centres were reviewed by a group in 1977, which recommended adoption of Polyvalent Adult Education Centres in the adult education programme for workers in urban areas. In pursuance of this decision, Shramik Vidyapeeths was set up in the states.

vi) *Education Commission (1964-66)*

The appointment of the Education Commission (1964-66) was a significant event in the history of education in India. Among several measures, it recommended that high priority be accorded to ending illiteracy. It urged that adult education be promoted both through "selective" as well as "mass approach" and stressed on the active involvement of teachers and students and the wider use of the media for the literacy programme.

The Education Commission also stated that in the world of science and technology, the main objective should be to relate it to life, needs and aspirations of the people so as to make it an instrument of socio-economic and political change.

vii) ***Functional Literacy for Adult Women (FLAW)***

The scheme of Functional Literacy for Adult Women (FLAW) was started in 1975-76 in the experimental ICDS project areas. It was gradually expanded along with the expansion of ICDS upto the year 1981-82.

Till then, 300 ICDS projects were approved. Sanctions were also given for FLAW scheme in these project areas. However, the Planning Commission decided to stop the expansion of FLAW scheme in ICDS project areas mainly due to constraint of resources.

The aim of the FLAW scheme was to enable illiterate adult women to acquire functional skills along with literacy, to promote better awareness of health, hygiene, child-care practices and to bring about attitudinal changes. The target age group was 15-45, with greater attention to those in the 15-35 age group.

viii) ***National Adult Education Programme (NAEP)***

The first nation-wide attempt at eradication of illiteracy was made through the National Adult Education Programme launched on October 2, 1978. It was a massive programme, which aimed at educating 100 million non-literate adults in the age group of 15-35 years within a time frame of five years.

The objectives of the National Adult Education Programme were not merely to impart literacy in the conventional sense, but also to provide learners with functional awareness which were conceived as three integral components of the skills of reading, writing and arithmetic. Functionality implied the ability to utilise and apply the skills acquired with a view to promoting efficiency of the neo-literate. The social awareness component aimed at knowing, understanding and taking action on issues which effect the individual, community and society.

ix) ***Rural Functional Literacy Project (RFLP)***

This was a major centrally sponsored scheme started in 1978 for rural areas. The erstwhile 144 Farmers' Functional Literacy Projects and 60 Non-formal Education Projects were merged into it. Further, projects were added and the number of projects throughout the country in 1987 were 513, each having upto a maximum number of 300 adult education centres and each centre having 25-30 learners.

x) ***State Adult Education Programme (SAEP)***

The states also similarly took up centre based projects under the state plan funds on the lines of RFLPs.

xi) ***Adult Education through Voluntary Agencies***

To ensure greater participation of voluntary agencies, the Central Scheme of Assistance to Voluntary Agencies was revived in April 1982. Under this scheme, registered societies were sanctioned Centre-based projects for functional literacy and post-literacy, where they were allowed to fund projects in a compact area.

Table 1

Urban-Rural Differential in Literacy Rates –India: 1961-91

Year	*Age Group*	*Literacy*		*Difference in rural /urban areas (% age points)*
		Urban Areas	*Rural Areas*	
1961	5 and over	54.43	22.46	31.97
1971	5 and over	60.22	27.89	32.33
1981*	5 and over	4.85	34.04	30.81
1981*	7 and over	67.20	36.00	31.20
1991**	7 and over	73.08	44.69	28.39

Source: Towards a Literate India, National Literacy Mission, New Delhi.

* Excludes Assam

** Excludes Jammu & Kashmir.

In spite of these programmes, literacy level did not improve. There was also disparity the achievement of literacy. For example, there is a large urban-rural differential in literacy rates. This differential is of the order of about 30 percentage points and has continued to remain so over the last several decades as may be seen from the Table 1.

The above Table 2 shows the literacy rate of the rural and urban areas of Cuttack District. It can be easily inferred from the above table that literacy rate is high in urban area than in rural area. Usually in any place the urban area has a high literacy in comparison to rural area. There is also a marked disparity in the literacy level between males in comparison to the females.

Figure

Literacy Rate of Rural and Urban Areas of Cuttak District

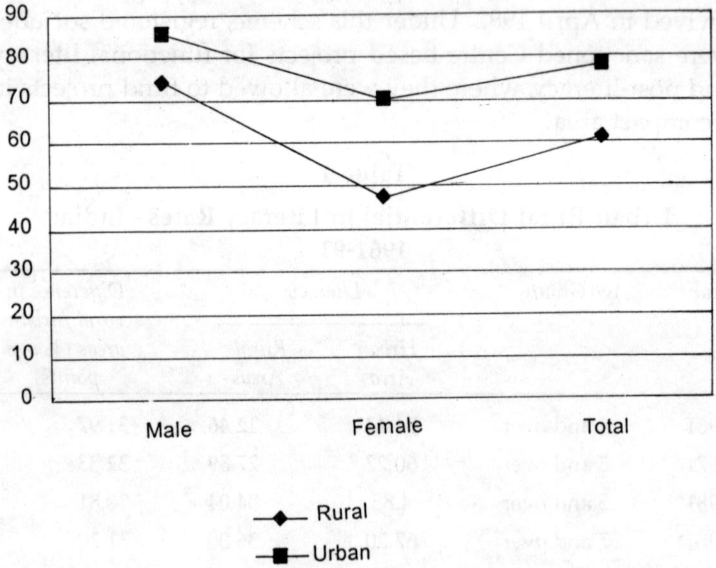

Table 2

Literacy Rate of Rural and Urban Areas of Cuttack District - 1991

Area	*Total*			*SC*			*ST*		
	Male	*Female*	*Total*	*Male*	*Female*	*Total*	*Male*	*Female*	*Total*
Rural	74.24	47.02	60.89	58.21	27.93	43.35	30.09	06.65	18.66
Urban	85.61	70.57	78.99	67.08	42.39	55.64	50.64	21.72	38.42

Source: Cuttack District Statistical handbook.

Table 3

Population, Literates & Literacy Rate of Orissa

Year	*Population*			*Literate Population*			*Literacy Rate*		
	Male	*Female*	*Total*	*Male*	*Female*	*Total*	*Male*	*Female*	*Total*
1951	7242892	7403054	14645946	1978705	334726	2313431	20.62	4.55	12.57
1961	8770586	8778260	17548846	3042004	759241	3801245	34.68	8.65	21.66
1971	11028036	10906791	21944615	4229124	1500164	5729288	38.35	13.75	26.12
1981	13309786	13060485	26370271	6268643	2758567	9027205	47.10	21.11	34.23
1991	16064000	15596000	31659736	10134778	5408693	15541764	63.09	34.68	49.09
2001*	18612340	18094580	3670920	12118256	7935529	20053785	75.95	50.97	63.61

Source: District Handbooks 1951-91.
* Provisional.

Table 4

Population, Literates & Literacy Rate in Cuttack District

Year	*Population*			*Literate Population*			*Literacy Rate*		
	Male	*Female*	*Total*	*Male*	*Female*	*Total*	*Male*	*Female*	*Total*
1951	1248351	1279886	2528237	487231	102310	487231	38.6	7.99	23.31
1961	1532583	1530489	3063072	699090	213461	912551	45.7	14.4	29.8
1971	1927033	1900645	3827678	959679	434720	1394399	49.8	22.9	36.43
1981	2346690	2282110	4628800	1363907	738760	2102667	58.4	32.4	45.4
1991	2801612	2701695	5503307	1784764	1151850	2936614	63.7	42.63	53.36
2001*	1208000	1133000	2341000	912000	662000	1574000	85.46	66.19	76.13

Source: District Handbooks 1951-91.

* Provisional.

Table 5

Ratio of Literates to Population, Total, Rural and Urban in Orissa (1981 & 1991)

Year	*Total*	*Rural*	*Urban*	*UR Difference*
1981	34.23	31.49	54.77	23.28
1991	40.97	37.76	61.70	23.94
2001	63.61	60.44	80.95	20.51

Source: Athreya & Chunkath, (1996), *Literacy & Empowerment*, Sage, New Delhi, P-56

Ratio of Literates 1981

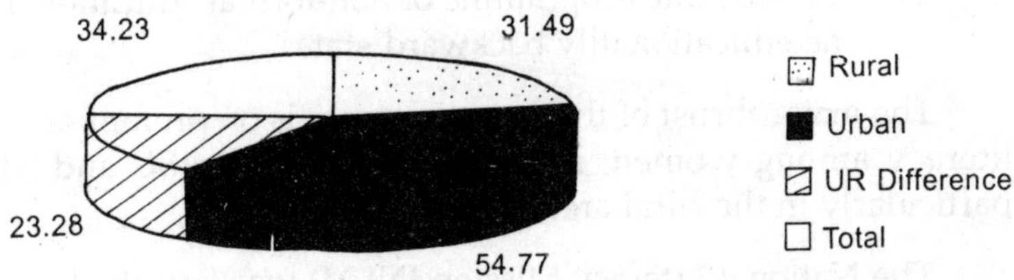

Figure

Ratio of Literates 1991

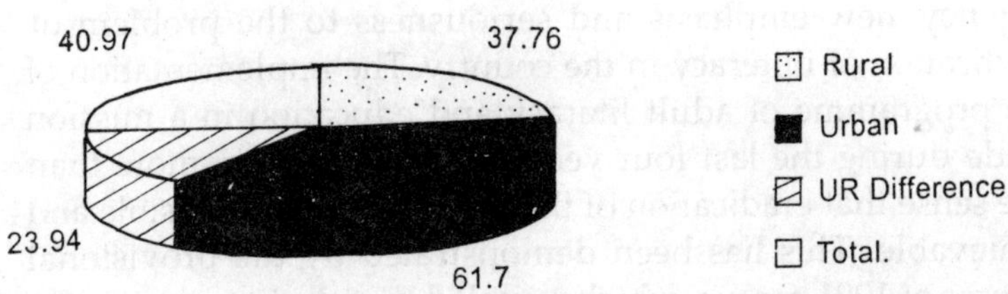

Figure

STEPS TAKEN FOR ERADICATION OF ILLITERACY

A two-pronged approach of universalisation of elementary education and universal adult literacy has been adopted for achieving total literacy. The National Policy on Education (1986) has given an unqualified priority to the following three programmes for eradication of illiteracy, particularly among women:

a) Universalisation of elementary education and universal retention of children upto 14 years of age.

b) The National Literacy Mission which aims at making non-literate persons in 15-35 age group literate.

c) A systematic programme of non-formal education in the educationallly backward states.

The major thrust of these programmes is on promotion of literacy among women, members belonging to SC and ST particularly in the rural areas.

The National Literacy Mission (NLM) was launched as a societal and technology Mission on 5th May, 1988 with the objective of imparting functional literacy to 80 million illiterate adults in 15-35 age group by 1995. Built on an objective assessment of the strength and weaknesses of the National Adult Education Programme it has imparted a new sense of urgency, new emphasis and seriousness to the problem of eradication of illiteracy in the country. The implementation of the programme of adult literacy and education in a mission made during the last four years has confirmed in more than one sense that eradication of illiteracy is possible, feasible and achievable. This has been demonstrated by the provisional figures of 1991 census, which revealed that the literacy rate for the population aged 7 years and above in the country increased from 43.56% in 1981 to 52.11% in 1991, registering an increase by 8.55%. The country achieved for the first time the distinction of having larger number of literate persons (352 millions) than that of the illiterate one (324 million). After experimenting with successive alternative models of literacy programmes, we have settled down to one, which is area-specific, time bound, volunteer based, cost-effective and outcome-oriented. This has given us lot of hope and faith that illiteracy is not a fatality and can be overcome in a time bound manner with planned, concerted and coordinated efforts. Even though the emphasis under NLM is on imparting functional literacy to illiterate adults in the age group 15-35, potential learners in the age-group 9-14 and above the age of 35 have also been enrolled in most of these campaigns.

NATIONAL LITERACY MISSION (NLM)

National Literacy Mission has been conceptualised and built on an objective assessment of the strengths and weaknesses of the earlier programmes emanating from the evaluation study reports mentioned earlier. The creation of a mission for literacy represents a national political commitment on the need to harness social forces and channelise the energies of people towards meeting the ultimate objective of effecting a qualitative change in their own lives. Conceptually, the mission focuses on:

1. a new sense of urgency, seriousness and emphasis with fixed goals, clear time-frame and age-specific target groups;

2. firm belief that adults can be made literate according to certain predetermined norms within a stipulated time limit (200 hours) and that it is not too late to learn;

3. emphasis on the close nexus between literacy of adult parents and enrolment of school going children, on the one hand, and literacy and infant mortality, immunisation and child care on the other;

4. a special mission which believes that literacy is not the concern of one ministry or department or agency but is the concern of the entire nation and all sections of society;

5 emphasis on institutionalisation of post-literacy and continuing education in a big way;

6. a technology mission also in the sense that besides emphasis on improvement of teaching/learning environment, it lays stress on improvement in the content and process of teaching-learning on a continuing basis;

7. envisages creation of an effective mission management system to ensure achievement of the mission objectives within a broad framework of flexibility, delegation, decentralisation and accountability;

8. emphasis is not on mere enrolment of learners but on attainment of certain predetermined norms and parameters of literacy, numeracy, functionality and awareness.

NLM Objectives

The mission seeks to impart functional literacy to non-literate persons in 15-35 age group. In qualitative terms, functional literacy implies:

1. Self-reliance in 3 R's.

2. Participation in the development process.

3. Skill improvement to improve economic status and general well being.

4. Imbibing values of national integration, conservation of environment, women's equality and observance of small family norms etc.

The NLM seeks to achieve these objectives through the following:

i) by creating an environment conducive to teaching-learning process, provision of good and relevant teaching-learning materials and facilitating teaching-learning by good training, media and communication;

ii) by improving the pace of learning and injecting confidence among the learners about their potential to learn and that the process is the drudgery;

iii) by integrating basic literacy with post-literacy and continuing education; and

iv) by developing the quality of human resource at all levels such as instructor, supervisor, project officer etc. through orientation and training.

Literacy Curriculum

NLM has defined the desired level of competencies in the 3 R's as follows:

Reading

1) Reading aloud, with normal accent, and at a speed of 30 words a minute, a simple passage on a topic of interest to the learner.

2) Silent reading at 35 words a minute, of small paragraphs in simple language.

3) Reading with understanding the road signs, posters, simple instructions and newspapers/broadsheets designed for neo-literates.

4) Ability to follow simple written passages relating to one's working and living environment.

Writing

1) Copying, with understanding at a speed of 7 words a minute.

2) Taking dictation at 5 words a minute.

3) Writing with proper spacing and alignment.

4) Writing independently, short letters and applications, and filling in forms of day-to-day use to the learner.

Numeracy

1) Reading and writing numerals 1-100.

2) Doing simple calculations (without fraction) involving addition and subtraction upto 3 digits, and multiplication and division by 2 digits.

3) Working knowledge of metric units weights, measures, currency, distance, area and unit of time.

4) Broad idea of proportion and interest (not involving fractions) and their use in practical situations.

CHARACTERISTICS OF TOTAL LITERACY CAMPAIGNS

In Kerala, the experiment of total literacy was launched in the Ernakulam district by voluntary agencies. Its success encouraged the adaption of the Total Literacy Programme in the State. This was a cooperative venture by government, political parties, NGOs and individual leaders. In April 1991, Kerala was declared the first totally literate state in India. The example of Kerala shows that eradication of illiteracy is very low-income countries is possible in non-revolutionary situations. The essential elements in Kerala were the political priority attached to this objective and the mobilization and cooperation of government, political parties and civil society organization.

The TLC model is now accepted as a dominant strategy of eradication of adult illiteracy by almost all States / UTs. This strategy has been reviewed and endorsed by the National Development Council and also by the conference of chief ministers of states convened by the Prime Minister on February

15, 1994. TLCs have certain features, which make them unique and distinguish them from other government programmes:

1) These campaigns are area-specific, time-bound, volunteer-based, and cost-effective and outcome oriented. The thrust in TLCs is on attainment of predetermined norms of literacy and numeracy. The learner is the focal point in the entire process and measurement of learning outcome is continuous, informal, participative and non-threatening.

2) The campaigns are implemented through district level literacy committees, which are registered under the Societies Registration Act as independent and autonomous bodies to provide a unified umbrella under which a number of individuals and organisations work together. The leadership to this body is provided by the district collector/chief secretary and Zilla Parishad (district council). All sections of society are given due representation in the planning and implementation of the programme. On the basis of the Ernakulam experience, an organisational structure for a district TLC has been evolved. The structure rests on three pillars of (1) participatory people's committees; (2) full-time functionaries and area coordinators; and (3) a support system provided by government officials. In itself, this may not seem significant, but it exemplifies an interactive and a communicative process management and implementation.

3) The campaign approach to total literacy is characterised by large scale mobilisation through a multifaceted communication strategy. The success of the campaign rests substantially on the effectiveness with which all sections of society are mobilised.

4) No targets are fixed from the top. The targets emanate from the grassroot level on the basis of a detailed

door-to-door survey conducted by the volunteers. This survey is not only a head counting exercise, but also a tool of planning, mobilisation and environment building.

5) The campaign is delivered through volunteers without any expectation of reward or incentive.

6) The management information system in a campaign is based on the twin principles of participation and correction. It has, to be accountable, credible and instead of being enrolment oriented, it has to be outcome oriented.

7) To enable every learner to achieve measurable levels of literacy, the new pedagogy known as "Improvement Pace and Content of Learning (IPCL)" has been translated in the shape of a set of multigraded and integrated teaching-learning materials and training. The learner is placed at the focal point in the entire process, which, through compact duration and continuous ongoing evaluation, helps to heighten the learner's motivation and improve the pace of learning.

8) Training of all functionaries involved in the campaign is crucial to the success of the campaign. Training has to be primer-specific, participative, communicative and a tool of continuous correction, upgradation and human resource development.

9) Though the TLC is meant to impart functional literacy, it also disseminates a 'basket' of other socially relevant messages such as enrolment and retention of children in school, immunisation, propagation of small family norms, promotion of maternity and child care; women's equality and empowerment, peace and communal harmony etc.

In order to ensure smooth implementation of aims and objectives of the TLC programme and to organise various activities at different levels, the following listed committees are to function:

1) Zilla Sakhyarata Samiti (District Literacy Committee)—The Collector and District Magistrate is the chairman of this Samiti. It is the apex body for project formulation of TLC and its monitoring and evaluation in the district.

   The aims and objectives of this Samiti are to work for promotion of Literacy among the people of the district in age group 9-35 years and to create environment conducive to literacy. It will maintain liasion between various Government and Non-government agencies for fulfillment of its objectives.

2) *District Executive Committee*: The District Collector is the Chairman of this Committee and members are drawn from among the existing members of District Literacy Committee. It is responsible for planning, executing and monitoring the TLC in the district.

3) *District Level Sub-Committees*: Various sub-committees have been formed under the district Executive Committee to ensure implementation of different aspects of the project. The following sub-committees have been constituted.

   a) *Planning and Survey Sub-Committee*: It is responsible for conducting survey for identification of illiterates, volunteers, Master Trainees and Resource persons. It will ensure tagging of illiterates with volunteers. It will chalk out plan and programme of the Project.

   b) *Environment Building Sub-Committee*: This committee is responsible for environment building, publicity and motivation for the project.

   c) *Academic Sub-Committee*: It is responsible for production and distribution of teaching and learning materials for Adult Literacy. Non-formal Education and Primary Education aspects of the programme.

d) *Training and Orientation Sub-Committee*: It is responsible for all type of training and orientation programme for Resource persons, Master-trainer, Volunteers and Volunteer for both Adult literacy and Non-formal Education. If required it will also organise training and Orientation for Primary Schools Teacher for improvement of teaching, better enrolment and to reduce drop-out rates in Primary Schools.

e) *Monitoring and Evaluation Sub-Committee*: It is responsible for designing suitable formats for monitoring and evaluation of the programme collection, compilation and analysis of data.

f) *Sub-Committee for Women*: It is responsible for overall development of women illiterates. It will also ensure proper enrolment of girl students in Primary Schools.

g) *Finance Sub-Committee*: It is responsible for financial transactions relating to the project. It will mobilise all resources, both external and internal, for smooth implementation of the project. The Collector and District Magistrate of the district is the chairman of this Sub-Committee.

Sakhyarata Samitis (Literacy Committees) have been formed at Sub-divisional level under the chairmanship of Sub-collector, at Block Level under the chairmanship of Block Chairman; at Gram Panchayat level under the chairmanship of the Sarpanch and at the Village levels.

Staffing

The entire government machinery associated voluntary

organisation and enthusiastic public will be involved to organise the project. One full-time project coordination will be there for the campaign with eight programme coordinators to assist the District Level Sub-Committees and Sub-divisional level Literacy Committee. There shall be one Assistant Programme Coordinate for each Block/NAC/Municipality level to implement the programmes. These functionaries will be responsible for organising the meetings of various committees, sub-committees, keep liaison with officials and non-officials and submit performance reports to respective committees from time to time.

The District Mass Education Officer will be above the Management of the Project.

State Resource Centre (July, 1976)

It is designed to give resource support to foundational education outside the formal system. The initial focus was on non-formal primary education for 6-14 age group and youth education, including literacy, mainly for the 15-25 age group and also including higher age-groups. The National Adult Education Programme (NAEP) in 1978 made the SRC's to work only towards eradication of adult illiteracy.

The principal functions of SRC's are:

1) Preparation of teaching-learning materials, keeping in view the objectives of functional literacy as spelt out by NLM.

2) Preparation of training materials, namely, teachers' guides, teaching aids, audio-visual materials.

3) Organisation of training programmes for official and non-official adult education functionaries as well as staff of District Resource Units.

The roles of SRC's are essentially related to their overall functions of providing resource support to adult literacy programmes. Some of them are:

a) stimulator of literacy-action.

b) mobiliser of people in the interest of literacy.

c) enabler for those engaged in literacy action.

d) builder of networks for literacy promotion.

e) researcher and evaluator, and

f) courageous innovator in education in the interest of the oppressed and illiterate.

Role of UNICEF in Orissa

UNICEF, Orissa Office, and Department of School and Mass Education, Govt. of Orissa, have started a programme called "Anandmayee Education". This programme will qualitatively enhance the schools, teachers and education and will also try to achieve 100% admission to schools of all children in 5+ age, 100% retention and a minimum of 80% success rate. This programme started from 1994 in 8 districts of Orissa in the first phase. These districts are Bolangir, Keonjhar, Mayurbhanj, Phulbani, Ganjam, Gajapati, Dhenkanal and Angul.

The main motto of this programme is to transform education to joyful experience for children. It will bring a change in the mode of teaching and other related activities by teachers and improve the student-teacher relation so that children will not leave school and they will read better.

Objectives

1) Universalisation of primary education.

2) Helping children to attain maximum educational level.

3) To bring success in attaining minimum educational level for children and encouraging teachers to teach in a joyful way so that children do not leave schools.

4) Entertaining the schools and making more attractive the pattern of education learning.

5) Make the teachers more concern towards the girls, scheduled castes/tribes children.

6) To ban child labour.

7) To help the children 5+ years of age in 1995 in completing Higher Primary Level of education in 2000.

8) To make the Village Education Committee stronger so as to take its patronage in bringing the children at 5+ age to schools and continue their education in schools.

9) Making the Village Education Committee more effective.

10) To bring active and close cooperation between teachers and parents.

Modern society has a large number of voluntary associations for socio-economic and cultural development of the society. These associations are different from primary social groupings such as family, friendship clique of an informal group of workman etc. These associations have certain characteristic features which are (a) they are consciously assured to marshal social power, (b) they possess relatively explicit aims or goals, (c) they are composed of functional positions and roles that are distinct from the individuals occupying them and (d) explicit rules govern relations between roles. In general, voluntary associations fill up the blanks left in social organisations i.e. those areas which are neglected by formal organisations in society like political authorities, local bodies, bureaucracy etc. paving way for the welfare of the people and strengthening the value consensus of society. According to Putnam, "Civil associations contribute to the effectiveness and stability of democratic government. Internally, associations instill in their members habits of cooperation, solidarity and public-spiritedness".[13] This voluntary association is not confined to any particular profession or others but works for the welfare of general people at large. It does not serve the interest of its members only but also serves the interest of non-members.

Voluntary Associations work for the deprived and underprivileged persons in the society so as to bring in social welfare and development. They are always forthcoming to pursue their work not only for the poor and downtrodden, but also wherever there is a discrepancy of basic amenities to modern life. They do not have partisan bias but try to encompass all political parties so as to facilitate their work process and this later part is much evident. "Such associations are widely regarded in modern democratic theory as the social foundation for plural political interests, as the cement of the 'civil society' that sustains the liberal state. Associationalism, however, treats such self-governing voluntary bodies not as 'secondary associations' but as the primary means of organising social life. In this doctrine, a self-governing civil society becomes primary, and the state becomes a secondary (if vitally necessary) public power that ensures peace between associations, protects the rights of individuals and provides the mechanisms of public finance whereby a substantial part of the activities of associations are funded".[14]

In democratic arrangement "associationalism may be loosely defined as a normative theory of society, the central claim of which is that human welfare and liberty, are both best served when as many of the affairs of society as possible are managed by voluntary and democratically self-governing associations".[15] Voluntary association in a way can be said to represent the traditionally excluded groups such as women, tribals and ethnic minorities, poverty stricken persons – who have been deprived of their welfare. The people who compose the voluntary associations know very well what is lacking in the social conditions and how to ameliorate the ill-health of the society as they come from the very same social circumstances in which the 'affected' persons reside. (We use 'affected' in the sense that they are poor, illiterate, ill-health and know not the resources the state provides for their benefits). The voluntary association channels the grievances of such persons and articulate, aggregate and represent their interests for the welfare of the whole society. It is "only with sustained, organised pressure from below, in civil society, can political and social equality be advanced, and the quality, responsiveness, and legitimacy of democracy thus be deepened."[16] For instance India has adopted a 'socialist pattern of society' and socialism advocates the control of production by society, and not by man, and here society refers to the community of 'freely-associated men'. From this we can infer the importance of association to human society. "Society, among human beings, can be defined by the existence of relationships involving mutual expectations and understandings, with the possibility of mutually oriented actions".[17] Hence human society is based on inter-dependency and associations in this regard smoothens the life of the individuals.

Voluntary associations help in furthering networks among people both from within and outside. The members of a particular voluntary association, who may have come from diverse fields and professions, join together as a single unit and work for the collective goals of the society. The members of a voluntary association meet often and interact with each other. This gives rise to a closer relationship between them which may be mutually beneficial to them. When a person gets a benefit from another person he develops a soft attitude towards him and the element of trust and faith combined with loyalty grows in him for that person. Even if a person may be having a negative opinion on another person and disliking him, repeated face-to-face contact through associations can develop a friendly attitude between them and there is every possibility for that person to change his view. "According to Tocqueville (1968) and Mill (1910) networks of voluntary activity create trust and cooperation. Mill regarded voluntary associations as a means of "mental education" and Tocqueville believed them to be "the great free school" of American democracy".[18] Associations contribute to the growth of democratic values of equality, tolerance, moderation, willingness to compromise and respect for opposing views thereby promoting a democratic culture and consensus among people. To some extent rich associational life supplements the role of political parties by stimulating political participation and maximising their utilisation of political rights as a democratic citizen. They train people to behave in an organised and disciplined way. Voluntary associations also establish contact among themselves so as to smoothen their work process and also to cover a vast area. "Putnam (1993) regards network of civic engagement to be at the very core of his concept of 'social capital'. Strong networks enable communities to solve collective action problems by breeding cooperation and easing coordination. Secondary associations such as Church groups, labour unions, school groups and fraternal organisations are especially important manifestations of community interaction".[19] This interaction further leads to cooperation and coordination in personal life. "Associations might thus gradually create a network of formal and informal relations, which would enable society to enjoy both diversity in social governance and a substantial measure of coordination".[20] Voluntary associations make dense the inter-personal relations and networks among people and facilitate the process of associational life for the individuals. "Associational life helps 'foster sturdy norms of generalised reciprocity and encourage(s) the emergence of social trust' (Putnam, 1995, p. 67), which in turn, helps resolve dilemmas of collective action and smooth economic and political negotiations. In addition associations 'broaden the participant's sense of self, developing the 'I' into the 'We' (Putnam, 1995, p. 67). They thus foster what Tocqueville (1969) termed 'self-interest properly understood', as well as a wider sense of community and social purpose".[21] Voluntary associations thus provide a binding force to the society and "see the need for activism and cooperation to create a 'civil society' for the poor".[22]

Voluntary associations, apart from contributing to the reduction of human suffering, instill in the minds of the people the idea of cohesiveness and participation in public works leading to common good. They try to associate the participation of as much of people as possible capable of pursuing a welfare work and this leads to the awareness and enlightenment of common people about certain issues or programs on which they may be having no idea. According to David Held, "citizenship is to be conceived as full participation of individuals in the community they belong to".[23] As Amartya Sen says that 'institution building' and 'participatory growth' are two major requirements of democracy, particularly in Indian democratic scene. Voluntary associations help in the fulfillment of these two requisites thereby strengthening democracy. They bring about a certain degree of social transformation through a democratic process based on 'consensual and reconciliatory' means as Yogendra Singh writes.[24] Participation is defined as "the pressure from groups in the society for having a part in the decision making of the system".[25] People having an organised structure in the form of a voluntary association put pressure on the government for the implementation of such policies and also the existing welfare and poverty alleviation policies leading to social justice and economic equality. The vast majority remain as isolated individuals but when they are collectively represented through a voluntary association they pose a challenge to the local elite and influential persons who hamper the pace of social justice and economic equality for their selfish and parochial interests. Participation in its real and practical sense has two equally important aspects : contributive and distributive.[26] The social section contributing maximum to the decision making process will naturally receive maximum out of the fruits of social efforts.[27] Thus voluntary associations play both the role of contributive and distributive in the civil society. They infuse the process of socialisation and participation among people to reap benefits for people themselves. The draft 6th Five –Year plan of India stated "Critical for the success of all redistributive laws, policies and programs is that the poor be organised and made conscious of the benefits intended for them".[28] The voluntary associations undertake the work of unionising people, particularly the underprivileged people, for achieving their benefits which may otherwise be diverted by the local influential persons for their own use. In this way these associations also function as watchdog against corruption and misappropriation by initiating a process of re-socialisation in the society. This feature of voluntary associations acting as 'watch-dog' got a boost when the Supreme Court, the apex judicial body in India, allowed third party petitions by voluntary social workers and associations on matters of social concern. They can approach the Court, on behalf of the affected people, for redressal of certain grievance(s) and this has "set in motion a new democratisation process in India".[29]

Voluntary associations also act as a recruiting and training agency for new political leaders or they act as an agency for political socialisation. Of course this training is given on a non-partisan basis to local democratic institutions so as to acquire the technical and administrative skills along with the normative standards of public accountability and transparency. These skills of a member help the association in motivating and mobilising people, publicity campaigns, debating issues and achieving success in their voluntary work. Such type of training becomes useful particularly to those persons who do not get the opportunity of political exposure. This again becomes important at a time when no new political leaders are experimented in the electoral fray by the political parties. "Voluntary associations after all are generally created to further some purpose beyond abstract social capital formation. They pursue goals both political and non-political. They mobilise people's interests and advance their visions of the good life and the common good. These are important functions in any society. They are arguably essential to a democracy".[30] Hence voluntary associations perform a multifarious function promoting the essentials of good social and civilized life. "Associational institutions are in keeping with the fundamental principles of western liberalism: they are libertarian and consistent with fundamental human rights. Associational governance would lessen the tasks of Central Government to such an extent that greater accountability of both the public power and of the developed associational agencies would be possible. The main political objective of modern associationalism is to decentralise and develop as much of the affairs of society as possible to publicly funded but voluntary and self-governing".[31] Considering the potentiality and role of voluntary associations, Deepak Lal proposes "to channel all foreign aid and domestic public expenditure on social programs and on 'safety nets' to alleviate destitution and conjunctural poverty through NGOs (national and international charities)".[32] as it has the comparative informational advantage of private agents with local knowledge. Basing on a study by World Bank in Latin American countries, he says the non-governmental organisations certainly have a vital role to play in promoting the social indicators in India.

The TLC is to be adopted by each district of India. The district administration with the involvement of voluntary associations and on a participatory approach from general mass will implement it so as to achieve full literacy in the district.

A district is declared as totally literate when about 85 percent of the illiterates become literate in the targeted age group. To maintain a continuity in the literacy programme and to prevent the relapsing of the neo-literate, the post-literacy campaign is undertaken.

With these aims and objectives, the TLC was started in Orissa. It represents a studied disciplined and well-planned thrust to campaigning for literacy. The TLC operates at two stages, Stage I will comprise TLC for 15 months and Stage II will comprise of post-literacy for another 15 months. Kit's containing one slate, exercise note book, pencil, calcium chalk pencils, learning books in three parts called Primers and a bag to carry these things are supplied by the Government to the learners. The Primers contain lessons on (a) literacy (reading, writing and comprehension) (b) numeracy, (c) functionality & (d) social awareness. Simple and familiar words are introduced in the first primer, simple sentences, addition and subtraction in the second primer and longer sentences, functionality lessons, division and multiplication in the third primer. A learner is declared literate when he completes the two formative tests and one summative test in each primer and passes the final test, called T-9. The Instructors who will teach the learners will be supplied with cloth blackboard, chalks, duster and an attendance register. Registered Voluntary Associations i.e. those registered under the Societies Registration Act, 1860 by the Government for not less than three years and recommended by local bodies are eligible to get the materials free of cost and funds for propaganda respectively from Government. The teaching programme is totally on a voluntary basis and no financial funding is provided by Government to the Associations. Children in the age group of 9-14 years who are unable to attend schools due to very poor economic conditions or family compulsion are also covered under TLC, though it is not a formal provision.

For better implementation of TLC policy, the Government apart from involving the voluntary associations, also appoint some Master Trainers (MT's) and Voluntary Teachers (VT's) on purely voluntary basis. The MT's are the school teachers employed in the local primary, middle and high schools. The MT's select a number of educated persons as VT's. These MTs and VTs then get necessary training from Government officials engaged in literacy activities. The VTs then start the learning centres and teach the illiterates. The MTs supervise the whole learning process and give a monthly report to the concerned official. Apart from this report, the Government requests the local area committees to give a report on the progress of literacy activities. It should again be noted that the MTs and VTs do not get any remuneration for imparting teaching to the illiterates. Only at the time of training they get a token amount of Rs.10/- only.

Table 6

Number of MT's and VT's in the selected area.

Area	*MT's*	*VT's*
Cuttack Municipality (Urban)	640	13793
Tangi Block (Rural)	57	1117

Source : District TLC Control Room Office, Cuttack.

Though the TLC policy was started earlier in some districts of Orissa, in Cuttack district it was initiated in March, 1996 and from then onwards it is continuing. The voluntary associations work under the basic framework and guidelines prepared by the Government departments engaged in TLC policy i.e. Department of Mass Education, Govt. of Orissa and the Ministry of Human Resources Development, Govt. of India. The number of illiterates present in the area has been identified by the Government through a survey. The members take the list of the identified illiterates and proceed on their work on literacy.

There are some registered voluntary associations in Cuttack rural area selected for our study. But none of these are getting themselves involved in TLC programme. They are engaging themselves in other developmental and welfare programmes of the Government like poverty alleviation programme, employment assurance programme, relief work at the time of natural calamity like flood, drought etc. We enquired to some of the voluntary associations about their active non-involvement in TLC programme and they responded that they are only involved in persuading the illiterates to attend the learning centres and cooperating in propaganda. But on our query on the active non-involvement of formal voluntary associations in rural area to local people, MT's, VT's and Government Official, we shockingly learnt that TLC does not offer any financial grants and aids to the voluntary associations. Hence these associations are not actively involving themselves in this programme.

TLC programme in rural area is mainly carried on by the VTs and MTs with the assistance of the Government Officials. The VT's directly get in touch with the illiterates and teach them. During the beginning of this teaching process there comes in the role of informal associations like the elder persons of the village congregating in one place and having discussions, the youths gathering in play grounds, the farmers and agricultural labourers meeting at common places during lunch time and in the evenings and such other gatherings of people which have been transformed into informal associations with the passage of time. Many of the members of these informal associations are themselves illiterate and they express their desire to attend the learning classes. This is how TLC programmes begins in Cuttack rural area.

In urban area the members of voluntary associations, with the assistance of the Government, themselves take a keen interest in the promotion of literacy. They themselves impart teaching to the illiterates and induce them to attend the learning centres.

Table 7

Mobilisation/Motivation

Particulars	*Urban*			*Rural*
	Voluntary association	*Women association*	*Total*	*Voluntary association*
Visiting houses of illiterates	60	40	100	100
Propaganda	46	32	78	88
Opinion Leader's cooperation	60	40	100	100
Convincing the illiterates	60	40	100	100
Cooperation of Political party activists	28	20	48	100
Cooperation of Govt. officials	38	20	58	100
Media	80	20	100	100

Source : Field Study.

Table 7 depicts the methods adopted by the members of voluntary associations, both formal and informal, in motivating and mobilising the illiterates towards generating interest for literacy and attending the learning centres. They visit the houses of the identified illiterates and meet them personally, particularly the female illiterate. The female illiterate generally has their inhibitions for learning at a later stage of their life. And secondly they are, in a way compelled to do the household work. Hence visit to the houses of the illiterates is a primary step for the members. They convince the illiterates about the importance of literacy and how they can reap the benefits of literacy. The members cite common examples of daily life like knowing the actual price of an item printed on the cover, expiry date of medicines, etc. Various propaganda measures like street plays, pictorial pamphlets, street meetings are conducted by the members for awareness of importance of literacy. They take the active cooperation of Opinion Leader's of the locality in order to persuade the illiterates of that particular locality. In these activities the women associations in urban area also participate. The media also played a significant role in motivating the illiterates and it also helped the members of the voluntary associations. The media had the audio-visual effect and the members in their visits to the houses of the illiterates and in the meetings at street-corners referred to the literacy campaigns and advertisements telecast in the television and broadcast in Radio programmes. Newspaper advertisements and newspaper reports of successful literacy campaigns in other places also helped in motivating the illiterates to attend the learning centres. Sometimes the illiterates demand for certain services from the Government like streetlights, roads or pond clearing as a condition for attending the learning centres. The members in turn, request the Government officials to comply with the demands and the illiterates start coming to the learning centres.

The members of the voluntary associations take part in the street-plays and sometimes they engage a professional artist for the purpose so as to have a greater impact upon the illiterates. The street-plays are mainly based on day-to-day experience and the part of literacy in facilitating such activities. In one of the plays an illiterate lady receives a letter from her husband working in a distant city is unable to read it and had to go to one of his friend's house situated in another village and a distance of 50 kms. so as to have it read. In another play a young girl dares to step out of her house to study and to learn. She refuses to be a slave to the reactionary forces at home and in society. It was seen that many women in the audience often nodded their heads as if in approval of the theme in the play. Surprisingly, such plays did not evoke much opposition from the men folk, perhaps as their services had also been enlisted in the cause of women.

The political party activists of the local areas also help the members of the voluntary associations in their noble endeavour. The party activists sometimes arrange the Panchayat Offices in the rural area and Ward Offices in urban area for the literacy work and also do not hesitate to move around with the members in convincing the illiterates. Often it is seen that the activists of different political parties do not have good relationship between them, and this is more particularly marked in rural area, but in the literacy activity they forget their differences and come together to help the volunteers in their effort to literate the illiterates. One political party activist remarked that literacy can considerably reduce their job of explaining and bringing awareness to the different policies and programmes of their party as people can *suo-motto* know about by reading the newspapers, party manifestos and pull-outs. The time saves in this way can be more fruitfully utilised in organising and strengthening the party activities. From this remark one can easily conclude how much true was Mill when he said "Universal enfranchisement must precede universal education". Mill stressed upon the 3R's of education i.e. reading, writing and arithmetic, which has also been adopted by the NLM in its TLC policy. In the urban area the co-operation of Government Officials is not much sought as the voluntary associations themselves undertake the literacy activities without relying on Government help. This is not seen in rural area and here the voluntary associations role is only limited upto motivating and mobilising the illiterates and the learning / teaching activity is undertaken by the Government volunteers.

From this it is inferred that voluntary associations, formal and informal, generate awareness regarding importance of literacy to the illiterates .It is also inferred that voluntary associations help involving people in the implementation of TLC policy.

Table 8

Learning Centres

Learning Centres	*Urban*			*Rural*
	Voluntary association	*Women association*	*Total*	*Voluntary association*
Slums	60	40	100	00
Suburbs	56	28	89	00
Near working place of illiterates	54	36	90	42
Community Centre	52	34	86	86
Front open space of buildings	00	00	00	100
Temple Courtyard	42	20	62	78
Others	24	14	38	40

Source: Field Study.

N.B.: Others include the houses of the member of voluntary associations, market areas, school building & below tree shade in villages.

The members having knowledge of the illiterates mainly choose public places for imparting teaching to them. In urban area the slums and suburbs are the places where the majority of illiterates reside. Their poverty forbids them to spend time on education and instead they spend it on earning by doing physical labour. These categories of persons are generally daily-wage labourers, rickshaw pullers, unskilled workers, etc. Children here are considered as an additional source of income, which supplements their parent's income for which they are sent to work as child labourers, instead of schools, to earn. The members in urban area set up the learning centres near the residence of illiterates so as to have an easy accessibility for them.

In the rural area the learning centres are held mostly in the front open spaces of buildings in villages, the community centre buildings in the villages. Some of the classes are also held in the houses of the MT's and VT's. Class in the daytime is held in the tree shades, which are near the working places of the learners. The temple courtyard is also used for learning classes both in urban and rural areas.

The classes are held according to the convenience of the learners, which is usually in the evening. The learners after finishing their daily work attend the learning centres in the evening. The members, without hesitation, come to teach the illiterates according to the suitability of the later.

Table. 9

The beneficiaries i.e. neo-literate came to know about TLC from - 33

Variables	*Urban*			*Rural*		
	Male	*Female*	*Total*	*Male*	*Female*	*Total*
Friends and Relatives	52	36	88	56	36	92
Voluntary associations	60	40	100	60	40	100
Political Party activists	26	20	46	60	40	100
Govt. Officials	42	28	70	60	40	100
Media	40	26	66	48	34	82
Propaganda	52	32	84	60	40	100
Opinion Leader	60	40	100	60	40	100
Employer	32	24	56	24	28	52

Source: Field Study.

In rural area the role of local political party activists and Government officials in promoting awareness about TLC is significantly more compared to urban area. All the respondents came to know about TLC from their Opinion Leader also. Propaganda and Media also contributed to the awareness of TLC. Networks among the illiterates have also helped in the promotion of awareness regarding TLC, both in urban and rural areas.

Table 10

Mode of teaching the illiterates

Mode	*Urban*			*Rural*
	Voluntary association	*Women association*	*Total*	*Voluntary association*
Volunteers of associations	60	40	100	00
Instructor	40	30	70	00
Facilitator	30	14	44	00
Voluntary Teachers	60	40	100	100

Source : Field Study.

Table 10 shows the mode of imparting teaching to the learners in urban and rural areas selected for our study. In rural area the mode of imparting teaching is solely through VT's. In urban area there are a number of methods adopted by the members for imparting teaching. The members of the voluntary associations in urban area themselves teach the illiterates according to the suitability of the learners. Some of the voluntary associations appoint an instructor for this purpose who is paid on honorarium. The Instructor teaches the learners and his honourarium also acts as a stimulus for his work. Sometimes the associations seeks the cooperation of the facilitators who impart the teaching to the learners. The facilitators are neither the members of the association nor are they paid any honorarium for this purpose. These facilitators solely do it on a voluntary basis. Persons known to the members of the association is requested by the later to undertake the activity and they when accept the request of teaching the illiterates are known as facilitators. Here engaging facilitators depends on the network and acquaintance of the members of the voluntary association. Apart from these methods, voluntary teachers are also engaged in the promotion of literacy activity.

Table 11

Sources of funding of the association

Funding	*Urban*			*Rural*
	Voluntary association	*Women association*	*Total*	*Voluntary association*
Govt. Kits and Funds	60	40	100	100
Membership contribution	60	40	100	10
Private Donation	30	14	44	00
Others	38	32	70	00

Source : Field Study.

N.B.: Others include grants from parent national associations, fund raising through entertainment and charity programs, sale proceeds of handicraft materials, and foreign donations.

Table 11 shows the various sources of funding for voluntary associations for conducting TLC program. In rural area funds in the shape of materials are provided by Government . There is a very low response for membership contribution in rural area . Urban area has high responses to the various sources of funding. Here the members do not depend on Government for funds but resort to other alternatives.

Table 12 shows the problems/constraints faced by the members of associations. In urban area motivating the illiterates is a problem. The targeted illiterates mainly belong to the lowest economic class, not even getting two-square meals a day. Their income is meagre for which they seek to broaden their work opportunities. It being impossible considering the constraints of time and energy the next logical outcome is to engage their children in myriad avenues of work opportunities as child labourers, thereby removing them from the educational scene.

The targeted mass i.e. the illiterates belong to the category of daily-wage labourers. They will loose their bread if they do not go to work even one day. They are themselves illiterate and hence do not know the value of literacy and education. Many of these labourers consume country-liquor and exhaust their money and time. Again the illiterate husbands forbid their wives to attend the learning centres and become suspicious of the motives of the members of associations. The women folks themselves have the problem of family management and family is their first priority. They have to cook food, look after the elders and the children and have to do the other household works of the family. Many of them are also engaged as daily labourers.

Table 12

Problems faced by members during the implementation of TLC policy

Problems	*Urban*			*Rural*
	Voluntary association	*Women association*	*Total*	*Voluntary association*
Motivation/convincing	56	38	94	76
Infrastructure availability	52	36	88	90
Funding	60	40	100	100
Retention	44	34	78	44
Red-tapism	58	38	96	00
Caste dimension	52	32	84	94
Child Labour	50	36	86	08

Source : Field Study.

Common question that all the members faced, both in rural and urban area, was 'What is the use of literacy ? Can you give us Government employment if we become literate ?' Moreover the illiterates feel that, by being literate and educated, persons become averse to perform physical work as workers/ labourers. Problem also arises in convincing the illiterates about the continuing need of being literate when they have accommodated themselves to a particular mode of life style according to the nature of their work.

There is the problem of a proper teaching/learning place both in rural and urban area. The inhabitants of the locality/ village, due to inadequacy of space in their house, are unable to provide a room to the volunteers for teaching purpose. The authorities are providing rooms in the Government schools but sometimes these are located at a distance, which makes a learner hesitant to attend. Again there is the problem of electrical lights as classes are usually held in the evenings and without light it becomes difficult to teach. There is also the problem of urinal facilities, particularly for female learners.

Funding for TLC programme becomes a major problem for the associations, both in urban and rural areas. Government does not provide them any financial help for literacy projects. It only supplies the kits and the members of voluntary associations in urban areas allege that this also suffers from red-tapism. However, in rural area this allegation is not noticed. The volunteers who teach the illiterates are also not paid any amount towards their transportation to the learning centre. This inhibits many women volunteers to teach the illiterates for the period of 15 months at least.

Caste factor is also posing a problem to the members, both in urban and rural area. A group of learners attending classes are unwilling to be taught by a VT who belong to a caste other than their own. Cases of this sort have been reported and it is ameliorated by arranging a VT of that caste. In the rural area a case of this sort happened which was about to assure grater proportion when the voluntary teacher was changed. The villagers of that village belonged to the higher caste and the voluntary teacher belonged to the scheduled caste category. The villagers at first did not know about it and initially they attended the literacy classes with much enthusiasm. However, later they came to know that the voluntary teacher was a SC person and this was sufficient for the villagers to start the trouble. They stopped coming to the literacy class and then prohibited the VT to enter their village. When the VT insisted on coming to the village and explained about the futility of the caste system, he was ill-treated and threatened with dire consequences. The matter was reported to the BDO and he immediately interchanged the VT and assigned him a SC village. The matter settled and the ego of the higher castes was satisfied. The BDO remarked that probably it is because of illiteracy that things of such sort tend to happen.

Red-tapism on the part of the Government in the supply of primer books is also alleged by the members of the voluntary associations in the urban area. Even though they inform about the need of such books in an advance they seldom get the books in time. In such situations the members repeat the old primer books to the learners which often becomes boring both for the volunteers and the learners. In such instances it is also seen that some of the learners stop coming to the learning centres and some even have also discontinued in between. Red-tapism also has a corollary problem of retention of the learners.

Table 13

Problems experienced by the neo-literate/learner in TLC

Variables	*Urban*			*Rural*		
	Male	*Female*	*Total*	*Male*	*Female*	*Total*
Poverty	60	40	100	60	40	100
Time constraint	60	34	94	56	22	78
Employment constraint	60	40	100	24	10	34
Delay in primer book supply	42	28	80	00	00	00
Lack of light & urinal facility	56	38	94	54	36	90

Source : Field Study.

Table 13 depicts the problems of neo-literate/learners. Poverty is the main cause, which hampers the learners from attending the classes. They often engage in some activities by which they can earn more. This leads to time constraint on their part. Lack employment opportunities and delay in primer book supply is a problem faced in urban area only. Learners of both areas face the problem of proper light facility in the classes held in the evening and urinal facility.

Table 14

Satisfaction and effectiveness in the implementation of TLC policy as responded by the members

Variables	*Urban*			*Rural*
	Voluntary association	*Women association*	*Total*	*Voluntary association*
Satisfaction	34	20	54	70
Effectiveness	60	40	100	100

Source : Field Study

Table 14 shows the satisfaction and effectiveness of TLC policy. The members in urban area have a lower degree of satisfaction due to the problems they face during the implementation of TLC policy. In rural area the satisfaction level is a bit high even though they face certain problems. This is because in rural area the members expect that Government may bring changes in the TLC policy for better implementation. With regard to effectiveness of TLC policy, members are of the opinion that it is highly effective and giving positive results.

Table 15

Satisfaction and effectiveness in the implementation of TLC policy as responded by the neo-literate/learner

Variables	*Urban*			*Rural*		
	Male	*Female*	*Total*	*Male*	*Female*	*Total*
Satisfaction	24	18	42	48	36	84
Effectiveness	52	36	88	56	40	96

Source: Field Study

Table 15 shows the responses of the neo-literate/learner

both in urban and rural area with regard to the satisfaction and effectiveness of the TLC policy. Many respondents are not satisfied with the TLC policy due to certain problems/ constraints, which are discussed above. However, regarding the effectiveness of TLC policy a higher percentage of respondents give positive responses.

The success of TLC policy implementation in a major way lies more in the active participation of the Voluntary Associations than the erratic irregular and unresponsive involvement and participation of the state. Eradication of illiteracy can be achieved with the active cooperation of the various voluntary associations than the state intervention and undertaking.

Table 16
Impact of Literacy on the Society as responded by the members of Voluntary associations.

Problems	*Urban*			*Rural*
	Voluntary association	*Women association*	*Total*	*Voluntary association*
Literate	60	40	100	100
Awareness	60	40	100	100
Trust building	46	38	84	88
Cooperation	42	36	88	96
Employment opportunities	42	32	74	22
Superstition break-down	34	36	70	54
Political participation & Voting	60	40	100	100
Small family adoption	54	36	90	84
Better Governmental Performance	36	40	60	100
Representative accountability	60	38	98	100
Judiciary remedial measures	14	10	24	18
Prevention to exploitation	60	40	100	100

Table 16 depicts the impact of literacy on the society, how literacy promotes personal development thereby leading to the socio-economic and political development of the society.

Literacy results in a literate population. It brings in awareness among people to many undiscovered thing and facts for them. They become aware of their rights and privileges. It exposes them to the economic avenues in the era of Globalisation and Liberalisation in India. A number of members of voluntary associations opine that literacy brings in expansion of trust and cooperation among people in spite of the segmented division of the society based on caste, religion and language. It enables people to understand the values of a good social existence and a harmonious relationship among them. A literate gains the capability of rationalisation and this further helps in the breakdown of blind beliefs and superstitions. It brings in more political participation and a higher percentage of voting. Literacy enables them to write applications to authorities and representatives so as to provide remedial measures. Last but not the least, it is a definite means to bring an end to their exploitation which occurs due to their ignorance. The burgeoning population problem for India can be slowed down if a woman is literate. She comes to know about the means of adopting a small family and enlightens her husband, who also happen to be an illiterate. Literacy also provides employment opportunities, particularly in urban area as some of the voluntary associations themselves provide/arrange interest free loans to the neo-literate, which he has to repay, and can start his own business. This helps in economic development. Very few members are of the opinion that literacy can bring judicial remedial measures by the neo-literate on social, environmental and other problems.

From the above it is also inferred that literacy promotes the fuller development of an individual.

REFERENCES

1. The Constitution of India, Publications Division, Govt. of India, New Delhi, 1992.

2. Bhola (1998), *Campaigning for Literacy*, UNESCO, Paris, p. 44.

3. Sen & Dreze (1998), *India – Economic Development and Social Opportunity*, Oxford University Press, Delhi, 1998, p. 106.

4. Shivkumar, A.K. (1998), 'Rewriting Future through Literacy', *Times of India*, New Delhi, 4.2.98.

5. Sen & Dreze (1998), *INDIA-Economic Development and Social Opportunity*, Oxford University Press, Delhi, p. 20.

6. *ibid.*, p. 104.

7. *ibid.*, p. 104.

8. Singh, Yogendra (1993), *Social Change in India – Crisis & Resilience*, Har-Anand Publication, New Delhi, pp. 72-3.

9. Ghosh, Jayati (1998), "Development Strategy in India" in Bose, Sugata & Jalal, Ayesha (eds.), *Nationalism, Democracy & Development*, OUP, New Delh, p. 169.

11. Sen, Amartya and Dreze, Jean (1998), *op.cit.*, p. 37.

12. Parikh, Kirit S. (1998), "Food Security: Individual and Nation," in Ahluwalia, I.J., & Little, I.M.D., (eds.), *India's Economic Reforms and Development*, OUP, New Delhi, 1998, p. 259.

13. Putnam, Robert D. (1993), *Making Democracy Work*, Princeton University, New Jersey, pp. 89-90.

14. Hirst, Paul (1994), "Associational Democracy", in Held, David (ed.) *Prospects for Democracy*, Polity Press, Cambridge, 1994, p. 117.

15. *ibid.*, p. 112.

16. Georgina Waylen (1994), 'Women and Democratisation: Conceptualising Gender Relations in Tansition Polities', *World Politics*, No. 16, (April), pp. 327-54.

17. Martin Shaw (1996), "Global Society and Global Responsibility," in Fawn, Riek & Larkins Jeremy, *Internal Society after the Cold War*, Millennium Publishing Group, p. 53.

18. Newton, Kenneth (1997), 'Social Capital and Democracy', *American Behavioral Scientist*, Vol. 40, No. 5, March / April, Sage Publications, p. 577.

19. Brehm, John & Rahn Wendy (1997), 'Individual level Evidence for the causes and consequences of Social Capital', *American Journal of Political Science*, Vol. 41, No. 3, July, p. 1005.

20. Wt. Streek & P. Schmitter (1984), *Community, Market, State and Associations*, European University Institute Working Paper, No. 94, Florence.

21. Berman, Sheri (1997), 'Civil Society and Political Institutions', *American Behavioural Scientist*, Vol. 40, No. 5, March / April, Sage Publications, p. 564.

22. Hirst, Paul (1994), "Associational Democracy" in Held, David., (ed.) *Prospects for Democracy,* Polity Press, Cambridge, 1994, pp. 115.

23. Held, David (1989), *Citizenship and Autopnomy: Political Theory and the Modern State,* Stanford University Press, pp. 202, 43.

24. Singh, Yogendra (1993), *Social Change in India*, Har Anand Publications, New Delhi, p. 25.

25. Almond & Powell (1972), *Comparative Politics: A Developmental Approach*, Amerind Publications, New Delhi, p. 35.

26. Singh, Birkeshowar Prasad & Singh, Sakhendra Prasad (1981), 'Development Administration in India: Some Essential Prerequisites'. *The Indian Journal of Political Science, Vol. XLII,* No. 1, p. 49.

27. Singh, Sakhendra Prasad (1979), 'Participatory Policies and Development in Rural India : The Real Challenge' *Quarterly Journal of Local Self-Government Institute,* (Bombay), Vol.XX, No.1, p. 424.

28. *Draft Five Year Plan: 1978-83,* Govt. of India, Planning Commission, New Delhi, p. 15.

29. Singh, Yogendra (1993), *Social Change in India*, Har Anand Publications, New Delhi, p. 125.

30. Edwards, Bod & et al., (1997), 'Science capital and the Political Economy of our Discontent", *American Behavioral Scientist*, Vol. 40, No. 5, p. 554.

31. Hirst, Paul (1994), 'Associational Democracy' in Held, David; (ed.), *Prospects for Democracy*, Polity Press, Cambridge, p. 116.

32. Lal, Deepak (1998), "Economic Reforms and Poverty Alleviation" in Ahluwalia, I.J. & Little, I.M.D. (eds.) *India's Economic Reforms and Development*, OUP, New Delhi, 1998, p. 246.

5
CONCLUSION

Human beings as 'individuals'; individuals in competition with one another; freedom of choice; politics as the arena for the protection of individual interests, the defense of 'life, liberty and estate' the democratic state as the institutional mechanism for the articulation of the legal framework for the pursuit of private initiatives in civil society and public concerns in the 'process of government': all these are preoccupations of the liberal democratic tradition.[1] While Marx and Engel's did not deny that people had unique capacities, desires and an interest in free choice, they attacked the idea that the starting point of the analysis of political life and its most desirable organizational form can be the individual, and his or her relation to the State. As Marx put it, "man is not an abstract being squatting outside the world. Man is the human world, the State, society".[2] Individuals only exist in interaction with and in relation to others; their nature can only be grasped as a social and historical product. It is not the single individual, isolated individual who is active in definite relations with others and whose nature is defined through these relations. An individual, or a social activity, or an institution can only be properly explained in terms of its historically evolving interaction with other social phenomena, a dynamic and changing process of inextricably related elements.

The preceding pages shows how social capital influences the formulation and successful implementation of public policy, particularly the national literacy policy of total literacy campaign. Adult education is a necessity in order to achieve overall social development. Human capital and social capital, to a large extent, determine the level of social development in general, and economic development in particular. Well-planned programme and designs based on successful implementation of such literacy policy needs to be applied on the national scale in order to eliminate illiteracy. The model of Ernakulam Total Literacy campaign was thought to be the best model to achieve literacy in the national scene and so the planners revised plans to implement the model in all district of India. The success of this model in Kerala lies to a greater extent in the effective mobilization of social capital of the communits. It led to a meaningful community participation for its success. The presence of social capital is not constant everywhere. It varies from place to place and person to person. The components of social capital may be very high in one area whereas it might be low in some other area, as has been found by Putnam in his study of Italy and of the American Society. Similarly other scholars have also undertaken empirical analysis to find out the role of social capital in a given society leading to a better democratic governmental performance in the respective states.

In our empirical study we have examined and analysed the functioning of civil society and their involvement in public policies particularly the national literacy policy, Total Literacy Campaign (TLC). Wherever the formal voluntary associations/ NGOs are reluctant to associate themselves in the implementation of the TLC programme, the informal organisations and groups of people have come out and rendered their service for the community welfare. This happened more in the rural area than the urban area of Cuttack district. Involvement of the civil society has contributed a lot to the success of the TLC programme, which is being implemented in the Cuttack district. However, some suggestions have been derived both, from the members of formal and informal voluntary associations, and the neo-literates or beneficiaries covered under the TLC programme. The suggestions are :

Table 1

Suggestions derived from the members of voluntary associations for the improvement of the TLC policy

Suggestions	*Urban*			*Rural*
	Voluntary association	*Women association*	*Total*	*Voluntary association*
Follow-up programmes	60	40	100	94
Awareness to other issues	30	36	66	62
Solving unemployment	50	40	90	92
Mandatory provision for Govt. Employees.	52	36	88	88
Incentives	56	36	92	94
Education a Fundamental Right	54	38	92	76
Women's reservation	22	40	62	40
Abolition of upper-age limit	60	40	100	100
Pictographic letters	50	34	84	80
Opening libraries	36	26	62	50
Networking	60	40	100	88
Strengthening of welfare policies	52	30	82	96

Table 1 shows the suggestions derived from the members of voluntary associations, both in urban and rural area, for the improvement of the existing TLC policy. As is found from the above the members complain that proper follow up programmes are not undertaken by the Government to maintain the literacy level achieved among the illiterates. Government has policy of Post-Literacy campaign but it is not properly implemented. Associations also do not get any material, financial or moral support from Government to implement post-literacy campaign. Improper implementation of this policy erodes the literacy level and again the neo-literate tend to forget the newly gained literacy skills. In this circumstance the members opined that proper follow up programmes should be undertaken by the Government to maintain the literacy level.

The members are of the opinion that only making the illiterates literate will not bring in social development *suo-motto*. Along with literacy they should be taught simultaneously about other issues concerning health and hygiene, legal issues, mass participation in the democratic process, etc. These issues can bring in meaningful social development expeditiously. Although these are included in the action-plan of TLC policy, it is not properly implemented. Illiterate mass is notbenefited by only knowing letters and numerical if other related issues are not made known to them.

India has a vast reserve of unemployed educated youths. So also is the case with Orissa state. These unemployed educated youths, who have no other source of income, can be fruitfully engaged in the literacy program by the Government and a small stipendiary amount be paid to them so that they will have an enthusiasm to teach the illiterates. In this process, two problems viz. Illiteracy, and to some extent unemployment can be ameliorated.

The members suggest that Government should make it mandatory for its employees to make at least a certain number of illiterate persons literate and this achievement should be a part of their Career Confidential Report (CCR), incremental benefit and promotional opportunities. With compulsion and benefits a large number of them will be genuinely interested for the literacy campaign.

According to the members, the learners who are attending the literacy classes should be given some incentives by the Government which can act as an attraction for them to become literate. This further can also help to retain the learners.

Another suggestion for attaining total literacy is to make education a Fundamental Right upto primary level at least. By this every citizen can get an opportunity to be educated without incurring any cost. This will be particularly beneficial to the children of poor family and can cease the incidence of perpetual illiteracy.

Women's reservation in Legislature is also regarded as a positive step towards women literacy by the members of the women association. They opine that the women legislators can better understand the problems a women faces and hence will work for the betterment and empowerment of women at large. It is to be mentioned here that some of the members of the women associations in urban area themselves aspire for legislative membership.

Another suggestion which emerged from the members was regarding the abolition of the upper age limit i.e. 35 years in the TLC policy. Many elderly persons belonging to 35 years of age and above are attending the learning centres so as to be literate. They are overcoming the inhibition of an advance age and their involvement becomes a source of inspiration for the younger generation who are illiterate. In this context it becomes highly irrelevant, on the part of the Government, to put an upper age limit. An illiterate is an illiterate no matter whatever be his age.

Other suggestions which emerged are opening libraries, introducing pictographic letters and distributing colourfull books to the learners. The library should contain books meant for the neo-literate only and there should be at least one library per municipal ward/Gram Panchayat.

Networking among the neo-literate to maintain the literacy achievement and also to utilise the neo-literate further, as far as possible, to teach the illiterate is lacking. By this the neo-literate can feel a sense of satisfaction that they have achieved something.

Another suggestion which is derived for the members is to strengthen the existing welfare and poverty eradication programmes. If these welfare policies achieve their target, at a large scale, then interest for literacy among the illiterates can sou -motto develop.

Table 2

Suggestions derived from the learners/neo-literate for the improvement of TLC policy

	Urban			*Rural*		
	Male	*Female*	*Total*	*Male*	*Female*	*Total*
Incentives	60	40	100	60	40	100
Literacy Allowance	60	40	100	60	40	100
Loan Facility	60	34	94	60	40	100
Permanent Learning Centre	54	30	84	40	22	62
Creche Facility	50	40	90	00	04	04

Table 2 shows the suggestions derived from the learners/ neo-literate, covered under TLC policy, in improving the TLC. Respondents want apart from continuing the learning centres, the above mentioned facilities. Many have responded positively to loan facility for their personal development by some commercial activities. Respondents in urban area suggest for a creche so that they can get time to attend the learning centre leaving their infants there.

From this it is inferred that in the light of experiences in the implementation of the TLC policy in Cuttack urban and rural areas, the national policy of TLC requires certain modifications for its smooth implementation and greater satisfaction among the learners.

The State is supposed to play a socially meaningful role from a cultural and ethical point of view. All sections of population have to be circumscribed by the State. Kothari cites the example of Mrs. Indira Gandhi's governance where "she appealed to the rural poor but relied essentially on a techno-managerial urban elite. Consequently, as discontent grew, she had no alternative but to protect her personal power by relying more and more on the techno-managerial elite".[3] He says we must realise how the myriad diversities in India have been undermined and their interests stifled for the sake of unity at the centre. He therefore, sees the hope for the future lying with non-party activists who operate in non-governmental organisations which are voluntary in character and outside the persuasive powers of the technocratic centre.[4] "This does not mean that Kothari wishes to replace the State, but in fact he would like a more viable state structure that would be sensitive to the civil society. To sensitize the State a new socio-economic coalition should be created through grass-root initiatives so that new institutional structures may develop".[5] D.L. Sheth also emphasises the nature of these grass-root initiatives in India and says it should be, both, beyond the governmental agencies and aspirations for power.[6] Thus these authors opined that any welfare for people at large can be brought in through collective non-party activism led by Voluntary Organisations.

Here it is pertinent to mention the desires of Mahatma Gandhi, the Father of Indian Nation, who had himself desired and advised that the Congress Party after India's independence should transform itself to a non-political social service organisation and completely disband its political activities so as to provide social and humane service to people without expecting any returns from them. Had it so happened then, there would have been an enormous influence of voluntary associations in India and the culture of associational life would have reached its zenith as Congress Party is the largest party in India and has a strong organisational structure even in a hamlet and has mass-appeal and mass-following. However, Congress Party has remained as political party till date.

For the growth of Associations, the Constitution of India has specific provision under Article 19 (1)© which states that "All citizens shall have the right to form associations or unions subject to reasonable restrictions".[7] This provision is guaranteed as a Fundamental Right.

In this perspective it can be said that voluntary associations

Table 3

Beneficiaries Enrolled in TLC Policy in the Areas Selected

Area	*General*			*SC*			*ST*			*Total*		
	Male	*Female*	*Total*	*Male*	*Female*	*Total*	*Male*	*Female*	*Total*	*Male*	*Female*	*Total*
Safa G.P	164	235	399	71	78	149	118	128	246	353	441	794
Kotasahi G.P	68	206	274	17	33	50	37	46	83	122	285	407
Tangi Block	2090	3047	5137	928	1215	2143	1720	2170	3890	9738	6432	16170
Cuttack Muncipality	-	-	-	-	-	-	-	-	-	5571	7032	12603

Source: TLC Control Room, Tangi Block & Cuttack Muncipality.

N.B.: In Cuttack Municipal Area the beneficiaries caste break-up was not available.

have an immense role in the civil society. They mostly undertake evangelical activities and act as a sort of bridging the gulf between State and civil society and between people themselves. "During the past two decades the voluntary movement has helped to connect people to their rulers. Literally hundreds of NGOs have become embedded in local communities across the country, and have reinforced the message of self-help, cooperation and civic solidarity to the villagers".[8] In an era of decentralisation of decision making, emphasis on local self governance, economic reforms and reliance on market, the civic engagement and voluntary associations provide solace to people, through collective action for common good. Voluntary associational life is an apt antidote to an overbearing bureaucracy and insolent politicians. When voluntary associations performed such a huge task within the sphere of the State bringing about its accountability, responsiveness, effectiveness and thereby increased legitimacy, the image of the state glorifies and citizens never think of resisting the state. It improves the performance of the state to govern in a conducive manner.

Kothari writes, "Voluntary action' should not be seen merely as another form of action.`Rather, it is woven into the very structure and ethos of Indian Society – more a way of life than a form of action. It is closely tied to the fundamentally plural nature of our society. In Indian pluralism is not just a characteristic of the political system as is the case in western politics, it is something ingrained in the very structure and organization of society".[9] In India, the voluntary spirit is much enthusiastic and people are eager to help the distress and the needy persons. Thus, if one says that voluntarism has been an enduring feature of India, it only means that many people at many places are engaged in multifarious action without being asked to do so by an external agent – political, bureaucratic or market propelled.[10] Conceptually, any action by an individual, an informal group, or a duly constituted organization, which is not prompted by external pressure or self-interest and has a purpose of collective welfare can be termed as 'voluntary action'. It is in this context, our empirical research has investigated how the civil society is cooperating and coordinating with the Government or in other words is a complement and not a duplicate. The civil society, while implementing the literacy policy, is thoroughly dedicated and it considers that its cause is more important than the cost of collaboration with the Government and this is more particularly marked in the urban area than in the rural area, where the formal associations are deeply involved at the implementation stage of TLC. In the rural area we find that it is rather the informal associations of peasants, youths, castes, and professionals who are implementing the TLC. It is not that in the rural area the formal associations are not involving themselves but it is limited upto the mobilization stage of the illiterates.

The members of voluntary associations, both in rural and urban areas, coordinate and cooperate with the Government authorities in making the TLC a success. It is not that prior to TLC there were no literacy programmes of the Government but the programmes lacked the commitment and enthusiasm of the illiterates and it remained merely as a Government sponsored welfare programmes. Formulation of policies and programmes can be done easily without any hindrance but it is only at the implementation where proper attention and strategy in required and more important is if we use the famous words of Lasswell, what is to be implemented, when is to be implemented and how is to be implemented. Literacy is an intangible thing but it certainly leads to many tangible things. It might not give immediate rewards like we find in other welfare and developmental programmes. Such as housing, persons, subsidy, etc. but it is definitely rewarding in the long run. Similarly, social opportunities of education and health care, which may require public action, complement individual opportunities of economic and political participation and also help to foster our own initiatives is overcoming our respective deprivations.[11]

In spite of the constraints and the problems in the TLC,

large-scale mobilization of community and voluntary resources is indispensable for a speedy and large-scale attack on illiteracy. Flexibility in the leaving programme so as to facilitate the learners to attend the learning classes is also another important feature found from the study.

Both the rural and urban areas have social segmentation on the basis of caste, religion, language and class but this segmentation has no negative effect on the working of voluntary associations. The members of the voluntary associations, even though they themselves come from diversified social environ, work together for the welfare of all people. It is not that the negative influence of segmentation has been overcome in the areas studied but in due course of the egalitarian work of the voluntary associations and the accommodative process adopted by them it is softening the social segmentedness.

"There are many structures that stand between the individual and the wider society of which he is a part. These mediating structures vary enormously from one type of society to another, and they also change in the course of the evolution of each type. Some of them are actual or potential obstacles to the development of civil society; others are necessary and desirable for its sustenance and well being".[12]

The voluntary associations are involved in a lot of social and economic development activities and they assist the Government in its implementation and also for modification of certain policies so as to suit the needs of the local people. In this process we find that policies and programmes are effectively implemented and positive results are obtained. Generally, people are a bit skeptical about the altruistic attitudes of the Government authorities but with the involvement and association of local level voluntary associations there is a smooth facilitation of the entire process.

They help to connect individuals to each other and to the wider society. "Two features of these institutions deserve special comment: They should be of different kinds, and each, within its own sphere, should enjoy a measure of autonomy in relation to the others and to the State. Civil society, in this conception, is pluralistic in principle; it rescits absorption by the State as well as by religion" .[13] For its supporters, civil society is both a process and a goal: it is through the development of civil society that political and economic frameworks in the region can be made more democratic, and it is the presence of a strong and effervescent civil society which will, in the end, be proof of the success of that enterprise.[14] Voluntary cooperation is easier in a community that has inherited a substantial stock of social capital in the firm of norms of reciprocity and networks of civil engagement.[15]

The hypotheses framed for the research study can now be put to test. Our first hypothesis, 'social capital facilitates coordinated actions' is found to be true. Social Capital brings in better communicative resources to the people and thereby facilitating their coordinated actions. This is proved by the Table nos. 2, 3, 4, 8 and 9 in chapter III. Our second hypothesis 'social capital helps in formulating public policy' is found to be partially true. The formulation of public policies is not independent of civil society in which voluntary associations (formal and informal) play active role. It provides a public space for free discussions on matters of public importance leading to interest, articulation and aggregation which are transformed into public and are formally prioritised and formulated by government. Here social capital indirectly plays a role in policy formulation. Besides, the process of implementation of public policies (in which the voluntary associations are closely associated) very often exposes shortcomings. The voluntary associations identify those lacking and suggest corrective measures to be incorporated in the existing policies so as to attain better and effective implementations of policies. So, second hypotheses is found to be partially true. It is implicit but has not been exhaustively dealth with. This is proved by Table 6 in chapter III and Table 1 in chapter V. our third hypothesis, 'the success of the implementation of the public policy depends to a large extent on the articulation and mobilisation of social capital' is found to be true. The TLC policy is set to be a success only due to the mobilisational capacity of social capital. This is proved by Table nos. 7, 8, 9, 10 and 11 in chapter IV. Our fourth hypothesis, 'human capital and social capital reinforce one another' is found to be true. Both social capital and human capital are having family resemblance. Human capital refers to skill, awareness, literacy etc. Hence, more the human capital better the quality of social capital. It helps in removing the ascriptiveness of the social capital, thereby making it universal. Therefore, there is an interface between the two. This is proved by Table nos. 14, 15 and 16 in chapter V. Our fifth hypothesis, 'social capital promotes the implementation of literacy policy' is also found to be true. Social capital due to its coordinate aspects helps in the better implementation of literacy policy.

The provisional census 2001 shows an increase of 14.51 percent in the state literacy rate during the decade 1991-2000. While the literacy percentage in All India Level was estimated at 65.28 per cent in the latest provisional census report, the rate of literacy was calculated at 63.61 per cent in Orissa. The literacy rate in the state in 1991 was 49.9 per cent as against the national average of 52.1 per cent. This increase in the literacy rate, which is higher than the rate of increase in the national average (the rate of increase at the State is 14.51 per cent while at the national level it is 13.18 per cent) was possible due to the central sponsored TLC policy. The TLC policy is being implemented in all the thirty districts of the state. While the male literacy rate of 75.95 per cent in the state in 2001 was nearer to the national average of 75.85 percent, the rate of female literacy is 1.19 per cent below the national average. The literacy rate among females stood at 52.97 per cent while that at the national average is 54.16 per cent.

From the provisional census 2001 we find that the literacy level has increased considerably and this became possible due to the people-centered TLC policy and a much enthused civil society. The findings of the census, further, throws light on the presence of social capital and its effectiveness on policy implementation. Prior to the TLC policy, there was no innovative programme of associating the civil society in the literacy policy implementation. This hampered the implementation process as it was solely a Government sponsored programme. The association of civil society and voluntary associations brought dramatic changes in the literacy scenario and made possible for a high literate population. An essential goal of public policy has been to ensure that the bulk of the young population had the capacity to read, write, communicate and interact in a way that is quite essential for modern industrial production. Literacy, in this perspective, can bring in the betterment of the people and, for this only, the civil society plays an active role in transforming the illiterates to become literates.

Literacy and basic education can facilitate public discussion of social needs and encourage informed collective demands (e.g. for health care and social security); these in turn can help expand the facilities that the public enjoys, and can contribute to the better utilization of the available services.[16] Greater literacy and educational achievements of disadvantaged groups can increase their ability to resist oppression, to organize politically, and to get a fairer deal. The redistributive effects can be important not only between different social groups or households, but also within the family, since there is evidence that better education (particularly female education) contributes to the reduction of gender-based inequalities.

Voluntary organisations are now being looked upon as bearers of new promises and possibilities. With the demise of state socialism and the crisis of welfare state and liberal democracy, voluntary organisations have become our new rallying points of hopes and aspirations. There is a growing realization on the part of many concerned that to think that either state or society should do everything for the realization of human well-beings is to prepare the ground for colossal human suffering and erosion of individual moral responsibility. The move towards voluntary organisations is part of the shift from a clinical dependence on state and recognition of the creativity of civil society and other-directed communicative action of concerned and sensitive individuals. This hope on voluntary organization is part of the refrigeration of hope on new social movements in the advanced industrial societies and the non-governmental organisations in the developing world. Civil society has traditionally been conceived of by its proponents as a site of resistance against two forces: that of the state and that of the market. In societies where the state apparatus and the nature of economic development are seen as creating forces of social inequality and exclusion, the exponents of civil society have argued that it can help constitute a space where critiques of these forces can be formulated and alternative trajectories of political and economic development propounded. For its supporters, civil society is both a process and a goal: it is through the development of civil society that political and economic frameworks in the region can be made more democratic and effective, and it is the presence of a strong and effervescent civil society which will, in the end, be proof of the success of that enterprise.[17]

Writing on the strengthening of the voluntary organisations, Kothari writes, "There is a growing concern that the state has not been able to function as an instrument of liberation and enfranchisement of the poor and the deprived, of the excluded and the various peripheralised 'minorities'. Actually, the activities, policies and programmes of the state have given rise to greater disparity and this disparity has been growing in all spheres. All projections indicate the serious units of the machinery of the government and other instruments of the state to function as purveyors of social change in any basic way. For the basic problem today is that the system, as it has developed, looks more and more to the entrenched elites and the prosperous sections for its support".[18] It is due to the fallacies of the state that increasing reliance is now being given to the civil society organisations. Kothari again writes, 'voluntary organisations, to become part of the democratic process, should contribute to it in as large a way as possible'.[19] Truly, replacement of the state by voluntary agencies appears to be too far-fetched in the context of developing nations, but at the same time we have to admit that involvement of voluntary agencies can certainly make the whole process of development more humane, understandable and pervasive through willing participation of the target-groups of development themselves. For this the civil society organization has to rely on the collective goodwill and strength of the people who remain the final *raison d' etre* of its existence.

REFERENCES

1. Held, David (1996), *Models of Democracy*, Stanford University Press, Stanford, p. 122.

2. Marx, K. (1970), *The Critique of Hegel's Philosophy of Right*, Cambridge University Press, Cambridge, p. 131.

3. Kothari, Rajni (1990), 'Integration and Exlusion in Indian Politics', *Economic & Political Weekly*, Bombay, Vol. 23, p. 2226.

4. Kothari, Rajni (1986), 'The Non-Party Political Process', *Economic & Political Weekly*, Bombay, Vol. 19, p. 221.

5. Gupta, Dipankar (1996), *Political Sociology in India—Contemporary Trends*, Orient Longman, New Delhi, p. 41.

6. Sheth, D.L. (1996), 'Grass-roots Initiatives in India', *Economic & Political Weekly*, Bombay, Vol. 19, pp. 259-62.

7. Resonable restrictions include interests of sovereignty and integrity of India, security of the state, friendly relations with foreign states, public order, decency or morality, or in relation to contempt of court, defamation or incitement to an offence.

8. Das, Gurcharan (1997), 'Civic Engagement', *Times of India*, New Delhi, dt.19.11.97.

9. Kothari, Rajni (1998), 'The Future of Voluntarism', in Dantawala, M.L. *et al.* (eds.), *Social Charge through Voluntary Action*, Sage, New Delhi, p. 182.

10. *ibid.*, p. *183*.

11. Sen, A. (2000), *Development as Freedom*, OUP, New Delhi, p. xii.

12. Beteille, Andre (1998), 'The conflict of Norms and Values in Contemporary Indian Society', in Peter L. Berger (ed.), *The*

Limits of Social Cohesion: Conflict and Mediation in Pluralist Societies, West View Press, p. 283.

13. *ibid.*, pp. 283-4.

14. Lizee, Pierre P. (2000), 'Civil Society and Regional Security: Tensions and Potentials in Post-crisis Southeast Asia', *Contemporary South-East Asia*, Vol. 22, No. 3, p. 551.

15. Putnam, Robert (1993), *Making Democracy Work*, Princeton Univ. Press, Princeton, p. 167.

16. Sen & Dreze (1998), *Economic Development and Social Opportunity,* Oxford University Press, Delhi, p. 14.

17. Lizee, Pierre P. (2000), 'Civil Society and Regional Security', *Contemporary Southeast Asia*, Vol. 22, No. 3, p. 551.

18. Kothari, Rajni (1987), 'Voluntary Organisation in a Plural Society', *Indian Journal of Public Administration*, Vol. XXXIII, No. 3, pp. 433-4.

19. *ibid.*, p. 452.

BIBLIOGRAPHY

Books

Action Aid (1995), *Role of NGOs in the Changing Scenario: A Symposium*, Action Aid, Madras.

Agnihotri, Anita & Sivaswamy, G. (1993), *Total Literacy Campaign in the Sundergarh District of Orissa*, Directorate of Adult Education, New Delhi.

Agora Project, (1996), *Democracy and Social Capital in Segmented Societies*, Department of Government, Uppsala University, Uppsala.

Ahmed, E., Dreze, J.P., Hills, J. & Sen, A.K. (eds.) (1999), *Social Security in Developing Countries*, Oxford University Press, New Delhi.

Alagh, Yoginder, K. (1986), *Some Aspects of Planning Policies in India*, Vohra Publishers, Allahabad.

Alberoni, F. (1984), *Movement and Institution*, Columbia University Press, New York.

Alliband, Terry (1983), *Catalysts of Development: Voluntary Agencies in India*, CT: Kumarian Press, Hartford.

Almond, C.A. & Coleman, J. (1960), *The Politics of Developing Area*, Princeton University Press, Princeton.

Almond, G. & Verba, S. (1963), *The Civic Culture*, Princeton University Press, Princeton.

Almond, G. & Verba, S. (eds.) (1980), *The Civic Culture Revisited*, Little Brown, Boston.

Anderson, J.E., (1977), *Public Policy-making*, Holt Rhinehart & Winston Ltd., New York.

Andrews, G. (ed.), (1991), *Citizenship*, Lawrence & Wishart, London.

Appleby, P.B. (1975), *Policy and Administration*, University of Albama Press, Albama,VS.

Annin, S. & Hakim, P. (eds.), (1988), *Direct to the Poor: Grassroots Development in Latin America*, Lynne Reinner, London.

Arato, Andrew & Cohen, Jean (1992), *Civil Society and Political Theory*, MIT Press, Cambridge.

Archer, David & Costello, Patnaik (1990), *Literacy and Power: The Latin American Battle Ground*, Earthscan Publications, London.

Archibugi, D., Held D., & Kohler, M. (edn.) (1998), *Re-imagining Political Community*, Polity Press, Cambridge.

Arendt, H., (1958), *The Human Condition*, Chicago University Press, Chicago.

Arya, Ved (1996), *Towards a Relationship of Significance*, Pradan, New York.

Athreya, V.B. & Chunkath, Sheela Rani (1996), *Literacy and Empowerment*, Sage, New Delhi.

Atkirson, A.B. (1983), *Social Justice and Public Policy*, MIT Press, Cambridge.

AVARD, (1992), *Government-NGO Interface in India's Development: A Country Paper I*, AVARD/ANGOC, New Delhi.

Avineri, S. (1972), *Hegel's Theory of the Modern State*, Cambridge University Press, Cambridge.

Axelrod, R. (1984), *The Evolution of Cooperation*, Basic Books, New York.

Baldwin, Peter (1990), *The Politics of Social Solidarity*, Cambridge University Press, Cambridge.

Barber, Benjamin (1984), *Strong Democracy*, Berkeley University Press, Berkeley.

Bardhan, P.K., & Srinivasan, T.N. (eds.) (1988), *Rural Poverty in South Asia*, Columbia University Press, New York.

Barrett, S. & Fudge, L. (eds.) (1981), *Policy and Action*, Methuen, London.

Baxamusa, Ramala, M. (1992), "Voluntary Organisations in Women's Development: An Assessment", in R.K. Punia (ed.), *Women in Agriculture, Education, Training and Development*, Vol. 2, Northern Book Centre, New Delhi.

Bentley, A. (1908), *The Process of Government*, University of Chicago Press, Chicago.

Berger, Peter, & Neuhers, Richard, J. (1996), *To Empower People: From State to Civil Society*, AEI Press, Washington D.C.

Bhola, H.S., (1984), *Campaigning for Literacy*, UNESCO, Paris.

Billis, D., (1993), *Organising Public and Voluntary Agencies*, Routledge, London.

Blair, H., (1996), 'Donors, Democratisation and Civil Society: Relating Theory to Practice' in Edwards, M.& Hulme, D. (eds.), *NGOs, States and Donours: Too Close for comfort* ? Macmillan, Basingstoke.

Bobbio, N. (1996), *Left and Right*, Polity Press, Cambridge.

Bobrow, D. & Drysek J. (1987), *Policy Analysis by Design*, University of Pittsburgh Press, Pihsburgh.

Brown, L.D. (1998), "Private Voluntary Organisations and Development Partnerships" in Khandwalla (eds.), *Social*

Development: A New Role for the Organisational Sciences, Sage, New Delhi.

Caroll, T.F. (1993), *Intermediary NGOs: The Supporting Link* in *Grassroots Development*, Kumarian Press, USA.

Carron, G. & Bordia, A., (eds.) (1985), *Issues in Planning and Implementing National Literacy Programmes I*, The UNESCO, Paris.

Carter, Stephen L. (1998), *Civility*, Basic Books, New York.

Castles, F.G. (1989), *The Comparative History of Public Policy*, Polity Press, Cambridge.

Castells, M. (1983), *The City and the Grassroots: A Cross-cultural Theory of Urban Social Movements*, Edward Arnold, London.

Chadha, P. (1995), *Development Management Need for Capacity-Building in Community Based NGOs*, PRIA, New Delhi.

Chambers, Simone, & Kymlicka, Will (eds.) (1999), *Alternative Conceptions of Civil Society*, Princeton University Press, Princeton.

Chand, Prem (1991), *Literacy Digest*, Directorate of Adult Education, Ministry of HRD, GOI, New Delhi.

Chandhoke, Neera (1995), *State and Civil Society: Explorations in Political Theory*, Sage, New Delhi.

Chandler, A.F.D. (1986), *Participation as Process: What we can learn from Grameen Bank, Bangladesh*, NORAD, Oslo.

Chuq, Beng Huat (1994), 'For a communitarian Democracy in Singapore', in Da Cunha, Derez. (ed.), *Debating Singapore*, Institute of South-East Asian Studies, Singapore.

Clark, J. (1991), *Democratising Development: The Role of Voluntary Organisation*, Kumarian Press, Connecticut, USA.

Clayton, A. (1996), *NGO's State and Civil Society Organisation: Summary of Workshop Discussions*, INTRAC, UK.

Colas, Dominique (1997), *Civil Society and fanaticism: Conjoined Histories*, Stanford University Press, California.

Comeman, James S. (1990), *Foundations of Social Theory*, Harvard University Press, Cambridge.

Cornia, G., Jolly, R. & Stawart, F. (eds.) (1987), *Adjustment with a Human Face*, Clarendon Press, Oxford.

Covey, J.G., & David, L.B. (1995), *Beyond Strategic Planning: Strategic Decisions is Non-profit Organisations*, Institute for Development Research, Canada.

Current Sociology, (1998), Special Issue on Voluntary Organisations, Vol. 46, No. 3.

D'Abrea, D.A. (1992), *NGOs in the Nineties*, Federation of Voluntary Organisations for Rural Development, Bangalore.

Dash, Shreeram Chandra (1997), *States of Our Union – Orissa*, Publications Division, Govt. of India, New Delhi.

Deshpande, Vasant (1981), *Developing Voluntarism*, Gramayan, Pune.

Deshpande, V. (1992), *Islands of Development: Role of Voluntary Action in Rural Transformation*, Society for Participatory Research in Asia (PRIA), New Delhi.

Development Support Initiative (1997), *Dossier on Civil Society*, Development Support Initiative, Bangalore.

Dewey, J. (1966), *Democracy and Education*, Free Press, New York.

Dogra, B, *et al*. (eds.) (1993), *NGOs in Social Change*, NFS – India, New Delhi.

Douglas, J. (1987), "Political Theories of Non-Profit Organisation", in Powell, W.W. (ed.). *The Non-Profit Sector: A Research Handbook*. Yale University Press, New Haven and London.

Dreze, J.P. & Sen, A.K., (1989), *Hunger and Public Action*, Clarendon Press, Oxford.

Dreze, J.P. & Sen, A.K., (eds.) (1990), *The Political Economy of Hunder*, Oxford University Press, Oxford.

Dreze, J.P. & Sen, A.K., (1998), *India—Economic Development and Social Opportunity*, Oxford University Press, New Delhi.

Dunn, Chris, & Hann, E. (eds.) (1996), *Civil Society: Challenging Western Models*, Routledge, London.

Dye, T. (1966), *Politics, Economics and Public Policy: Policy Outcomes in the American States*, Rand McNally, Chicago.

Edgeston, R.B. (1992), *Sick Societies: Challenging the myth of Primitive Harmony*, Free Press, New York.

Edwards & Hulme (eds.) (1995), *Non governmental Organisation: Performance and Accountability*, Earthscan Publications, London.

Ehrenberg, John (1999), *Civil Society: The Critical History of an Idea*, New York University Press, New York & London.

Evans, Peter, (1995), *Embedded Autonomy: States & Industrial Transformation* Princeton University Press, Princeton.

Forring ton, J. *et al*. (1993), *Reluctant Partners & NGOs, the State and Sustainable Agricultural Development*, Routledge.

Faellks, Keith (1999), *Political Sociology: A Critical Introduction*, Edinburgh University Press, Edinburgh.

Fawn, R. & Larkins, J. (eds.) (1996), *International Society after the Cold War*, Macmillan Press, London.

Ferguson, Adam (1980), *An Essay on the History of Civil Society*, Transaction Books, New Brunswick.

Fine, Robert & Rai, Shirin (1997), *Civil Society: Democratic Perspectives*, Frank Cass, London.

Fischer, F. & Forester, J. (eds.) (1993), *The Argumentative Turn in Policy Analyses*, UCL Press, London.

Foschi, M. & Lawler, E.J. (ed.) (1994), *Group Processes: Sociological Analysis*, Nelson-Hall.

Fukuyama, F. (1995), *Trust: The Social Virtues and the Creation of Prosperity*, Penguin, London.

Gambetta, D. (ed.) (1988), *Trust: Making and Breaking Co-operative Relations*, Basil Blackwell, London.

Gaskin, K., Vlaeminke, M. & Fenton, N. (1996), *Young People's Attitudes to the Voluntary Sector*, NCVO, London.

Gellner, Ernst (1996), *Conditions of Liberty: Civil Society and Its Rivals*, Penguin, London.

Ghai, Dharam (ed.), (2000), *Social Development and Public Policy: A Study of Some Successful Experiences*, Macmillan Press in Association with UNRISD, London.

Giddens, Anthony (1998), *The Third Way: The Renewal of Social Democracy*, Polity Press & Blackwell, Cambridge & Malden.

Gillespie, R. & Paterson, W.E. (1993), *Rethinking Social Democracy*, Cars, London.

Goldtarb, Jeffray, C. (1998), *Civility and Subversion: The intellectual in Democratic Society*, Cambridge University Press, Cambridge.

Green, David (1993), *Reinventing Civil Society*, Institute of Economic Affairs, London.

Gulati, Ravi, & Gulati, Kaval (1996), *Strengthening Voluntary Action in India*, Konark, New Delhi.

Gupta, Dipankar (ed.) (1991), *Social Stratification*, Oxford Univeristy Press, Delhi.

Gupta, Dipankar, (1996), *Political Sociology in India: Contemporary Trends*, Orient Longman, Hyderabad.

Gupta, R.L. (1994), *NGO Experiences in Social Security*, Friendrich–Ebert–Stiftung, New Delhi.

Hadenius, Axel (1992), *Democracy and Development*, Cambridge University Press, Cambridge.

Hall, John (ed.) (1995), *Civil Society: Theory History Comparison*, Polity Press, Cambridge.

Ham, C. & Hill, M. (1984), *The Policy Process in the Modern Capitalist State*, Harvester Wheatsheaf, Brighton.

Handy, C. (1988), *Understanding Voluntary Organisations*, Penguin, London.

Hardin, Russell (1982), *Collection Action*, Johns Hopkins University Press, Baltimore.

He, Baogang (1997), *The Democratic Implications of Civil Society in China*, St. Martin's Press, New York.

Heclo, H. (1974), *Modern Social Policies in Britain and Sweden*, Yale University Press, New Haven.

Held, David (1995), *Democracy and the Global Order; From the Modern State to Cosmopolitan Governance*, Polity Press, Cambridge.

Heidenheimer, A.J., Heclo, H, & Adams, C.T. (1983), *Comparative Public Policy*, St. Martin's Press, New York.

Hirst, Paul (1994), *Associative Democracy: New Forms of Economic and Social Governance*, Polity Press, Oxford.

Hirst, Paul (ed.) (1997), *From Statism to Pluralism: Democracy, Civil Society and Global Politics*, UCL Press, London.

Hirst, Paul, & Khilnani, Sunil (eds.) (1996), *Reinventing Democracy*, Blackwell Publishers, Oxford.

Hofferbert, R. (1974), *The Study of Public Policy*, Bobbs-Merrill, Oxford.

Hoggett, P., (1994), *The Future of Civil Forms of Organisation*, DEMOS, London.

Hogwood, B. & Peters, B. (1985), *The Pathology of Public Policy*, Clarendon, Oxford.

Honneth, Axel (198), *Social Action and Human Nature*, Cambridge University Press, Cambridge.

Huntington, S. (1993), *The Clash of Civilisations*? Council of Foreign Relations, New York.

Hyden, Goran (1995), *Assisting the Growth of Civil Society: How might it be Improved* ? Uppsala University, Uppsala.

Indian Journal of Public Administration (1987), Special Number on 'Voluntary Organisations and Development: Their role', Vol. XXXIII, No. 3, New Delhi.

Jain, P.S. (1989), *Perspectives on Voluntary Organisation*, Institute of Rural Management, Anand, Gujarat.

James, P.J. (1995), *Non-Governmental Voluntary Organisation: The True Mission*, Mass Line Publications, Kerala.

Jencks, Christopher (1992), *Rethinking Social Policy*, Harvard University Press, Cambridge.

Jenkins-Smith, H. (1990), *Democratic Politics and Policy Analysis*, Brooks/Cole Publishing Company, Pacific Grove.

Karlekar, Hiranmay (ed.) (1998), *Independent India: The first fifty years*, ICSSR and OUP, New Delhi.

Karlsson, Nicke (1993), *The State of State: An Inquiry Concering the Role of Invisible Hands in Politics and Civil Society*, Almqvis & Wksell International, Uppsala.

Kaviraj, Sudipta, (ed.) (1997), *Politics in India*, Oxford University Press, New Delhi.

Keane, John (1988), *Democracy and Civil Society*, Verso, London.

Keane, John (ed.) (1988), *Civil Society and the State*, Verso, London.

Kelling, G.L., & Coles, C.M. (1997), *Fixing Broken Windows*, Simon & Schuster, New York.

Khandwalla, P.N. (ed.) (1988), *Social Development: A New Role for the Organisational Sciences*, Sage, New Delhi.

Kohli, Atul (1990), *Democracy and Discontent: India's Growing Crisis of Governability*, Cambridge University Press, Cambridge.

Kohli, Atul (ed.) (1991), *India's Democracy: An Analysis of Changing State - Society Relations*, Orient Longman, Hyderabad.

Kooiman, Jan (ed.) (1993), *Modern Governance: New Government Society Interactions*, Sage, London.

Kortern, D.C. (1990), *Getting to the 21st Century: Voluntary Action and the Global Agenda*, Kumarian Press, USA.

Koselleck, Reinhart (1988), *Critique and Crisis: Enlightenment and the Pathogenesis of Modern Society*, MIT Press, Cambridge.

Kothari, Rajni (1976), *Democratic Polity and Social Change in India: Crisis and Opportunities*, Allied Publishers, New Delhi.

Kothari, Rajni (1985), 'Role of Voluntary Organisations in the Seventh Plan and the Development of the Weaker Sections', *in Seventh Plan and Development of the Weaker Sections: Questions, Challenges and Alternatives*, ISI, New Delhi.

Kothari, Rajni (1990), *Politics and the People – In Search of a Humane India*, Aspect & Ajanta Publications, New Delhi.

Kothari, Rajni (1990), *State against Democracy – In Search of Humane Governance*, Aspect & Ajanta Publications, New Delhi.

Kothari, R. (1994), "The NGOs, The State and World Capitalisation", in LRSA (ed.), *Action Groups Beginning or End of a Drama*, Legal Resources for Social Action, Tamil Nadu.

Lasswell, H.D. (1971), *A Pre-view of Policy Sciences*, Elsevier, New York.

Ledesma (1992), *Partners in Development – The Role of NGOs in Rural Poverty Alleviation in Asia*, ESCAP, SEARSOLIN, Phillipines.

Lerner, D. & Lasswell, H.D. (1951), *The Policy Sciences*, Stanford University Press, Stanford.

Lewis, J.P., *et al.* (1988), *Strengthening the Poor: What Have we Learned?*, Transaction Books for ODA, Washsington D.C.

Lind, Agneta & Johnston, Anton, (1986), *Adult Literacy in the Third World*, SIDA, Education Division Document No. 32, Stockhom.

Lindblom, C. (1968), *The Policy-Making Process*, Prentice-Hall, Englewood Cliffs, New Jersey.

Loury, Glenn (1977), 'A Dynamic Theory of Racial Income Differences' in Wallace, P.A. & Le Mund, A. (eds.) *Women, Minorities and Employment Discrimination*, Lexington Books, Lexington.

Madiath, A. (1994), *Powerful People – A Study of Community Organisation in Accord, Asha and Gram*, Action Aid, Bangalore.

Mahajan, Gurpreet (1998), *Identities and Rights; Aspects of Liberal Democracy in India*, Oxford University Press, Delhi.

Mahajan, Gurpreeet (ed.), (2000), *Democracy, Difference & Social Justice*, Oxford University Press, New Delhi.

Milbraith, Lester W. (1965), *Political Participation: How and why do people get involved in Politics*, Rand McNally, Chicago.

Malik, Iftikhar, H. (1997), *State and Civil Society in Pakistan: Politics of Authority, Ideology and Ethnicity*, St. Martin's Press, New York.

Mamdani, Mahmood, (1996), *Citizen and Subject: Contemporary*

Africa and the Legacy of Late Colonialism, Princeton University Press, Princeton.

Mamdani, Mahmood (1997), *Citizen and Subject: Decentralised Despotism and the Legacy of Late Colonialism,* Oxford University Press, New Delhi.

Manor, James (ed.) (1991), *Rethinking Third World Politics,* Longman, London & New York.

Markaff, John, (1996), *Waves of Democracy : Social Movements and Political Change,* Pine Forge Press, Thousand Oaks.

Mazmanian, D. & Sabatier, P. (eds.) (1981), *Effective Policy Implementation,* D.C Health, Lexington, Massachusettes.

Mc Adam, D., MaCarthy, J.D., & Zald, M.N. (edn.) (1996), *Comparative Perspectives on Social Movements, Political Opportunities, Mobilising Structures and Cultural Framings,* Cambridge University Press, Cambridge.

Midgley, J. (1986), *Community Participation, Social Development and the State,* Methuen, London.

Migdal, J., Kohli, A., & Shue, V. (eds.) (1994), *State Power and Social Forces,* Cambridge University Press, Cambridge.

Mohanty, M., & Mukherji, P.N., with Tornquist, O. (eds.) (1998), *People's Rights: Social Movements and the State in the Third World,* Sage, New Delhi.

Murthy, K.R.S., (1994), *Leadership Potential of NGO's,* Indian Institute of Management, Bangalore.

Narayana, E.A., (1990), *Voluntary Organisations and Rural Development in India,* Uppal Publishing House, New Delhi.

Norton, M. (1995), *The Voluntary Sector in India: Issues and Ideas for its Future,* Centre for Innovation in Voluntary Action, London.

Olson, M. (1965), *The Logic of Collective Action,* Harvard University Press, Cambridge.

Omvedt, Gail, (1993), *Reinventing Revolution: New Social Movements and the Socialist Tradition in India,* M.E. Sharpe, New York & London.

Ostrom, E. (1990), *Governing the Commons: The Evolution of Institutions for Collective Action,* Cambridge University Press, Cambridge.

Oz-Salzburger, Fania (ed.) (1996), *Adam Firguson: An Essay on the History of Civil Society,* Cambridge University Press, Cambridge.

Pandey, S.R. (1991), *Community Action for Social Change: Grassroots Organisations in India,* Sage, New Delhi.

Parsons, W., (1995), *Public Policy,* Edward Elgar, Aldershot.

Parry, Geraint (1994), 'Making Democrats: education and democracy', in Parry, Geraint, & Moran, Michael, (eds.), & *Democracy & Democratisation,* Routledge, London.

Peters, B.G. (1988), *American Public Policy: Promise & Performance,* Affiliated East-West Press, New Delhi.

Perez-Diaz, Vistor M. (1978), *State Bureaucracy and Civil Society,* Macmillan, London.

Planning Commission (1994), *Action Plan to Bring About a Collaborative Relationship between Voluntary Organisations Government,* Planning Commission/VANI, New Delhi.

Pressman, J.L. & Wildavski, A.B. (1973), *Implementation,* University of California Press, Berkeley.

PRIA (1989), *NGO-Government Relations: A Source of Life or a Kins of Death,* PRIA, New Delhi.

PRIA (1991), *Voluntary Development Organisations in India: A Study of History, Roles and Future Challenges,* New Delhi.

PRIA, (1994), *Report of the Workshop on Civil Society in the New Global Context: Implication for Voluntary Development Organisation,* PRIA, New Delhi.

Provinse, J.H. (1955), 'Cooperative Rice Field Cultivation among the Siang Dyaks of Central Borneo', in E.A. Hoebel (ed.), *Readings in Anthropology*, McGraw-Hill, New York.

Putnam, Robert (1993), *Making Democracy Work: Civic Traditions in Modern Italy*, Princeton University Press, New Jersey.

Putnam, Robert (2000), *Bowling Alone: The Collapse and Revival of American Community*, Simon & Schuster, New York.

Pye, Lucian (1966), *Aspects of Political Development*, Little Brown, Boston.

Ramaswamy, V. (1991), *Non-Government Organisations – A Perspective*, Friedrich – Ebert – Stiftung, New Delhi.

Rein, Martin (1976), *Social Science and Public Policy*, Penguin Books, Middlesex.

Ritchey-Vance, Marion (1991), *The Art of Association: NGOs and Civil Society in Colombia*, United States Inter-American Foundation.

Rose, R. (1993), *Lesson-Drawing in Public Policy*, Chatham House, New Jersey.

Rosenberg, J. (1994), *The Empire of Civil Society: A Critique of the Realist Theory of International Relations*, Verso, London.

Rudebeck, Lars (ed.), (1992), *When Democracy makes sense: Studies in the Potential of Third World Popular Movements*, AKUT, Uppsala.

Rudebeck, L. & Tornquist, O., with Rojas, V. (ed.) (1998), *Democratisation in the Third World: Concrete Cases in Comparative and Theoretical Perspective*, Macmillan, London.

Rudolph, L.I. & Rudolph, Susanne (1987), *The Modernity of Tradition: Political Development in India*, Orient Longman, Hyderabad.

Rudolph, Lloyd, & Rudolph, Susanne H. (1987), *In Pursuit of Lakshmi*, Orient Longman, Delhi.

Sanyan, Bishwapriya, (1994), *Cooperative Autonomy: The Dialectics of State NGOs Relationship in Developing Countries*, International Institute for Labour Studies, Geneva.

Scherer, Ross (ed.), (1980), *American Denominational Organisation: A Sociological View*, William Carey, Pasadena.

Schleifer, J.T. (1980), *The Making of Tocqueville's Democracy in America*, University of North Carolina Press, Chapel Hill.

Schwedler, Jillian (ed.) (1995), *Towards Civil Society in the Middle East?*, Lynne Rienner, Boulder & London.

Seligman, Adam (1992), *The Idea of Civil Society*, Free Press, New York.

Sen, Amartya (2000), *Development as Freedom*, Oxford University Press, New Delhi.

Sen, A., & Dreze, J. (1996), *Indian Development: Selected Regional Perspectives*, Oxford Univ. Press, Delhi & Oxford.

Serrano, I.R. (ed.), (1994), *Civil Society in the Asia Pacific Region*, CIVICUS, USA.

Singh, Harjinder (ed.), (1977), *Caste among Non-Hindus in India*, National Publications, Delhi.

Smillie, I. & Helmich, H. (eds.) (1993), *Non-Governmental Organisations and Governments: Stakeholders for Development*, OECD Development Centre, Paris.

Sorensen, Georg, (1993), *Democracy & Democratisation: Processes & Prospects in a Changing World*, Westview Press, Boulder, Co.

Stephen, F., (1990), *NGOs Hope of the Last Decade of this Century*, SEARCH, Bangalore.

Stnobr, T.G. & Graff, H.J. (eds.), (1987), *National Literacy Campaigns: Historical and Comparative Perspectives*, Plenum Press, New York.

Tandon, R. (1993), *Advocacy by NGOs in India: Some Reflections*, PRIA, New Delhi.

______________, *The Role of Voluntary Action in Contemporary Context – Implications for Institutional Development*, PRIA, New Delhi.

Tandau, Alfred (1996), *Policy Implementation in India: A Case Study*, Vikas, New Delhi.

Tarrow, Sidney, (1994), *Power in Movement: Social Movements, Collective Action and Politics*, Cambridge Univ. Press, Cambridge.

Tester, K., (1992), *Civil Society*, Routledge, London & New York.

Tharakan, Michael, P.K. (1990), *The Ernakulam District Total Literacy Campaign: Report of the Evaluation*, Mimeo, Centre for Development Studies, Trivandrum.

Thomas, A. (1992), "Non-Governmental Orgnisations and the Limits to Empowerment" in Mackintosh, M., *et al.*, (eds.), *Development Policy and Public Action*, Oxford University Press, UK.

Thorlind, Robert (1988), *Decentralisation and Local Government Performance: questioning the Civil Society / Social Capital Paradigm through a Comparison of Different Types of Politicisation in West Bengal and Bangladesh*, Seminar for Development Studies and the Nordic Institute for Asian Studies, Uppsala & Copenhagen.

Tismaneanu, Vladimir (1990), *In Search of Civil Society: Independent Peace Movements in the Soviet Bloc*, Routledge, London.

Uggla, Fredik (1995), *Making Civil Society Work-Promoting Democratic Development: What can States Donors do ?*, Uppsala Studies in Democracy, No. 9, Department of Government, Uppsala University, Uppsala.

UNESCO (1976), *The Experimental World Literacy Programme: A Critical Assessment*, The UNESCO, UNDP, Paris.

Van De Berge, Pierre, L. (1969), 'Pluralism and Polity: A Theoretical Exploration' in Leo Kuper and M.G. Smith (eds.), *Pluralism in Africa*, University of California Press, Berkeley.

Van Tils, J. (1988), *Mapping the Third Sector*, The Foundation Centre, New York.

Verba, Sidney, Schoolman, Kay L., & Brady, Henry E. (1995), *Voice and Equality: Civic Voluntarism in American Politics*, Harvard University Press, Cambridge.

Wade, R. (1988), *Village Republics: Economic Conditions for Collective Action in South India*, Cambridge University Press, Cambridge.

Weber, M. (1964), *The Theory of Social and Economic Organisation*, Free Press, Toronto.

Weiner, Myron (1962), *The Politics of Scarcity, Public Pressure and Political Response in India*, University of Chicago Press, Chicago.

White, G. (1994), *Civil Society, Democratisation and Development*, Mimeo, Institute of Development Studies, U.K.

Wood, Ellen M. (1995), *Democracy against Capitalism: Renewing Historical Materialism*, Cambridge University Press, Cambridge.

World Bank (1992), *Governance and Development*, World Bank, Washington D.C.

World Bank (1994), *Governance: The World Bank's Experience*, World Bank, Washington D.C.

World Bank (1999), *World Development Report*, Oxford University Press, New York.

Wright, E.O. (ed.) (1995), *Associations and Democracy: The Real Utopias Project*, Vol.1, Verso, London.

Wuyts, M., Mackintosh, M. and Hewitt, T. (eds.) (1992), *Development Policy and Public Action*, Oxford University Press with Open University, Oxford.

Yin, R. (1994), *Case Study Research: Design and Methods*, Sage, London.

Zachariah, M. & Sooryamoorthy, R. (1994), *Science in Participatory Development—The Achievements and Dilemmas of a Development Movement: The case of Kerala*, Zed Books, London & New Jersey.

Articles

Acharya, Ashok (1997), 'Civil Society and Liberal Norms', *Seminar*, 456.

Allison, Lincoln (1998), 'Sport and Civil Society', *Political Studies*, Vol. XLVI, pp. 709-26.

Bandyopadhya, D. (1997), 'People Participation in Planning: Kerala Experiment', *Economic & Political Weekly*, 27 September.

Beteille, Andre (1996), 'Civil Society and its Institutions', The First Fulbright Memorial Lecture, United States Educational Foundation in India, Calcutta.

Bhatt, Anil (1995), 'Voluntary Action in India', *Economic and Political Weekly*, Vol. 30, No. 16, pp. 870-76.

Bhat, M.K. (1997), 'NGOs from Charity to Civil Society', *Development Support Initiative*, Bangalore.

Birnbaum, Karl E. (1991), 'Civil Society and Government Policy in a New Europe', *The World Today*, Vol. 47, No. 5, pp. 84-5.

Blaney, D.L., & Pasha, M.K. (1993), 'Civil Society and Democracy in the Third World: Ambiguities and Historical Possibilities', *Studies in Comparative International Development*, Vol. 28.

Bradford, Neil (1998), 'Prospectus for Associative Governance:

Lessons from Ontario, Canada', *Politics and Society,* Vol. 26, No. 4, pp. 539-7.

Brown, L.D. & Tandon, R. (1994), 'Institutional Development for Strengthening Civil Society', *Journal of Institutional Development,* Vol. 1, No. 1.

Bryant, Christopher G.A. (1993), 'Social Self-organisation, Civility and Sociology: a comment on Kumar's 'Civil Society', *British Journal of Sociology,* Vol. 44, No. 3, pp. 397-401.

Calhaun, Craig (1993), 'Civil Society and the Public Sphere', *Public Culture,* Vol. 6, No. 5, pp. 267-80.

Candler, G.G. (2000), 'The Professions and Public Policy: Expanding the Third Sector', *International Political Science Review,* Vol. 21, No. 1, pp. 43-58.

Castles, F. & Merrill, V. (1989), 'Towards a General Model of Public Policy Outcomes', *Journal of Theoretical Politics,* Vol. 1, pp. 177-212.

Chattopadhyay, G.P. (1996), 'Organisational Development for NGOs: Some Speculations', *Renewal,* No. 2, June.

Chaubey, Geeta (1997), 'Literacy in India: An Examination', *IASSI Quarterly,* Vol. 16, No. 2, pp. 13-26.

Cho, Hee-Yeon (2000), 'Civic action for global democracy: a response to neo-liberal globalisation', *Inter-Asia Cultural Studies,* Vol. 1, No. 1, pp. 163-167.

Clarke, G. (1998), 'Non-Governmental Organisations and Politics in the Developing World', *Politics Studies,* Vol. XZVI, pp. 36-52.

Clark, J. (1995), 'The State, Popular Participation, and the Voluntary Section', *World Development,* Vol. 23, No. 4.

Coats, Dan (1996), 'Can Congress Revive Civil Society?', *Policy Review,* Vol. 75, Jan./Feb.

Cohen, Jean (1988), 'Discourse Ethics and Civil Society',

Philosophy and Social Criticism, Vol. 14, Nos. 3 & 4, pp. 315-37.

Cohen, J., & Rogers, J. (1992), 'Secondary Associations and Democratic Governance', *Politics and Society*, Vol. 20, pp. 393 – 472.

Colas, Alejandra (1997), 'The Promises of International Civil Society', *Global Society*, Vol. 11, No. 3, pp. 261-77.

Coleman, J. (1988), 'Social Capital in the creation of human capital', *American Journal of Sociology*, Vol. 94, pp. 95-120.

Coleman, W.D. & Perl, A. (1999), 'Internationalised Policy Environments and Policy Network Analysis,' *Political Studies*, Vol. XLVII, pp. 691 – 709.

Curric, Bob (1998), 'Public action and its Units: Re-examining the politics of hunger alleviation in eastern India,' *Third World Quarterly*, Vol. 19, No. 5, pp. 873–92.

D' Abreo, D.A. (1995), 'The Role of Voluntary Sector in Development', *Link*, Vol. XIII, No. 1, April.

Dahrendorf, Ralf (1996), 'Economic Opportunity, Civil Society, and Political Liberty,' *Development and Change*, Vol. 27, pp. 229 – 49.

Dean, Jodi (192), 'Including Women: The consequences and side effects of feminist critiques of civil society', *Philosophy & Social Criticism*, Vol. 18, No. 3/4.

Dembownski, Hans (1999), 'Courts, Civil Society, and Public Sphere', *Economic and Political Weekly*, 9th January, pp. 49 – 56.

Diamond, Lorry (1992), 'Economic Development and Democracy Reconsidered', *American Behavioural Sciences*, Vol. XXXV, No.4/5

Diamond, Lorry (1994), 'Rethinking Civil Society: Toward Democratic Consolidation', *Journal of Democracy*, Vol. 5, No. 3, pp. 4–18.

Dirks, R. (1980), 'Social Responses during Severe Food Shortages and Famine', *Current Anthropology,* 21.

Dowding, K. (1995), 'Model or Metaphor? A critical review of policy network approach', *Political Studies,* Vol. 43, pp. 136–58.

Dreze, J. & Loh. J. (1995), 'Literacy in India and China', *Economic and Political Weekly,* November 11.

D' Souza, K.C. (1995), 'Enabling Organisations for Human Development: HRD in the Voluntary Sector ', *Renewal,* No. 1, September.

Edwards, Bob, & Foley, Michael W. (1997), 'Social Capital, Civil Society and contemporary democracy', *American Behavioural Scientist,* Special Issue, Vol. 40, No. 5.

Elbridge, P., & Raton, N. (1988), 'Voluntary Organisations and Popular Movements in Bihar', *Lokayan Bulletin,* 6:4, New Delhi.

Evans, Peter (1996), 'Government Action, Social capital and Development: Creating Synergy across the Public– Private Divide', *World Development,* Vol. 24, No. 6.

Fenton, N, Passey, A., & Hens, L. (1999), 'Trust, The Voluntary Sector and Civil Society', *International Journal of Sociology and Social Policy,* Vol. 19, No. 7/8, pp. 21-42.

Fine, Ben (1999), 'The Development State is Dead – Long Live Social Capital', *Development and Change,* Vol. 30, pp. 1–19.

Flyubjerg, Bent (1998), 'Habermes and Foucault: Thinkers for civil society ?", *British Journal of Sociology,* Vol. 49, N. 2, pp. 210 – 33.

Foley, M.W. & Edwards, B. (1996), 'The Paradox of Civil Society', *Journal of Democracy,* Vol. 7, No. 3, pp. 38 – 52.

Fowler, Alan, F. (1991), 'The role of NGOs in changing State – Society, Relations: Perspectives from Eastern and Southern Africa', *Development Policy Review,* Vol. 9, pp. 53 – 84.

Fowler, Alan, F. (1998), 'Authentic NGO Partnerships in the New Policy Agenda for International Aid: Dead End or Light Ahead?' *Development and Change*, Vol. 29, pp. 137 – 59.

Frantz, T.R. (1987), "The Role of NGOs in the Strengthening of Civil Society ", *World Development*, Vol. 15.

Garain, S. (1993), "Grassroots Levels Workers", *The Indian Journal of Social Work*, Vol. LIV, No. 3.

Gellner, Ernst (1991), 'Civil Society in Historical Context', *International Social Science Journal*, Vol. 43, No. 3, pp. 495 – 510.

Giner, Salvador (1985), 'The Withering Away of Civil Society', *Praxis International*, Vol. 5, No. 3, pp. 247 – 67.

Gitlin, Todd (1990), 'The Uncivil Society', *New Perspectives Quarterly*, pp. 46 – 9.

Graf, W. (1995), 'The State in the Third World', *Socialist Register*, 1995.

Greeley, Andrew (1997), 'Coleman Revisited: Religious Structures as a Source of Social Capital', *American Behavioural Scientist*, Vol. 40, No. 5, pp. 587 – 604.

Gruhn, Isebill, V. (1997), 'NGOs in Partnership with the UN: A New Fix or a New Problem for African Development?', *Global Society*, Vol. 11, No. 3, pp. 325 – 37.

Gupta, A. (1987), "Bank – NGO – Poor Interface in Backward Regions: Alternatives for Action", *Indian Journal of Public Administration*, Vol. XXXIII, No. 3.

Gupta, Dipankar (1997), 'Civil Society in the Indian Context', *Contemporary Sociology*, Vol. 26, No. 3.

Habermas, J. (1981), 'New Social Movements', *Telos*, 49, pp. 33–7.

Hadenius, A. & Uggla, F. (1996), 'Making Civil Society Work, Promoting Democratic Development: What can States and

Denors do?', *World Development*, Vol. 24, No. 10, pp. 1621 – 39.

Hall, Peter A. (1997), 'Social Capital in Britain', *British Journal of Political Science*, Vol. 29, pp. 417 – 461.

Hansra *et al.* (1995), 'Role of Voluntary Organisation in Rural Development', *Kurukshetra,* February.

Hardt, Michael (1995), 'The Withering of Civil Society', *Social Text,* Vol. 14, No. 4, pp. 27-44.

Harris, Margaret (1998), 'A special case of voluntary associations? Towards a theory of congregational organisation', *British Journal of Sociology,* Vol. 49, No. 4, pp. 602-18.

Heidenheimer, A. (1985), 'Comparative public policy at the cross roads', *Journal of Public Policy,* 5, pp. 441 – 65.

Heredid, R. (1988), 'Problems and Possibilities of Development Work among Tribals: A Participatory Evaluation of a Voluntary Agency in India', *Community Development Journal,* Vol. XXIII, No. 1.

Heredia, Rudolf (2000), 'Subaltern alternatives on caste, class and ethnicity', *Contribution to Indian Sociology,* Vol. 34, No. 1, pp. 37–62.

Hill, K.Q. (1997), 'In Search of public policy theory', *Policy Currents,* 7, pp. 1–9.

Honneth, Axel (1993), 'Conceptions of Civil Society', *Radical Philosophy,* Vol. 64, pp. 19–22.

Horch, H.D. (1994), 'On the Socio-economic of Voluntary Organisations', *Voluntas,* Vol. 5 :2.

Jacob, Margaret C. (1991), 'The Enlightenment Redefined: The Formation of Modern Civil Society', *Social Research,* 58:2, 475–95.

Jain, Devaki (1985), 'Voluntary agencies and their role', *Indian Express,* New Delhi, 1st July.

Jain, L.C., (1987), 'The Role of Non-Government Organisations in Development', paper prepared for the *Workshop on Poverty in Indian – Research and Policy*, University of Oxford, October 3 – 7.

Janoski, Thomas & Wilson, John (1995), 'Pathways to Voluntarism: Family Socialisation and Status Transmission Models', *Social Forces*, 74 : 1, pp. 271 – 292.

Jordan, G. (1990), 'Sub Governments, Policy Communities and networks', *Journal of Theoretical Politics*, 2, pp. 319 – 38.

Jordan, Tim (1995), 'The Unity of Social Movements', *The Sociological Review*, 1995, pp. 675 – 92.

Kamrava, Mehran, & Mora, Frank, O. (1998), 'Civil Society and Democratisation in Comparative Perspective: Latin America and the Middle East', *Third World Quarterly*, Vol. 19, No. 5, pp. 893 – 916.

Kapoor, K. (1996), 'Voluntary Action: Survival, Politics and Transformation', *Social Action*, Vol. 46.

Karat Prakash (1984), 'Actions Groups/Voluntary Organisations: A Factor in Imperialist Strategy', *The Marxist*, Vol. 2 (April / June).

Karsim, H. (1994), 'Policy networks, networks and European Union Policy making: A Sceptical View', *Western European Politics*, 17, pp. 15 – 27.

Khan, M.B.A. (1996), 'Growth Problems of an NGO: A like case of a Voluntary Organisation', *Renewal*, December.

Knoke, D., & Prersky, D. (1984), 'What relevance do Organisation Theories have for Voluntary Associations', *Social Science Quarterly*, 65, pp. 3 – 20.

Koehn, P. (1983), 'The Role of Public Administration in Public Policy making: Practice & Prospectus', *Public Administration and Development*, January/March.

Kothari, Rajni (1984), 'The Non-Party Political Process', *Economic and Political Weekly*, February 4.

Kulkurni, S. (1986), 'Volags and the New Policy', *Lokayan Bulletin*, Vol. 43 : 4.

Kumar, Krishna (1993), 'Civil Society: an inquiry into the usefulness of an historical term', *British Journal of Sociology*, Vol. 44, No. 3, pp. 375 – 395.

Laitin, David D. (1995), 'The Civic Culture at 30', *American Political Science Review*, Vol. 89, pp. 168 – 73.

Lanzet, P. (1996), 'People's Participatory Processes: A Learning and Training Support for People and NGO's in Development', *Renewal*, No. 2, June.

Leach, M. (1988), 'Becoming A "People Sector': Indian Voluntary Agencies at a Crossroads', *Community Development Journal*, Vol. XXIII, No. 2.

Leftwich, Adrian (1993), 'Governance, Democracy and Development in the Third World', *Third World Quarterly*, Vol. 14, No. 3.

Lemarchand, Rene (1992), 'Uncivil States and Civil Societies: How Illusion became reality', *Journal of Modern African Studies*, Vol. 30, pp. 177 – 91.

Levi, Margaret (1996), 'Social and Unsocial Capital: A Review of Putnam's "Making Democracy Work", *Politics and Society*, Vol. 24, No. 1, pp. 45 – 55.

Loury, Glenn (1987), 'Why should we care about Group Inequality?', *Social Philosophy and Policy*, Vol. 5, pp. 249 – 271.

Maithani, B.P. (1995), 'Voluntary Organisations as Partners in Promoting Participatory Development', *Kurukshetra*, February.

Massni, Vittorio (1985), 'Non-Governmental Organisations and Development', *Finance and Development*, Vol. 22, No. 3.

Markus, Maria (1985), 'Formation and Restructuring of Civil Society: Is there a general meaning in Polish Paradigm?', *International Review of Sociology*, Vol.21, No. 1-3, pp. 5 – 24.

Mayekiso, Moses (1992), 'Working-class Civil Society: Why we need it and How to get it', *African Communist*, Second Quarter, pp. 32 – 42.

Mies, M. (1983), 'Landless Women Organise: A Case Study of an Organisation in Rural Andhra', *Manushi*, 3.

Muller, Edward N., & Seligson, Mitchell A. (1994), 'Civic Culture and Democracy: The Question of Causal Relationships', *American Political Science Review*, Vol. 88, No. 3, pp. 635 – 52.

Najam, A. (1996), 'Understanding the Third Sector: Revisiting the Prince, the Merchant, and the Citizen', *Non-Profit Management and Leadership*, Vol. 7, No. 2, pp. 203 – 19.

Narayana, E.A. (1991), 'Managing Voluntary Organisations with Limited Finances and Unskilled Personnel', *The Indian Journal of Social Work*, Vol. LII, No. 3.

Nelson, Daniel, N. (1996), 'Civil Society Endangered', *Social Research*, Vol. 63, No. 2, pp. 345 – 68.

Newton, Kenneth (1997), 'Social Capital and Democracy', *American Behavioural Scientist*, Vol. 40, No. 5, pp. 575 – 86.

Nuna, S.C. (1996), "Centripetal Vs. Centrifugal Forces and the Role of NGOs", *Social Action*, Vol. 26.

Ostrom, E. (1994), 'Constituting social capital and collective action', *Journal of Theoretical Politics*, 6, pp. 527 – 62.

Oliveira, M.D. & Tandon, R. (1994), "An Emerging Global Civil Society", *Citizens Strengthening Global Civil Society*, CIVICUS, USA.

Paris, D.C. (1991), 'Moral Education and the "tie that binds" in liberal political theory', *American Political Science Review*, Vol. 85, No.3, pp. 875 – 90.

Phillips, Anne (1999), 'Who needs Civil Society?' A Feminist Perspective', *Dissent*, Vol. 46, Winter, pp. 56 – 61.

Portes, Alejundra & Landolt, Patina (1996), 'The Downside of Social Capita', *American Prospect*, No. 26 (May/June).

Pratt, B., & Adrian, S. (1994), 'Multilateral Agencies and NGOs: A Position Paper', *Occasional Paper Series*, Vol. 1, No. 1, The International NGO Training and Research Centre, Oxford.

Prindle, P.H. (1979), 'Peasant Society and Famines: A Nepalese Example', *Ethnology*, 1.

Punalekar, S.P. (1997), 'On Dialectics of Voluntary Organisations and Social Change', *IASSI Quarterly*, Vol. 15, No. 4, pp. 67 – 90.

Putnam, Rabert, D. (1993) 'The Prosperous Community: Social Capital and Public Life', *American Prospect*, No. 13 (Spring).

Putnam, Robert D. (1995), 'Tuning Out: The Strange Disappearance of Social Capital in America', *Political Science and Politics*, Vol. XXVIII, No. 4, pp. 664 – 83.

Putnam, Robert D. (1995), 'Bowling Alone: America's Declining Social Capital', *Journal of Democracy*, Vol. 6 (January), pp. 65 – 78.

Qureshi, M.A. (1998), 'The World Bank and NGOs: New Approaches', *Lokayan Bulletin*, 6:4.

Raj, S.L. (1996), 'The Emerging Political Scenario and the Role of NGOs', *Social Action*, Vol. 46, No. 1.

Ramachandran, V. (1995), 'Equality among Unequal Parties Relationship between NGOs and Government', *The Administrator*, Vol. XI.

________________, (1996), 'NGOs in the time of globalisation', *Seminar*, November.

Ramachandran, Vimala (1999), 'Adult Education: A Tale of Empowerment Denied', *Economic and Political Weekly*, April 10, pp. 877 – 82.

Reddy, G.N. (1992), 'Training Voluntary Workers as Agents of Development', *Social Change*, Vol. XXII, No. 4.

Roy, B. (1995), 'Voluntary Action: Where do we go from here?', *Lokayan Bulletin*, 12:3.

Roy, S. (1994), 'NGOs too need a Code', *Anubhuti*, Vol. XV, No. 1 & 2.

Sabatier, P. (1991), 'Towards better theories of the policy process', *Political Science and Politics*, 24, pp. 147 – 56.

Sales, Arnaud (1991), 'The Private, the Public and Civil Society: Social Realms and Power Structures', *International Political Science Review*, Vol. 12, No. 4, pp. 295 – 312.

Schmidt, James (1995), 'Civil Society and Social Things: Setting the Boundaries of the Social Sciences', *Social Research*, Vol. 62, No. 4, pp. 899 – 932.

Schmidt, James (1998), 'Civility, Enlightenment and Society: Conceptual Conusions and Kartian Remedies', *American Political Science Review*, Vol. 92, No. 2, June, pp. 419-27.

Seligson, Amber L. (1999), 'Civic Association and Democratic Participation in Central America: A test of the Putnam's Thesis', *Comparative Political Studies*, Vol. 32, No. 3, pp. 342-62.

Sengupta, Chandan & Roy, M.N. (1996), 'Sociological Impact of Total Literacy Campaign: The case of Midnapore', *Economic & Political Weekly*, February, 24.

Sharma, K.L. (1996), 'The Indian State and the NGOs', *Social Action*, Vol. 26.

Shaw, Martin (1994), 'Civil Society and Global Politics: Beyond a Social Movements Approach', *Millennium: Journal of International Studies*, Vol. 23, No. 3, pp. 647 – 67.

Sheth, D.L. (1984), 'Grassroots initiatives in India', *Economic and Political Weekly*, Vol. 19, pp. 259-62.

Sheth, D.L., & Sethi, Harsh (1991), 'The NGO Sector in India: Historical Contest and Current Discourse', *Voluntans*, 2.

Shils, Edward (1992), 'The Virtue of Civil Society', *Government and Opposition*, Vol. 26 (Winter), pp. 3–20.

Sinha, A. (1994), 'Reshaping NGO Roles in the Era of Panchayati Raj', *Exchanges*, No. 7.

Smith, R. (1992), 'The Role of the Voluntary Sector in Tackling Poverty', *Community Development Journal*, Vol. XXVII, No. 3.

Smith, T.B. (1973), 'Policy Implementation Process', *Policy Science*, M. 4.

Sollis, P. (1992), 'Multilateral Agencies, NGOs and Policy Reform', *Development in Practice*, Vol. II, No. 3.

Srikanth, H. (1996), 'State, NGOs and Urban Community Development', *Social Action*, Vol. XXVI.

Srivastava, G. (1996), 'People's Empowerment and the NGO Role Transformation', *Search Bulletin*, Vol. IX, No. 1, Jan. - March.

Stoker, Gerry (1988), 'Governance as Theory: Five Propositions', *International Social Sciences Journal*, No. 158.

Sundavaraman, Sudha (1996), 'Literacy Campaigns: Lessons for Women's Movement', *Economic and Political Weekly*, May, 18.

Swilling, Mark (1992), 'Socialism, Democracy and Civil Society: The case for Associational Socialism', *Theoria*, Vol. 79, pp. 75–82.

Tandon, R. (1996), 'Changing Context and Challenges for Voluntary Action', *Social Action*, Vol. 46, No. 1.

Tarrow, S. (1996), 'Making Social Science Work Across Space and Time: A Critical Reflection on Robert Putnam's "Making Democracy Work"', *American Political Sicence Review*, Vol. 90, No. 2, June.

Taylor, Charles (1990), 'Modes of Civil Society', *Public Culture*, Vol. 3, No. 1, pp. 95-118.

Throgmorton, J.A. (1991), 'The rhetoric of policy analysis', *Policy Sciences*, 24, pp. 153-79.

Tornquist, Olle (1991), 'Community and Democracy: Two Indian Cases and One Debate', *Bulletin of Concerned Asian Scholars*, Vol. 23, No. 2.

Upendranath, C. (1995), 'The Changing Role of the State in Welfare and Implication for NGOs', *Exchanges*, No. 10.

Uphoff, N. (1993), 'Grassroots Organisations and NGOs in Rural Development: Opportunities with Diminishing States and Expanding Markets', *World Development*, Vol. XXI, No. 4.

Vepa Ram, K. (1974), 'Implementation: The Problem of Achieving Results', *Indian Journal of Public Administration*, Vol. 20, May/June.

Walzer, Michael (1991), 'The Idea of Civil Society', *Dissent*, Vol. 38 (Spring), pp. 294-98.

Walzer, Michael, (1999), 'Rescuing Civil Society', *Dissent*, Vol. 46, Winters, pp. 62 – 67.

Weiner, Richard R. (1991), 'Retrieving Civil Society in a Post Modern Epoch', *Social Science Journal*, Vol. 28, No. 3, pp. 307-23.

White, Gordon (1994), 'Civil Society, Democratisation and Development (I): (Learning the Analytical Ground', *Democratisation*, Vol. 1, No. 3.

__________ (1995), ____________ (II), Two Country Cases', *Democratisation*, Vol. 2, pp. 56-84.

Wood, Ellen M. (1990), 'The Uses and Abuses of "Civil Society", *Socialist Register*, pp. 60–84.

Yee, A. (1996), 'The casual effects of ideas on policies', *International Organisation*, 50, pp. 69-108.

APPENDIX-I

The Constitution (Eighty-third Amendment) Bill, 1997

A Bill Further to amend the Constitution of India

Be it enacted by Parliament in the Forty-eighth Year of the Republic of India as follows: Short title & commitment

1. 1) This Act may be called the Constitution (Eight-third Amendment) Act, 1997.

   2 It shall come into force on such date as the Central Government may, by notification in the Official Gazette, appoint.

2. After article 21 of the Constitution, the following article shall be inserted, namely: Insertion of new Article 21A Right to Education

   "21A, (1) The State shall provide free and compulsory education to all citizens of the age six to fourteen years.

   (2) The right to free and compulsory education referred to in Clause (1) shall be enforced in such manner as the State may, by law, determine.

   (3) The State shall not make any law, for free and compulsoryeducation under clause (2), in relation to the educational institutions not maintained by the State or not receiving aid out of State funds."

3. Article 35 of the Constitution shall be renumbered as clause (1) of that article and after clause (1) as so renumbered and before the *Explanation*, the following clause shall be inserted, namely:

"(2) The competent legislature shall make the law for the enforcement of right to free and compulsory education referred to in Clause (1) of article 21A within one year from the commencement of the Constitution (Eighty-third Amendment) Act, 1997.

Provided that a provision of any law to free, and compulsory education in force in a State immediately before the commencement of the Constitution (Eighty-third Amendment) Act, 1997 which is consistent of Article 21A, shall continue to be in force until amended or repeated by a competent legislature or other competent authority or until the expiration of one year from such commencement, whichever is earlier".

4. Article 45 of the Constitution shall be omitted. — Omission of Article 45

5. In Article 51A of the Constitution, after Clause (j) the following clause will be added, namely — Amendment of Article 45

"(k) to provide opportunities for education to a child between the age of six and fourteen years of whom such citizen is a parent or guardian."

APPENDIX-II

The Members of the following Voluntary Associations of Cuttack City and Tangi Block were interviewed and the Questionnaire was administered for the purpose of the research.

1) Ashakiran, Laxmi Bazar Chhak, Jobra, Cuttack.
2) Centre of Alternative Training, Evaluation Research (CATER), Kalyani Nagar, Cuttack.
3) Chetna, Bepari Sahi, Buxibazar, Cuttack.
4) The Citizen, Tulsipur, Cuttack.
5) Lutheran World Services, Keonjhar Colony, Cuttack.
6) East Coast Honorary Organisation, Arunodaya Nagar, Cuttack.
7) The Educationist, Jagatpur, Cuttack.
8) International Indecency Prevention Movement, Bidanasi, Cuttack.
9) Jeevanjyoti, Naya Bazar, Cuttack.
10) Mahila Vikas Samity, Kalyani Nagar, Cuttack.
11) Maitrayee Samaj, Tulsipur, Cuttack.
12) Universe, Buxi Bazar, Cuttack.
13) YMCA, Buxi Bazar, Cuttack.
14) Orissa Urban Rural Service, Peyton Sahi, Cuttack.

15) Rural Development Society, Auronodaya Nagar, Cuttack.

16) Satabdira Surya, Pithapur, Cuttack.

17) Maa Jagulei Sangathan, Tangi.

18) Young Women's Christian Association, Mission Road, Cuttack.

19) Samaj Kalyan Samity, Shelter Chhak, Cuttack.

20) Nari Seva Sadan, Buxi Bazar, Cuttack.

21) Vasundhara, Bidanasi, Cuttack.

22) Utkal Mahila Samity, Gamadia, Cuttack.

23) Yuba Jyoti Mahila Samity, Ramagarh, Cuttack.

24) Mangala Mahila Samity, Jholasahi, Cuttack.

25) Lioness Club, Cuttack.

INDEX

❑❑❑